SHORT COURSE SERIES

WORLD
TRADE
PRESS®

Professional Books for International Trade

DATE DUE

JUL 1 4 2005		

International Business Plans

Charting a Strategy for Success in Global Commerce

Robert L. Brown, M.B.A., J.D., Ph.D.

Alan S. Gutterman, M.B.A., J.D., Ph.D.

Editor:

Dr. Jeffrey Edmund Curry

(AUDENCIA Nantes Ecole de Management)

World Trade Press
1450 Grant Avenue, Suite 204
Novato, California 94945 USA
Tel: +1 (415) 898-1124
Fax: +1 (415) 898-1080
USA Order Line: (800) 833-8586
E-mail: sales@worldtradepress.com
www.worldtradepress.com
www.worldtraderef.com
www.globalroadwarrior.com
www.howtoconnect.com

A Short Course in International Business Plans
Charting a Strategy for Success in Global Commerce
By Robert L. Brown, M.B.A., J.D., Ph.D. and Alan S. Gutterman, M.B.A., J.D., Ph.D.
Short Course Series Concept: Edward G. Hinkelman
Cover Design: Ronald A. Blodgett
Text Design: Seventeenth Street Studios, Oakland, California USA
Desktop Publishing: Brian Duffy

Disclaimer
This publication is designed to provide general information concerning aspects of international
trade. It is sold with the understanding that the publisher is not engaged in rendering legal or
any other professional services. If legal advice or other expert assistance is required, the services
of a competent professional person or organization should be sought.

Library of Congress Cataloging-in-Publication Data
Brown, Robert, M.B.A., J.D., Ph.D. and Alan S. Gutterman, M.B.A.,
J.D., Ph.D.
A short course in international business plans : charting a startegy for
success in global commerce / Robert L. Brown, Alan S. Gutterman.
p. cm. -- (The short course in international trade series)
ISBN 1-885073-62-3 (alk. paper)
1. Business planning. 2. International business enterprises -- Planning.
I. Title: International business plans. II. Gutterman, Alan S., 1955- III.
Title. IV. Series.
HD30.28.B7817 2003
658.4'012--dc21

                                        2003042258

Printed in the United States of America

INTRODUCTION

A Short Course in International Business Plans is a practical guide to the research, development and writing of an international business plan. Emphasis is placed upon the purposes, issues, content and format of the plan itself.

Two assumptions are made. The first is that you have already made the decision to "go global," whether as a start-up enterprise or as an expansion of an existing domestic business. The second is that you have already chosen, at least preliminarily, the international market or markets of best opportunity. If you have not yet decided upon your target market(s), we recommend that you consider reading *A Short Course in International Marketing*, also by World Trade Press.

BUSINESS PLANS VS. INTERNATIONAL BUSINESS PLANS

Domestic and international business plans share a similar structure and cover many of the same issues, such as descriptions of the company, its key players and plans for expansion. International business plans, however, are unique in the way these issues are addressed. In every instance, the development of a business plan for cross-border materials sourcing, manufacturing, marketing and/or sales requires unique research, expertise and emphasis.

That said, do not abandon any prior efforts at writing a domestic business plan. In many cases, your domestic plan can serve as a starting point. This book will alert you to the key differences and let you know where the emphasis needs to be placed. We'll expand your horizons and your business plan in the process.

CULTURE SHOCK

The authors have operated for many years in the international arena and have tried to understand with humility and interest the unique cultures of the world. We recognize that not every culture works the same way. We also acknowledge that we were brought up in the United States and that our perspective is that of North Americans. We have made every attempt, however, to make this book relevant to businesspeople from any country wanting to do business in any country. We believe that the fundamental issues of planning are the same regardless of where you are from and where you are going.

SAMPLE BUSINESS PLANS

This book contains a number of sample business plans that cover a spectrum of industries and business situations. While they are detailed to the particular business, they will present an excellent picture of the type of detail expected in a modern international business plan. As such, they are not forms with lots of "fill-in-the-blanks." Rather, the blanks are already filled in so the reader is provided with a more complete idea of what a plan actually looks like once it is finished.

WRITE YOUR PLAN

Although it may be tempting to avoid the labor and time needed to develop and write a plan, we know from our own experience that it is better to plan than to enter a new market without making the effort. Lack of planning typically leads to failure. Follow the guidelines and write your plan; we want you to succeed!

TABLE OF CONTENTS

CHAPTER 1

Why Write An International Business Plan?

TACTICS WITHOUT STRATEGY IS THE NOISE BEFORE DEFEAT. – SUN TZU

THIS BOOK IS ABOUT PREPARING AN INTERNATIONAL BUSINESS PLAN—a formal written plan for a company that seeks to gain benefit from foreign markets for new customers, raw materials, manufacturing partners, capital or labor. Countless opportunities await, but there are many pitfalls too. The time you spend in creating a solid business plan will help you anticipate the tough spots, modify your approach and climb to the peak of success in the international marketplace. A wise business leader is one who formulates a strategy that accounts for the considerations of going global.

FAQs of an International Business Plan

- QUESTION: Why write a business plan at all?
- ANSWER: A business should never be started or operated without a clear plan of what the owners intend to do and how they intend to accomplish their goals. Not having a business plan is equivalent to driving through a new area without a map.
- QUESTION: If I already have a domestic business plan, why make an international one?
- ANSWER: The need for a business plan is even more acute when a company is looking for opportunities in international markets. Many of the basic building blocks for an international business plan are similar to those for a domestic one, but in the global environment, a company will encounter new and different issues with additional risks.
- QUESTION: What will an international business plan accomplish for me?
- ANSWER: For any business, a plan will settle or fix your vision into a working commercial model both for internal management purposes and for use in persuading external resources—e.g., investors, bankers or potential business partners—of the realized and potential value of the business. If properly formulated, it will define your company's goals, identify meritorious features and potential pitfalls and establish operational policies, structure and procedures. For an international business, a plan will also cover features of cross-border and cross-cultural trading that your company will need to address in order to benefit from the advantages of, and survive in, the global arena.

Global Facets of a Company

Is your company "global enough" to warrant an international business plan? Global companies come in many sizes. Perhaps you think that a global company has to be a giant multinational corporation with franchises in every major metropolitan area around the world. Consider whether any of the following situations might fit your company:

- A processed food business in Hong Kong specializing in favorite local dishes decides to export its products to California to tap into the Asian population there and the general popularity of Chinese culinary delicacies.

- A manufacturer of popular dolls in Spain contracts with local distributors in other Spanish-speaking countries for promotion and sale of the dolls in those countries. The manufacturer is able to capitalize on the favorable demographics and opportunities for using its own promotional assets (e.g., TV commercials) in new markets of Spanish-speaking consumers.

- A producer of an animated television series in Japan localizes the content for distribution in English-language markets. Or vice versa!

- A Nigerian watchmaker uses parts imported from Switzerland.

Each of these companies is linked to the global economy and can benefit from an international business plan. The development of an international business plan—whether simple or complex—can be important to the realization of international success for a giant conglomerate as well as for a small company.

Achieving International Advantages

Having made the decision to "go global," your company must next consider how it is going to proceed to achieve the many advantages offered in the international trade arena. A company might seek to reduce its costs and risks, expand into new markets, procure reliable and less expensive sources of supplies and materials, improve production and technical abilities or enlarge its available labor pool.

Building an international company is similar to building a house. You begin with a vision. Your vision is translated into a plan. Your plan serves as the basic guideline for turning the vision into a real home with a strong foundation, secure walls and a protective, leak-proof roof. Likewise, an international business plan is the blueprint of a global company. It is an essential tool by which a company can identify desirable opportunities of cross-border operations and set short-term and long-term company goals for achieving perceived international trade advantages.

REDUCE OPERATIONAL COSTS

Primary reasons for entering a foreign market are to take advantage of *perceived* market opportunities and to reduce the costs of operation and production. Without a plan, however, opportunities can turn out to be more costly than the anticipated benefits.

What is so attractive about moving into another country? Perhaps you think that you will be able to reduce labor costs by tapping into the large pool of low-wage workers available there. Maybe the foreign country allows foreign investment in land and building facilities. If so, these resources might be available at less expense than in your own country, which would reduce your company's capital costs. Some countries offer incentives to attract business investment, such as exemptions from local taxes and tariffs or reduced licensing and documentary fees.

But what about the extra costs of doing business in another place—a faraway place? Will you move your whole operation or run two facilities? How do you coordinate and divide responsibilities? What about the expense of training, travel, moving, import and export, business registration, operational licenses and protection of the expanded use of trademarks, patents and other intellectual property? Do you have a plan to find and implement the advantages in such a way as to overcome the additional burdens?

REDUCE RISK BY DIVERSIFYING MARKETS

A company's international business plan may seek to establish global operations that are aimed at diversifying the company's market opportunities in order to reduce the risk of dwindling demand. By entering a new foreign market, a company can increase sales, extend its customer base and gain protection against variations in buying cycles that might occur in the company's home market. For example, a company that sells clothes used in warm weather, such as swimsuits, can follow the summer around the world to create a steady, year-long demand.

Plan in advance to avoid potential disaster when demand falls below sustainable levels—whether because of market saturation, outmoded products or otherwise. Foreign markets can provide good opportunities for selling older, more mature products that have become obsolete in technologically advanced markets. A network of global facilities can allow a company to divert products and supplies quickly to regions where demand is booming.

REDUCE RISK BY DIVERSIFYING SUPPLIERS

Companies that use raw materials will benefit from an international business plan that addresses the risk associated with relying on a single supply source. Materials that are scarce or even non-existent in a company's home country may be abundant and inexpensive in a foreign market. Assume that a company sells quarried stone. It can obtain varieties from quarries in various parts of the world to ensure a reliable supply regardless of disruptions at any single source because of uncontrollable events ranging from inclement weather to labor disputes to political or civil upheaval.

If you plan in advance, your business need not be limited when materials become unavailable or prohibitively expensive in one market. Instead, you will know how and where to pursue reliable sources in other countries. Risk reduction strategies might include shipping materials from a foreign country for manufacture elsewhere or finding a manufacturing facility within the foreign country where the materials are easily available. To assure access to products that are unavailable in Japan unless imported, Japanese automobile manufacturers have a long history of building production plants in other countries. This is particularly true if there is also a significant local market for Japanese cars.

INTEGRATE GLOBAL LEARNING

Education and environmental scanning is an important strategic tool for every business, regardless of its size or scope of operations. For a company that can afford the investment, cross-border operations can be a powerful learning tool for enhancement of operations and product development activities. Setting up business operations in a foreign market is an excellent way to observe how other companies deal with the unique technological, social, cultural and political factors that impact demand in that market. In addition, global operations can provide direct access to companies that have developed internationally recognized practices in key functional areas, such as new product development, manufacturing and supply chain management. Compiling and integrating this information into your business will strengthen and enhance its market standing, and therefore make global learning a key component of your business plan.

ACCESS GLOBAL TALENT

A company that participates actively in foreign markets often gains access to valuable human resources in those markets. Many countries, such as India, have a large pool of well-educated scientists and engineers who can provide high quality services at tremendous cost savings to firms located in higher-priced markets, such as the United States and Western Europe. By establishing a foreign branch office or strategic relationship, such as a joint venture, a company may attract local managers who are interested and experienced in international business. This creates a pool of talent that thinks globally and tangibly supports the company's development of new markets and resources. If your business might benefit from global talent, your international business plan should provide for the recruitment and utilization of such resources, which in turn may significantly reduce product development costs.

Adapting to the International Business Environment

Your international business plan is a useful tool for achieving the advantages of going global. However, it is at least equally significant as a guideline to focus your company on how it will need to adapt its business to account for the differences it is likely to encounter in the international business environment as compared to its domestic markets. The world offers significant business opportunities, but these opportunities are accompanied by significant challenges.

The greatest challenges stem from attempting to deal with the distinctive, and often quite different, nature of the business environment. For example, a company looking to set up manufacturing facilities in a foreign country may encounter government controls, difficulties in making an effective transfer of core technologies, poorly educated or trained local workers, financial restrictions and a lack of inputs and supplies that meet rigid quality standards. You must have a plan of action for handling a new environment if your company is going to enter and stay successfully.

LESSON: The following scenario almost ruined one company's efforts to set up an overseas manufacturing facility. Government controls on foreign investment required that the company set up a new joint venture with a local partner. Problems began immediately. The company first discovered that the local partner's employees lacked the technical background to absorb the technology licensed to the joint venture. It next encountered resistance from the local employees being trained. When they were assigned to the joint venture, they felt that they were being cast adrift from their main company and were reluctant to accept training in new techniques.

Another major problem was uncovered when the company learned that the industrial infrastructure was inadequate. As a condition to forming the joint venture, the government required that supplies be purchased from local companies; but local inputs fell far short of the quality required for finished goods being exported for sale in the company's home market. Some were even unavailable and had to be imported. Unfortunately, the importing process was very slow because of a lack of import financing and the need to satisfy local bureaucratic requirements. As a result, production cycles were delayed, increasing costs significantly.

A further blow to the company's efforts developed when several factors combined to cause a substantial change in market demand. Initially encouraged by government incentives that supported a strong demand in the local market for the goods being produced, the company was faced with a sudden shift in government strategies toward agricultural production. Such policy shifts are not uncommon in developing countries and can create havoc with a company's business. In addition, rising inflationary pressures led to credit controls that reduced the financial resources of potential buyers, including several government-owned businesses. Finally, the cost advantages of entering the foreign market were further reduced by a flow of low-priced imports from other countries.

ACCOUNT FOR MACROECONOMIC EFFECTS

A major risk of going global is increased exposure to macroeconomic conditions in other countries. An important feature of any international business plan is the development of policies and procedures that take into account the likely consequences of another country's macroeconomic problems. For example, inflation in a foreign country can lead to radical changes in monetary policies, including devaluation of the local currency. Other macroeconomic conditions can adversely impact the availability of capital to local banks and firms from external sources, such as the World Bank, the International Monetary Fund and other multilateral agencies that release funds only if a country has met specific standards. In such cases, a firm would be unwise to risk a substantial investment without a contingency plan or long-term goal in mind.

ANTICIPATE POLITICAL TRANSFORMATIONS

A change in the political landscape of a foreign market can lead to different governmental attitudes toward core business and investment issues, such as protection of private property and labor relations and requirements. These changes can result in adoption of new laws and regulations that increase the costs associated with using local resources and cause delay in commercial production. By means of an international business plan, a company can anticipate and set procedures in advance to deal with political transformations.

BEND TO SOCIOECONOMIC CONDITIONS

Socioeconomic conditions define the marketplace and the unique cultural norms that exist within a particular country. Foreign companies must always carefully consider how their products and marketing activities will be perceived in the local market, and their business plan must allow for product and service adaptations to ensure acceptance around the world. For example, a company marketing birth control products or food supplements for infants must consider whether those items might clash with social values in a local country, might be unaffordable or might be misused because of poor education. Differences in social classes and languages in foreign countries may dictate adjustments in advertising and packaging, as well as in personnel management and human resource practices.

For some companies, a useful strategy is to establish autonomous facilities or enter into joint ventures with local partners in order to gain a better understanding of the demands and customs of consumers in those countries. Selection of a local partner who has already established a significant customer base or distribution chain may also be an advantage. In order for such strategies to succeed, however, the company must plan its entrance into the foreign market with circumspection. It will need to select local managers who understand the local market, train them in the specifications and functionality of the company's products and demand standards of quality and customer service at least equal to those in the company's home market.

Making the Vision an Internal Reality

Most people who want to start a business begin with an idea—a vision—and a belief that it can be accomplished. The "how" might be a little fuzzy, but there is a strong commitment to make it happen. The vision must now become a structured reality. It is time to make a business plan.

ESTABLISH A SPECIFIC METHODOLOGY

The business plan is a means of converting a vision into a specific methodology. It helps the entrepreneur clarify how the idea will be achieved. It forces the company to determine the specifications of the new goods or services, how they will be marketed, how the company will be managed, where the money will come from, where it will be spent and who will be hired to make the company successful.

If you have never prepared a business plan, you might view it as a waste of time. You can also become particularly frustrated after having revised a plan for the third, fourth or perhaps tenth time. However, when you finish you will probably be glad that you completed the task. You will most likely have learned a great deal. If you are not happy with your efforts, your business plan is probably not finished.

ADVISORY: A business plan may be unpleasantly revealing. One of the authors worked for several months on a business plan with an entrepreneur. At the end of the process, the businessman discovered that the product was good, but he could not get it to market at an acceptable price. He moved on to other projects. Although disappointed by what he found, he was happier to have uncovered the truth at an early stage rather than after having spent a lot of time and money—both his and others—on a project that was doomed to failure.

BUILD A FOUNDATION FOR GROWTH

The utility of a good business plan will continue after the drafting is done. A primary use of a business plan is to serve as a guide for the growth and development of the business. Each and every important activity of the business must have a relationship to the plan. If it doesn't, the company is drifting and troubles are not far in the future.

MEASURE PERFORMANCE

A good business plan also will serve as a company report card, allowing managers to compare what actually happens to what was predicted when the plan was first written. Unforeseen events will undoubtedly affect the business, sometimes creating profitable gains and other times causing havoc. But, if the company's actual performance deviates significantly from the plan, management will need to reevaluate the goals and methodology to determine which factors have not been recognized or properly considered.

Convincing the Rest of the World

A business plan will most likely be given to third parties outside of the company for various reasons, including:

- To raise money from potential investors and bankers, who will review the business plan to see how you intend to generate profits in order to pay them not only the initial sum invested or loaned, but also interest or dividends.

- In the start-up stage, to persuade key managers and employees of the value of the venture and to convince them that it is viable and worthy of their long-term commitment.

- In the franchising context, to serve as the primary disclosure document in the offering circular required to be filed and provided to franchise participants.

- To identify the nature and scope of the business for prospective domestic and foreign business partners, who will review the plan when determining whether a basis exists for a joint venture, or for a long-term manufacturing or distribution arrangement.

Accordingly, keep in mind what elements outside parties will need to see in your company's business plan. After all, they will use the plan as a means of understanding the strengths and weaknesses of your company. A good business plan will thoroughly address the issues most commonly considered by third parties who might evaluate your business, including:

- Products offered
- Managerial acumen
- Demands of the marketplace
- Risks posed by actual and potential competitors
- Strategic plans for innovation, marketing and financing
- Overall business environment in which your company will be operating and plans for surviving within that environment

Business Plan: Myth And Reality

Conventional thinking about business plans is flawed. The primary reason for writing a business plan is not to raise money, but rather to flesh out ideas and to look for weak spots and vulnerabilities. A party that may be a source of capital (investor, banker, venture capitalist) will want to examine your business plan carefully, of course, but the major issue is: Does this concept seize an opportunity with the necessary drive and skills of its people? Here are ten top keys to a successful business plan:

1. By writing the business plan, you should begin to comprehend the discipline needed to capture the opportunity. The dream—the idea—must be grounded in reality.

2. Use the plan to clarify your goals and confront both positives and negatives. This is the most valuable outcome of writing a business plan. You will develop a clearer understanding of your purpose and the strengths and weaknesses of the concept.

3. Stress implementation of the plan. The plan must describe how key objectives will be attained. For operational success, the plan must state the details as to "how" things will be accomplished. These statements are crucial.

4. Make the plan workable by distilling your goals to one-page action summaries for each section of the plan: "Plan your work and work your plan." The key is how you make the plan work for you after it is developed.

5. Recognize and include, as part of the management team, professionals whom you will need to retain, such as an accountant, lawyer, marketing expert, etc. If your firm is going to be a small start-up, these professionals may be contracted for service. If you have a larger enterprise, then plan for the inclusion of people with these talents and abilities. Create a management team that has complementary skills to get the job done.

6. Schedule regular meetings with management to discuss ONLY the plan, nothing else. Set key goals for each core business area. Develop brief strategy statements for the next three-month period. Then go back and fill in the financial figures. Whether the enterprise is small or medium in size, or simply a concept on paper, active discussion of your plan is a sound approach to generating realistic financial projections.

7. Discipline yourself to maintain balanced attention to all areas. Don't focus only on the financials or marketing. Seize opportunities to improve continuously by stressing the strengths of all areas and commitments to overcome weaknesses.

8. Plan for both positive and negative contingencies. Anticipate the unexpected. What if a new competitor enters the market? Engage in contingency planning so that, when there is a crisis, you can be proactive and undertake planned action rather than being simply reactive.

9. Audit your plan each month to maintain progress control. The plan must be a working document, not simply paper to gather dust on a shelf. Creativity, energy and drive keep a business on track to succeed.

10. Update your plan every six months—that way you extend it another year. It helps guide your decisions and records your reasons for doing what you are doing. It keeps you focused on your mission and goals. It's your roadmap to success.

Bruce H. Kemelgor, Ph.D.
College of Business & Public Administration
University of Louisville (Kentucky, USA)

CHAPTER 2

Basic Plan Elements and Variations

IT IS A BAD PLAN THAT ADMITS OF NO MODIFICATION.

– PUBLIUS SYRUS

THE PREPARATION OF AN INTERNATIONAL BUSINESS PLAN is a challenging task, primarily because a plan typically needs to serve a variety of purposes. While nearly every plan will include a number of basic elements, the actual content will depend on such factors as what business you are planning, how you intend to use the plan and who will be asked to review and evaluate the plan. In fact, it is quite common to prepare a single plan and then subsequently alter the contents to the extent needed for a specific purpose. A business plan is mainly developed for two reasons: (1) to clarify your own vision, and (2) to sell your company to potential investors, bankers and partners. Write your international business plan with both goals in mind and cover all the issues necessary to accomplish your objectives.

Contents and Characteristics of a Useful Business Plan

Although there are no formal requirements when selecting the contents of an international business plan, you can follow established guidelines of successful businesses to ensure that you have collected all essential information and considered all relevant issues. Although a business plan can be organized in a variety of ways, and there are no hard and fast rules, there are some guidelines that can be followed.

ELEMENTS OF A BUSINESS PLAN

The following structure is suggested as a starting point:

- Introduction or Executive Summary
- Business
- Product or Service
- Marketing
- Management
- Financials
- Supplemental Materials

Each of the above elements is covered separately in detail beginning at Chapter 6.

EMPHASIS AND STRUCTURE

The purpose of the plan will dictate the emphasis and structure of its contents. For example, if the plan is prepared for circulation to investors who might not be familiar with the company, an Introduction and general background description of the business of the company will be relevant. Similarly, when a plan being used to expand a current operation is provided to investors, less emphasis is usually given to projections of future financial performance, as compared with financial statements from prior years. On the other hand, a business plan intended strictly for internal use generally need not include a lengthy Introduction or discussion of the historical development of the company.

Structural differences to be borne in mind in relation to the audience are as follows:

- FOR INVESTORS, the plan needs to include a disclosure document containing additional information regarding the terms on which the company is seeking to raise new funds.

- IN A FUND RAISING CONTEXT the plan should pay special attention to national securities and banking laws that may apply in each country where the document is distributed.

- AN INTERNAL BUSINESS PLAN will generally not include as much background information on the industry and the company.

- IN AN INTERNAL PLAN projections may be more detailed than in a document provided to investors. The plan must be sufficiently specific to handle potential problems in the event that the projections are not met, and detailed projections and forecasts are critical as planning and measurement tools for managers and employees.

LENGTH AND DETAIL

The length and detail of your business plan will necessarily vary depending on the nature of the business and how you intend to use the plan. For example, if the market is well established and the managers have a strong track record and extensive experience in the industry, the business plan can be shorter, with less analysis and explanation. On the other hand, a longer and more detailed plan might be appropriate for a start-up business or one that is involved in an emerging market with rapidly changing technical and demographic characteristics. If your company is making its first tentative steps into the international market, your business plan might be quite short with an emphasis on investigating opportunities through means that are cost- and time-efficient using your current managerial resources and business contacts.

The Global Factor

To seek the advantages and opportunities described in Chapter 1, your company will need a business plan that is focused on global issues. It is true that the basic building blocks of a business plan are the same regardless of whether the company is operating in a single country or across national borders. But there are significant factors not present locally that must be accounted for on the international level. For this reason, an international business plan is different than a domestic business plan. Here are some of the key differences:

- **DOMESTIC:** A domestic plan must acknowledge the need for market segmentation based on demographic differences within a single country.

- **INTERNATIONAL:** An international plan must account for the unique cultural, language and other differences in each of the targeted countries.

- **DOMESTIC:** A domestic plan needs to provide for compliance with the legal requirements for business operation in the company's home country only.

- **INTERNATIONAL:** An international plan must take into account different regulatory policies and practices with respect to foreign participation in the local economy. The plan must include entry strategies for each new target market.

- **DOMESTIC:** A domestic plan must take into account local culture, politics, weather, geography and other factors that affect market demand and supply in the company's home country.

- **INTERNATIONAL:** An international business plan must take into account local culture, politics, weather, geography and other factors that affect market demand and supply in each of the countries of operation. This is inherently more complex than dealing with different markets within a single (domestic) country. Furthermore, it is often more difficult to obtain and analyze information on local country markets. As such, the company must anticipate a broader range of problems than if the company was active only in its domestic market.

- **DOMESTIC:** A domestic business plan tends to be simply product- and sales-oriented. That is, it will focus on what products will be developed and how they will be sold within a domestic market.

- **INTERNATIONAL:** An international business plan is by nature more complex as it seeks to take advantage of different opportunities offered by different countries. As such, it is likely to take into account product development, raw materials purchase, manufacturing, marketing and sales in multiple countries. The variations may seem endless: develop the product in one country, acquire the raw materials in a second, manufacture the product in a third, transport through a fourth and sell and distribute in a fifth country. Alternatively, the final product might be shipped back to the original country of development.

Matching the Plan to the Nature of the Business

All companies with global goals and objectives, regardless of size or line of business, need some form of game plan, but the focus of the plan will shift depending on the particular business and industry situations.

ESTABLISHED DOMESTIC COMPANIES

An established domestic company, with a recognized line of products and well developed local distribution channels, must identify its reasons for going global before altering its business plan. The international provisions of the plan will depend on the opportunities that the company wants to seize. Perhaps the domestic market is saturated, in which case the international business plan can focus on identifying and penetrating foreign markets where the company's existing products are likely to be quickly accepted with minimal adaptation. If the established company is looking to foreign countries in order to reduce costs of manufacturing and raw materials, an international plan can be created to explore and acquire the best avenues of cost-savings while still concentrating sales activities on the home country market.

PRODUCT BUSINESSES

Companies that sell products such as consumer goods, computer hardware and machinery at wholesale and retail levels can use foreign countries as new markets for their products as well as for new sources of labor and materials. For ultimate success, the company's international business plan will need to account for the characteristics that are unique to product-driven businesses. If products will be sold in a new market, the plan will need to provide for product adaptations that may be required in order to meet national consumer and safety compliance laws, cultural tastes, transport restrictions and other factors for successful entry into the foreign market. If products will be made using foreign labor or materials, the international plan will cover such concerns as quality control, compliance with national labor laws, cross-border transport issues for finished products (or raw materials), brand identity and intellectual property protection. A business that has significant research and development capabilities might create a plan by which it will actually invent new products for a foreign market based on its assessment of needs and opportunities in that market. For successful entry into the foreign market, the company will make marketing plans based on the company's own brand identity and local distribution capabilities.

SERVICE BUSINESSES

Service providers are one of the fastest growing sectors of international trade. The success of convenience stores and restaurant franchises, such as McDonald's in multiple national markets is well documented. Moreover, as standardization increases in the area of information technology, companies are providing a bundle of technical consulting services to clients around the world. Accountancy, consultancy and law firms have all gotten into the act, often relying on local specialists to provide domestic advice and a network of offices to offer "real-time" services in other markets.

A service-based business faces unique challenges in doing business in new foreign markets, each of which calls for advance thinking that should be included in the international business plan. First and foremost, the company needs to determine the level of potential demand for the services in the new market. Second, the company needs to determine if the local environment is conducive to the company's core offerings. For example, the technical infrastructure of the country may not be mature enough to need or utilize the company's services. Finally, because a service business depends on the quality of its people as opposed to its goods, the company must be sure that it will be able to effectively service its clients with local employees.

E-BUSINESSES

With proper planning, almost every company can be an "e-business." One of the opportunities created by the growth of the Internet is the ability for businesses to market and sell goods to foreign clients and customers "online" without the need to set up and maintain local sales offices or contract with local distributors. However, for this strategy to succeed, the business owner must develop a plan to measure demand in foreign markets and the likelihood that clients and customers can be reached by online means, as opposed to more traditional promotional activities. Also, payment, shipping and export-import issues must be considered. In most cases, e-business is best viewed as an alternative to, not a replacement for, a "bricks-and-mortar" presence in the local market; at least until customers are comfortable with online ordering and communications. This, too, can be limited by the target market's infrastructure.

START-UP BUSINESSES

A start-up business confronts substantial risks, whether operations are limited strictly to domestic markets or extended to foreign nations. With a well-researched and carefully constructed international business plan, a firm might find that a global outlook will substantially increase the chances of success. For example, a fledgling business with limited financial resources may benefit from using low-cost manufacturers in foreign countries to produce goods that can be sold at attractive prices in the company's own domestic market. A new company also may seek out foreign markets where larger competitors have not yet become established. By building up a significant market share there, an entry barrier is created against competitors. The success of the product or service in a smaller foreign market can be used as a base for entering larger markets.

Five Key Features of a Viable Plan

There is no single method for producing a successful business plan. The attractiveness of a plan ultimately depends on the commercial viability of your company's products and/or services, and your ability to bring them to market and manage the operation. Nonetheless, it is worth reviewing the final draft of your business plan to see whether all or most of the following characteristics are present:

1. Provide readers with a clear sense of what your company intends to accomplish.

2. Have the plan cover an appropriate period of time, generally three to seven years, depending on the type of business and the objectives of the owners.

3. Include the three "Ms": manufacturing, marketing and management. For a service business, methodology replaces manufacturing.

4. Always quantify and qualify your statements.

5. Explain and document all financial projections, and make them realistic.

CHAPTER 3

Building a Plan: Fundamental Issues

THERE IS NOTHING MORE FRIGHTFUL THAN IGNORANCE

IN ACTION. — GOETHE

THIS CHAPTER COVERS THE FUNDAMENTAL ISSUES that need to be considered before, during and in final review of your international business plan. They are relevant when you are determining the scope and basic components of the plan, as well as when analyzing and planning for the risks inherent in doing business globally. Remember that for every plan there is a critical reviewer, whether it is an investor, an outside board member, an independent consultant or a senior manager in your company who has asked you to prepare a business plan. For just such a person—and regardless of why you are making the plan—always address these fundamental issues.

International Focus

Although domestic and international business plans have many of the same components, there is a distinct difference: an international plan is built on the fundamental premise that a company is looking at two or more countries as targets for potential sales and/or functional activities.

IDENTIFY THE GLOBAL FACTORS

Your plan will have an international focus only if you have identified the global aspects of your business. When preparing each section of the plan, be certain to ask the following questions:

- Can the company's products be adapted for use and sale in a foreign market? If so, which foreign markets?

- If there is potential foreign demand, have you done sufficient research to develop an appropriate marketing strategy in each target country?

- Has the company identified foreign partners that could assist in local manufacturing, operations and distribution?

- Does the company's organizational structure include resources for scanning foreign markets for new opportunities?

- What additional resources do you need for your domestic-focused company to implement a global strategy (e.g., new managers, capital, foreign offices, etc.)?

PLAN NOTE: As you write each section of the plan, ensure that you have considered global opportunities, established specific goals and included steps for achieving them.

Competitive Advantage

Of the billions of people on this planet, what makes you think that you can accomplish your business goals? Right now, there are probably dozens of other businesspeople in Palo Alto, Tel Aviv, New York, Tokyo, London and New Delhi thinking about business concepts similar to your own and targeting many of the same markets. Don't fool yourself into thinking you are the only one. Given that fact, how will you make your business succeed?

IDENTIFY IT

Identify your competitive advantages. This step is essential to success in global markets, and therefore, a key component in building a business plan. Compile a list of all competitive advantages that you can imagine. Include statements about relevant advantages in your plan and provide procedures and resources for implementing them in target markets.

Competitive advantages may be found in the potential opportunities that have attracted you to the international arena. One of the benefits of thinking globally is that it opens up a wide variety of strategies for identifying and securing access, for example, to low-cost labor and/or raw materials for manufacturing, by which you can gain a competitive advantage. However, identifying a competitive advantage on the international level is also particularly challenging, given that competitors are likely to arise from a number of different locations and competition is likely to be fast-paced and constantly changing.

You can gain competitive advantage by protecting your ideas and intentions, thereby slowing the progress of competitors. Take inventory of your intangible assets, such as patents, procedural manuals, trade secrets, other forms of intellectual property rights, exclusive distribution contracts and manufacturing agreements. All of these assets are valuable, provided you take measures to prevent competitors from using them.

PLAN NOTE: To share is human. You might have an exciting idea, so much so that you want to run out and shout it in the streets. But competitors will see the same opportunities that you do. To keep your competitive edge, you need to create barriers against other competitors who are trying to gain their own share of your intended markets. The first step is to make your plan a confidential document. Your plan, as well as all of your intellectual property rights, should be protected by means of nondisclosure agreements, company confidentiality training, memorandums and guidelines and registrations.

Your business plan also should provide for the establishment of barriers to competitors—that is, barriers that are legal (within the limits of fair trade). Special contractual arrangements can be made with suppliers and manufacturers to try to keep them from working with competitors. You need to plan to tap into intelligence from local market experts and to create a plan that is sufficiently flexible to allow for changes in markets, technology, locale, labor and other similar conditions to allow you to maintain competitive advantages.

Advance planning is important for protecting your competitive advantage. As part of your strategy, you will need to decide the time frame for your plan. Will you plan in advance for one year, three years, five years, ten years? You must consider such factors as how long it will take for your idea to be developed and presented to the market and how much time you will need to turn a profit. The protection barriers that you create will need to be sufficient to keep your competitors at bay, at least, until you have gained your intended share of the market.

Remember that a strategy to secure competitive advantage in one country may not hold up in another. For example, while companies in the E.U. are often able to rely on patents and other intellectual property rights to gain a head start over competitors, this strategy will not work well in countries where there is poor or non-existent enforcement of such rights. You will need to modify your plan's strategy to account for such differences, such as by introducing specialized marketing campaigns, training programs and promotional programs to raise brand value and awareness.

The Audience

Every entrepreneur or "intrapreneur" (an internal person proposing a new venture for an existing company) must write a plan with a specific audience in mind. The core information remains unchanged regardless of the audience; but you need to pay close attention to what the reader needs to know if your plan is going to help the reader, your company and you!

IDENTIFY IT

Start by taking good notes at the first meeting when the business plan drafting project is discussed. It's easy to become so focused on the general list of topics to be discussed in the plan that you forget about the primary reasons for preparing the plan. You need to determine who will be reviewing the plan and using the information included in it. Consider the following real-life situations:

- A mid-level manager is asked by the CEO to prepare a plan that includes recommendations for expanding company activities into foreign markets. In this case, the plan must not only make a case for entering specific markets, but also must lay out the steps that will need to be taken internally, such as upgrading the information system and hiring new managers with specific experience in each of the targeted markets.

- The board of directors has requested an annual budget and operating plan. If international activities are to be included, the plan must demonstrate global profitability and the company's strategy for dealing with country-specific risks.

- If sales activities in a specific market have already been approved, a manager may request a country-specific plan that is similar in scope and content to a plan that would have been prepared for activities solely in the company's domestic market. The plan would include extensive environmental and competitive analysis and detailed operating budgets for forecasting and monitoring purposes.

- You are asked to present a business plan to potential capital providers, including investors and commercial lenders. They are primarily interested in achieving a desired return on their investment. As such, the plan must contain detailed projections with reasonable assumptions that fall within the planning period of the provider. Many investors have investment horizons that are too short to support the long-term effort that may be required to build a global business.

◙ A potential business partner has asked you to provide a plan. The partner is a foreign firm interested in launching a joint venture to assist your company in entering a new market. In this case, the plan serves as a marketing tool to showcase the opportunities available to the partner. Specific details regarding revenues and expenses can be avoided until the relationship is formalized.

PLAN NOTE: After identifying your audience, review your business plan outline and determine which components will be most useful and which will be less helpful to the reader. Decide the emphasis of the plan, whether it is being developed for financial, marketing, long-term investment or operational purposes. Keep each core component in the plan, but write each with different stresses for different audiences.

A Clear Plan of Action

Managers often spend an inordinate amount of time describing the company's goods and services along with the tremendous market opportunities that they have identified. Marketing and management aspects are then dealt with in a cursory fashion, even though investors and consultants insist that a great idea is worthless without proper execution.

IDENTIFY IT

Plan for the three Ms: Manufacturing, Management and Marketing. In a service business, plan for Methodology, Management and Marketing. Don't overemphasize your product or service in your plan. It is only one component of your total business. Manufacturing or producing it, managing the business and marketing it are equally important. A great product or service alone is not enough. You have to get it to market at a profit, which requires a clear picture of the three Ms. In an international business plan, the three Ms carry even more significance because operating a global business requires attention to communications and logistics on a scale much grander than in a domestic business.

PLAN NOTE: While you can expect to spend significant time researching and writing the plan, you need to come to grips with the fact that your readers will probably take only a few minutes to determine if it's worth reading. So, be certain that the presentation is sharp, concise and progresses in an orderly fashion.
First of all, don't make readers flip pages to get to the heart of your plan. They won't. Include an executive summary. Most readers will not get beyond the summary, so make certain it is catchy and effective. A good summary increases the chance that the plan itself will be read. A bad summary can be fatal. Most advisors will tell you to write the executive summary last. This makes sense because you will learn a great deal from the discipline of writing the plan. If you save the summary until you have learned the lessons, you are in a better position to describe what you have learned about the business.

When putting your plan together, the following tips are useful:

■ GET TO THE POINT QUICKLY. You only have a few minutes to catch your reader's interest. Don't waste time.

■ MAKE SURE THE PLAN IS INTERESTING. Your plan must convey sufficient excitement about the business and opportunities to draw the reader in.

- **CHECK YOUR SPELLING AND GRAMMAR.** Read and re-read to make sure the plan is clear and free of errors. Be sure to run a spell check on your computer. Then have someone else read it. Nothing disturbs a reader more than sloppy drafting.

- **DON'T OVERWHELM THE READER.** Technical terms, acronyms and other jargon may be lost on the reader unless critical to the plan itself. The best plans are the easiest to understand, especially by readers who are unfamiliar with the industry.

- **MAKE SURE THE PLAN IS CURRENT.** Your credibility will suffer if research or financial information is out-of-date.

PLAN NOTE: A well composed Executive Summary can have an additional use outside of serving as an introduction to the business plan. It can serve as a "sell sheet" distributed to interested parties in lieu of the full plan. For entrepreneurs using online services to attract financing, it can also be posted on secure venture capital Web sites and forums.

A Great Team

The strength of a company is generally in its people. Management must have a clear vision and commitment. Carefully select each person for the talents that he or she brings to the table. This component of the plan is sometimes overlooked or treated minimally, but it can be a powerful indicator of whether the company is destined to succeed. Investors who are impressed with the team will be more likely to want to become a part of it. Experienced investors and venture capital firms often look at the management CVs first.

IDENTIFY THEM

In addition to identifying the staff that is already in place, you need to identify the positions that your company will need to fill. These might include research and development personnel, marketers, administrators, investors, labor and training managers, procurers and financial and legal advisors. This step includes an assessment of the talents, preferences and commitment of the key personnel already selected so that you can define their new roles in relationship to your global expansion and can also determine the missing links.

PLAN NOTE: A complete global business plan will describe the company's organization and its key players. The team that you have chosen can be a significant indicator of whether your business plan is worth the risk. Use your team's expertise to show that your impressive and exciting vision can become a reality.

At a minimum, the business plan will include a short description of the expertise and abilities of each core team member. Resumes are rarely offered in an internal business plan; but a plan that is to be presented to investors will normally include copies of the resumes of all key managers, engineers and scientists who will be involved in executing important parts of the strategy described. If your plan will include resumes, the information on the resumes needs to be restated in terms that show that the team has the requisite experience and skills to get the job done successfully.

Resumes are not just a listing of education and previous jobs. Focus on prior experiences and how they relate to the proposed business. Don't be afraid to list failures. Failures may be just fine as long as lessons were learned. Readers often understand their value.

A Well-Prepared Organization

Organizational analysis is a process of self-evaluation. Most companies regularly carry on organizational analysis so that management can quickly evaluate the potential value of new opportunities. Sometimes companies will ask outside consultants to give an independent, unbiased assessment of the organization to discover shortcomings not otherwise recognized by the company's own management. Global expansion makes little sense unless it provides an opportunity to address a specific organizational weakness or to build on a unique strength of the company.

Cover the following components of the company:

- Each of the main functional areas (e.g., for a manufacturer, these areas might be production, marketing, logistics and purchasing)

- The financial position of the company and the condition of its fixed assets

- The position of the company in its domestic market and any future trends that might make it prudent to seek new outlets for its products

- The managerial and technical skills of the company's existing workers

PLAN NOTE: When selecting the management team, take care that each team member's new job title is related to past experience. You cannot take someone with a purely engineering background and pass him off as the new marketing director simply to fill a slot on the organizational chart. If you don't have the right personnel to assemble the full team today, state in the plan how and when the expertise will be acquired. Many venture capital firms, for instance, provide managers to fill these gaps as part of their services.

Utilize the organizational analysis to develop specific company objectives for its global strategy. Deal with each objective in your business plan, including the purpose for pursuing it. For example, a company may find that it is expending excessive sums in trying to produce its products, which is dampening its profits and causing it to cut quality in order to hold prices at a competitive level. The company's objective may be to increase profitability by reducing variable costs through use of lower priced labor and raw materials available in foreign countries. If this is the case, emphasize it in the business plan.

Analysis of the Negatives

Every good business plan, including one prepared solely for internal use, will address potential problems and risks associated with achieving the positive goals in other parts of the plan. Identify these issues in the environmental analysis prepared for each new country market. In the case of an investor-focused plan, include the negative analysis in a separate "risk factors" section.

IDENTIFY THEM

Not every aspect of your journey to business success has been or will be smooth. For each problem, face it, describe it and tell how you learned from it or will overcome it. If there is competition, tell how you are better and will beat them. Don't let an investor or a senior manager wonder about a problem you skipped. The reader probably won't bother to ask, but will toss your plan aside as being unreliable or dishonest.

PLAN NOTE: Another way to intelligently deal with uncertainties is through alternative projections based on different assumptions. The best business plans include two or more sets of pro forma projections based on varying scenarios with respect to a key variable. These could include such variables as the level of demand in the new country or the failure of a country to adopt an anticipated technology as rapidly as the company may have expected. Although the SWOT process has become a bit dated, analysis of the Strengths, Weaknesses, Opportunities and Threats that face a company still goes on under other guises. Expect the best, plan for the worst.

Requirement of Confidentiality

If you reveal your business plan to the competition, you are likely to start a race to the marketplace. In some countries, laws may protect your rights, but don't count on it. Even if you can prove who was first and who has the rights to the plan, you will have spent a lot of cash and resources doing so. More importantly, you will already have lost your competitive edge.

IDENTIFY CONFIDENTIAL MATTERS

The information in the business plan is confidential and proprietary. It is a trade secret of your business. Likewise, your product or service research and development notes, memorandums and reports are trade secrets, and so are your marketing tools, customer and client lists, global expansion plans, contractual arrangements and other similar items that are not easily available to the general public. All of these items have value—property value. Carefully protect them against disclosure to competitors or the public at large.

Take particular care to ensure that the business plan does not include information that has been obtained from a third party, such as a prior employer or a competitor. Do not include proprietary and confidential materials belonging to a third party in your plan unless proper authorization for use has been obtained.

Also, carefully maintain the confidentiality of your company's proprietary information by implementing the following:

- Bind the business plan and include a cover with your company's name and primary address, the date of creation and a clearly visible legend stating, "Confidential and Proprietary Information." Make it obvious that disclosure is forbidden under all circumstances unless prior written approval of authorized persons is obtained.

- Emphasize the confidential nature of the plan to your company's directors, managers and all employees during their initial training and introduction to the company, in periodic follow-up training sessions and in exit interviews when such persons leave the company.

- Restrict distribution of the plan and retain all copies in safekeeping. Don't simply leave copies lying around or available on bookshelves.

- Limit the total number of copies of the plan. Require all company personnel to sign confidentiality agreements that specifically name the company's trade secrets, including the business plan.

- Require all recipients of the plan—potential marketers, licensees, franchisees, investors and so forth—to execute nondisclosure agreements that cover the information in the business plan, plus all additional information gained through meetings or discussions with the company's representatives.

- Maintain a record log of disclosure showing the person, date and purpose.

ADVISORY: Keep in mind that not everyone likes to be confronted with legal issues before even having had a chance to see the plan. Many venture capital firms, business "incubator" services or consultancies flatly refuse to sign such agreements because they say it ties their hands in their efforts to promote your plan. The prevailing attitude here is "If you want our help, you will have to trust us." If they are trusted firms with established records, you may wish to waive the non-disclosure process. If not, you will have to judge on a case by case basis.

Also, if you are considering floating your plan outside of your domestic legal system, be aware that intellectual property rights are not universally held in high regard. Someone may sign a non-disclosure agreement with the full knowledge that you could never enforce its restrictions should it be violated. If confidentiality is a major concern, check to see if such an agreement can be upheld in the local jurisdiction.

A Schedule for Implementation

Make your business plan a living and working document that serves as a guide for operation and direction of the company. As such, drafting of the plan itself must also be accompanied by implementation of procedures and practices to monitor the progress of the company against the action items and performance goals included in the plan. While these procedures need not be part of the plan itself, make sure they are clearly understood by all responsible persons within the organization.

MAKE IT A PRIORITY

Make the preparation and maintenance of your international business plan a high priority activity for the company and the members of the working group. Treat it in the same way as any other "mission critical" task within the organization, such as new product development or creation and execution of a marketing campaign.

Accompany the reporting and analyzing of business performance with incentives for timely completion of the tasks enumerated in the plan. Incentives are quite common when investors have been asked to supply capital to support a new initiative, such as launching operations in a new foreign market. For example, under an incentive program, managers might be rewarded with bonuses for exceeding projections. On the other hand, failure of the management team to meet projections may trigger a right in favor of the investors to impose restrictions on managerial discretion, and even to reduce salaries.

PLAN NOTE: The best way to be sure the plan is completed on a timely basis, and that the plan remains an important part of the ongoing strategic process of the company, is to establish a strict timetable for drafting and review among the working group members. Even before the business plan is complete, implementation will begin with the assembly of the working group described in Chapter 5. Once the plan has been drafted and approved by the relevant parties, prepare a calendar that lays out the milestones described in the plan and a schedule of meetings to review progress. In addition, make provision for periodic written reports that include financial and other business information for specified periods and detailed comparisons of operational results to the projections and goals of the plan.

Your implementation timetable might include all or most of the following elements:

- INITIAL MEETING Set up an initial meeting among senior managers to confirm the need for preparation of the business plan. This may sound a little silly, particularly when you are the senior management team. However, things have a way of falling through the cracks unless some sort of official directive has been issued.

- PRIMARY PURPOSE Determine the primary purpose of the plan and the specific issues that need to be covered as part of the plan. As discussed elsewhere, the emphasis of a business plan may vary depending on the company and the intended purpose. In the case of an international business plan, pay attention to the specific countries that need to be analyzed as new markets and/or sources for functional activities or raw materials.

- ASSEMBLE THE EXPERTS Depending on the purpose of the plan and the issues to be covered, assemble the group of experts and researchers who are best suited to collect the information and assemble it into a coherent plan. If operations in a particular part of the world are contemplated, recruit country experts along with local accounting and legal counsel.

- TIMETABLE Establish a strict timetable for preparation of the initial draft and for circulation of the drafts for comment and revision. Set time aside for the "editor" of the plan to sift through the drafts and reconcile any overlap of content among parts written by different drafters.

- IDENTIFY RESOURCES Identify ancillary resources that you may need in order to draft or execute the plan. For example, if overseas employees will have to be recruited, initiate contacts with local search agencies. In many cases, recruits can provide valuable input into the final stages of the business planning process. You will need to involve your outside accountants in preparation of historical financial information and projections of future performance.

- COLLATERAL MATERIALS Make sure that all collateral materials are prepared and ready to use in any formal presentations of the plan. Collateral materials include slide presentations and "sell sheets" (short summaries) that can be handed out at meetings. Don't forget that you often have to sell your plan to others, both inside and outside the company.

- GUIDELINES Establish guidelines for monitoring the progress of the plan and the company's ability to meet designated milestones. Ask the financial reporting department of the company to prepare comparisons of actual performance to projections so that any variances can be analyzed. Regular meetings of the working group must continue after the plan is completed. Also, plan to update the plan periodically. Whenever an update is contemplated, each section of the plan should be completely reviewed as if it had never been written before.

What a Business Analyst Looks for in a Business Plan

As a former entrepreneur accustomed to seeking investment capital, and later, as a business analyst for a seed stage investment firm, I have had the opportunity to gain a deep understanding of what investors really look for when funding a business opportunity. My goal is to pass along the basic nuts and bolts of what investors look for when evaluating new venture opportunities in the form of a business plan.

Bear in mind that you have to get past a business analyst before the money people in a venture capital firm take a look at your plan. For many entrepreneurs, coming up with the next million-dollar idea is not a problem. However, entrepreneurs struggle when it comes to writing a business plan that can effectively present their idea. I have heard rumors of entrepreneurs getting funding on an idea scribbled on a napkin, particularly during the early dot-com boom. That luxury is clearly not the case now since investors are now getting back to the fundamentals of sound business models. Now, more than ever, a thorough business plan is a necessity if you want to get investment capital.

So what do investors look for in a business plan? Typically, they look for answers to three basic questions:

1. How does the proposed opportunity solve a problem within a niche market?

2. Do the founding team members have the competency to make this venture work?

3. Can we realize a high enough return to make it worth our while?

These questions should be addressed in the executive summary, as well as in the body of the business plan. The executive summary should be no more than two pages and contain convincing statements within your business plan that address the three magic questions.

As a business analyst, the first thing I did when reading the business plan was to read the executive summary and then immediately turn to the section of the business plan that outlines the founding members domain expertise and core competencies. That way I get a quick feel of what problem is that the business solves and if the team members have the ability, if funded, to run and grow the company.

If those two questions are adequately answered, I will continue reading sections of the business plan that answer the final question: Can we realize a return on investment?

To determine if we can get a return on investment, we looked for several factors. The first is the company's marketing strategy. Business plans that mention a one million-dollar budget of television advertising are not appealing. This type of "push-marketing" is not as effective as a "pull-through" marketing approach. The key to pull-through marketing is to partner with a company that already has brand recognition and can pull your product or company into the market quickly. So it is important to establish partnerships and communicate those relationships in the business plan.

(continued next page)

What a Business Analyst Looks for (cont.)

The second factor we looked for in terms of return on investment is the monetization strategy. In other words, how is your company going to make money? Is the pricing structure reasonable? Is the number of potential customers reasonable? Is the amount of money required enough to generate the revenues projected?

The last important component for return on investment is competition and barriers to entry. An investor will always want to know how much competition is fighting for market share within the marketplace. If your company has a first-mover advantage to market a new product or service, investors will want to know if you have taken provisions to prevent competitors from quickly taking your hard-earned market share. This is called "creating a barrier to entry." There are several ways to creating a barrier to entry. One is through patents and trademarks to protect your company's technology or brand image. Another is to strategically align or partner with a company that is critical in the value chain to fulfill your company's product or service. This can make it difficult for other companies to break into the market.

In summary, regardless of how well your business plan is written, investors only fund valid opportunities. Many people ask me what we did if a business plan misspelled words or had grammatical errors. Misspelled words and grammatical errors won't kill a business plan, but it simply should not happen. Business plans are a reflection of your work and ability to pay attention to detail. Always have a fresh set of eyes proofread your business plan. Answer the three magic questions throughout your business plan with a powerful executive summary and you will be on the path to funding.

Lance Perkins

ADVISORY: Venture capital (VC) has served as a spur to the growth of many industries worldwide, but it comes with a price for the entrepreneur. VC firms will want to control a substantial part of a company's stock (think 40%) and have input into the operations of the business. Entrepreneurs often find it difficult to relinquish control of the project and may resist any and all operational input.

On the other hand, VC firms are usually composed of people that have already done what you are trying to do, so their experience may be both valid and useful. If you work with a VC firm be sure to take advantage of all the expertise they have to offer. This expertise may be more valuable than the capital they provide!

CHAPTER 4

Building a Plan: Global Expansion Issues

VISION IS THE ART OF SEEING THINGS INVISIBLE.

— JONATHAN SWIFT

ALL SUCCESSES (AND FAILURES!) START WITH AN IDEA. Successful ideas are developed over time, in large part by examining the issues that will affect their possible success or failure. A good international business plan will bring up these issues and answer key questions about how the organization is going to turn its idea into a success.

Therefore, before you begin drafting your international business plan, you and your senior managers need to do an analysis of the factors that will impact the proposed international expansion. Typically, this analysis is organized around four issues:

ISSUE 1: ENVIRONMENTAL FACTORS

Environmental factors are the external forces that flow primarily from outside the firm and create pressures, demands and opportunities for the business. This includes the business, industry and competitive environment that the company will face in each of the target markets.

ISSUE 2: FOREIGN MARKET ENTRY

Foreign market entry factors include all issues related to bringing the product or service to market in each targeted foreign market.

ISSUE 3: GLOBAL FINANCIAL ISSUES

Global financial issues relate primarily to financing the international venture, but also relate to international movement of funds, international payment methods, foreign exchange, repatriation of capital and receipt of profits.

ISSUE 4: LEGAL AND REGULATORY ISSUES

Legal and regulatory issues relate to the differences in laws and regulations of each of the proposed foreign markets and places of business operation.

The results of this analysis will provide the essential foundation stones of your business plan. If you have already completed such an analysis, then a quick review of this chapter will be helpful to check whether you have covered all issues.

Issue 1: Environmental Analysis

An environmental analysis is a thorough study of the risks and opportunities associated with moving into foreign markets in an effort to assess what the global business community has to offer your business. It is important in developing the company's own strategies and procedures for the conduct of day-to-day operations and expansion. The end product of this analysis can be seen in the specific functional goals of the company as written into the business plan.

To develop a well-considered and complete strategy, the analysis is made at the global level generally and then for each country and industry specifically.

- INTERNATIONAL All countries participate in the global economy as buyers, suppliers, competitors, capital providers and consumers. Changes in international markets can have a substantial effect on the local business environment confronting a new entrant. For example, changes in international pricing for major imports or exports can quickly alter the costs of operating in an individual country or throw a local economy into disarray. A similar problem can arise when there is a significant economic change in a bilateral alliance partner, such as might occur when a country's largest national trading partner enters a recession.

- NATIONAL National government strategies impact the business environment. Governmental advancement of and proactive interference with economic development is controversial. Many countries, particularly (but not exclusively) in the developing world, have chosen to adopt a wide range of governmental policies and compliance instruments that will be impacted by cultural and political factors. As such, managers entering a new foreign market must be prepared to expend the time and effort necessary to understand and interpret the national strategies in the target country and prepare for them in the business plan.

- INDUSTRY The traditional concern for competitive factors that applies to any market entry decision, domestic or foreign, becomes more complicated when going global because of the special conditions that exist within specific countries with different institutional histories. For example, managers may need to contend with competition from state-owned enterprises, business associations of commonly-owned firms engaged in related activities or small local producers. These entities may operate in informal sectors largely outside the regulations and restrictions imposed on foreign firms and larger domestic corporations.

The factors to be considered in the analysis cover a wide range of areas, including economics, politics, technology and competition, culture and social demographics. Among the questions to be asked and answered are the following:

- Are there business and economic opportunities for the company in other countries that warrant the required investment of capital and other resources?

- Can the company achieve an advantage over its direct and projected competitors by going global or is globalization required to keep up with the competition?

- Can the company gain access to new technologies in other countries and can it also protect its own proprietary position with respect to its intangible assets?

- What political, legal, financial and social risks must be overcome to enter a new market?

PLAN NOTE: The results of the environmental analysis are usually written into a business plan as part of the background information on each foreign market. This information is also useful in formulating a plan's strategy to deal country-by-country with such issues as business-government relations, entry strategies, marketing and strategic alliances. Thus, this analysis will form the basis of the specific business goals stated in the plan. Whatever you do, don't "pull your punches" or succumb to "political correctness" when describing the problems. The company's success may hinge on these environmental factors and they should be as accurate in their description as other information in the plan.

ECONOMIC FACTORS

Economic factors include natural resources, human resources, capital, infrastructure and technology. The characteristics associated with these different factors change as countries develop. Although there are some exceptions (e.g., natural resources will remain a dominant economic factor for oil-producing countries regardless of the overall stage of economic development), development tends to decrease the importance of natural resources. At the same time, the trend is to expand the pool of skilled labor, increase the income available for domestic consumption and investment, strengthen physical infrastructure and internal information flow and bolster technology.

■ NATURAL RESOURCES To create and maintain a viable international business plan, managers must monitor the development of natural resources and raw materials in targeted countries. What is the significance of natural resources to the local economy? What is the quantity and quality of available natural resources? If one or more resource is central to the local economy, a wise manager will consider whether there is an opportunity to utilize that resource in a global expansion strategy. Most likely, the foreign government will devote significant attention, and quite possibly, offer attractive investment incentives to industries in that sector. In addition, performance of that sector will probably influence overall economic conditions in the country, which may provide a useful means of forecasting local economic trends.

■ HUMAN RESOURCES Before committing to a new foreign market, an assessment of local labor is essential. Your business plan will fail if you forget to allow for education and training programs in countries where there is a scarcity of skilled labor. You may need to import skilled workers or managers and offer attractive incentives to keep them on the job. If a company intends to divert some of its own managerial resources into a new market, it also must plan how it will handle the tensions and misunderstandings that might arise among workers who are from different cultural, religious, educational and political backgrounds. Many countries offer real opportunities for foreign firms to gain access to a large pool of low-cost labor; but it is essential to plan for compliance with local labor laws, which are becoming more prevalent as a means of protecting domestic laborers from overreaching by foreign employers.

ADVISORY: Many developing countries have quotas on how many foreign managers can be brought in to set up operations, and there may be time limits on how long they can stay before being replaced by local managers. Foreign firms will be expected to supply the bulk of the management training and they may be required to pay the local managers at rates commensurate with the foreign managers. Market entrants are advised to research this HR (human resources) topic well in advance.

- CAPITAL Issues related to capital are two-fold: spending and receiving. Make your company's business plan clear as to what financial resources the company will need when entering a new market and what amount of return it can anticipate for its investment.

  In some countries, the government will offer attractive financing and incentives to new foreign investment. However, in many places, private and public domestic capital is scarce. Accordingly, foreign firms must come prepared to provide the necessary cash to fund their activities until they are self-sustaining. A company that sufficiently finances its global expansion will be able to seize market opportunities today with a view to long-term presence and profits.

  On the receiving side, the business plan should give a realistic picture of what the company can expect to gain. Do your homework on market demand and local purchasing power by examining income levels and savings rates in the target market, as well as the pattern of income distribution. Some questions:

  - Do consumers tend to limit their purchases to necessities or do they spend on luxuries?
  - Is the local currency stable and does the local population have confidence in its own financial institutions?
  - Is bank credit available to allow domestic companies to finance purchases of foreign equipment and goods?
  - How strong are local financial institutions, and are they privately or publicly operated?
  - What is the inflation rate, and how is inflation controlled?
  - Are there foreign exchange restrictions, making it costly and difficult to purchase raw materials or services overseas and import them into the country so that your operations will need to rely on whatever local resources might be available?
  - Will you need to alter the type and quality of your production technologies in the new market if you have to use local resources?

- INFRASTRUCTURE Virtual commerce may be the trend, but business is still conducted within the confines of a physical infrastructure. Every international business plan must consider whether the company's required infrastructure will be supported by the country's existing infrastructure, including such facilities and institutions as transportation, utilities and energy, postal and telecommunications. If any of these are lacking, you will need to plan to invest in systems that will allow you to operate in the targeted country. You may need to construct your own building or roads, maintain power generators and implement special satellite and communications systems. If a country has minimal facilities for compiling market research information, you will need to set up and maintain informal and personal communication networks to obtain reliable data on supply and demand, prices, technology, financing and government regulations.

- TECHNOLOGY An understanding of the state of technology in a targeted country is essential to a successful global expansion plan. If a company offers technology-based goods or services, the value of such items will depend on whether consumers can understand and use them in daily activities. Even if goods or services are not technology-based, the company is likely to rely on technology to increase the efficiency of its own manufacturing, marketing and operational functions.

A business plan must therefore account for the level of technical skill and knowledge among local workers and consumers, the sources of domestic technological development and the degree to which the specific country is reliant on technology imports. With advance planning, a company can anticipate the need to modify the technology content of its goods or services and to provide marketing and training programs. It might find new markets for technologies that have become obsolete in more developed countries. It may also be able to take advantage of a local technology transfer arrangement, which is a form of investment incentive sometimes offered when a country seeks to raise its technological base.

POLITICAL FACTORS

Political factors include stability, ideology, institutions and geopolitical links. Predictably, less developed countries tend to suffer from greater instability in the political process, less sophisticated public and private institutions and excessive dependence on a limited number of international linkages. The first two factors can significantly increase the so-called political risk to foreign investors while the later issue may limit the supply and distribution channels available to foreign investors who establish a base there.

- **STABILITY** Political stability refers to the degree of predictability in government policies and the continuity of the main political leaders in the country. In general, an unstable political environment is evidenced by authoritarian governments that change frequently, creating a business environment fraught with high risk and few guarantees for investors. In a stable government, the policies of the leaders are well-defined and the system of elections and legislative actions is accepted and transparent. If a company is considering entering a foreign market with a history of political instability, give careful analysis of the probability that changes might occur during the planning period and of the likely impact on the company. The adverse effects of political instability might be lessened or eliminated if a company's products are so essential or uniquely attractive to the foreign market that a change in control will have little impact on the business model.

- **IDEOLOGY AND NATIONAL STRATEGY** National ideology is the set of beliefs and assumptions about values that a country's population holds to justify and legitimize the actions and purposes of its institutions. Social attitudes, historical development foundations, economic maturation and similar factors should be assessed in considering whether a foreign company will be easily accepted and welcomed in a new market.

During the planning process, identify and analyze the ideological beliefs underlying a new market to anticipate the impact of those beliefs on the company as it enters the market. Are there restrictions on foreign participation and investment in the country? Has the country enacted regulatory requirements that increase costs and cause delays to foreign companies as opposed to domestic ones? Are local businesses afforded preferred access to domestic markets, sources of credit and other resources?

PLAN NOTE: Locating accurate, focused and unbiased sources on a country's ideology and national strategy can be difficult. Resources might include official government planning documents, speeches or presentations made by government officials and possibly the country's own published multi-year economic plans that include explicit goals and targets. Such plans were commonly produced in socialist countries during the 1960s and 1970s. However, a country's own plan must be viewed with caution because it might reflect what the political leaders prefer to publicize while in fact bearing little relation to the actual political and economic processes at work there.

Although each country has unique national goals, a business plan analysis of a country's strategy should, at minimum, focus on the following categories:

- *Economic growth*, usually measured by reference to the compound growth rate of GDP, is generally a key long-term goal and should be tied to strategies for the encouragement of domestic and foreign investment.
- *Rise in national income and standard of living*, resulting in increased consumption of domestic goods and services. Unfortunately, rising consumption can also cause conflicts with the need to invest disposable income to achieve long-term economic growth.
- *Equitable distribution of economic opportunities and resources*, which may require expansion of educational and other training programs and the use of income redistribution strategies.
- *Generation of new employment opportunities*, both as a method of furthering economic growth and as a basic social requirement.
- *Support to develop resources particular to one or more sector* of the country's economy or population, such as agriculture, industry, health, education or housing.
- *Preservation of national sovereignty* by establishing national security strategies and developing control over access to essential natural resources. For every ruling regime, preservation of its own authority often dominates some or all of the goals listed above.

Once you have completed the initial analysis, you should periodically measure national performance in relation to the country's stated goals and strategies, and again your business plan should be your guide. Various indicators can be used, in part, depending on what is available for each country. The most common are as follows:

- *Economic performance indicators,* including compound growth rate in real GDP, growth rates in specific sectors, annual inflation rates, savings and investment rates, generally expressed as a percentage of the country's GDP, balance of payments and employment rates.
- *Social performance indicators,* including literacy levels, infant and child mortality rates, life expectancies, years of education and completion rates, income distribution, incidence of specific diseases and average number of inhabitants in each household. In many countries, daily food consumption is an important factor, particularly where malnutrition has been a significant health problem.
- *Political performance,* including the degree of stability as indicated by the number of, and reasons for, changes in ruling regimes or important ministries, the number of significant events of civil disobedience, restrictions on basic freedoms and the transparency and certainty of the rule of law.
- *Historical development,* including social and economic problems that may have influenced the country's current goals and strategies, foreign invasions and occupations and political struggles for independence from colonial rulers.

PLAN NOTE: Mexico in the early 1980s faced rampant inflation and huge balance-of-payments and budgetary problems. It had little choice but to adopt short-term strategies that emphasized repair of credit markets, import restrictions and limited state spending. As a result, many long-term growth initiatives had to be deferred until preexisting problems, some of which were created by factors beyond the country's control, could be solved or contained.

■ POLITICAL INSTITUTIONS A country's political institutions are revealing of its ideology and stability. For this reason, review the activities of a country's political parties, government agencies, courts, labor unions, agricultural cooperatives, universities and industry associations. In addition, you should consider whether any particular groups within the country—perhaps members of a particular ethnic group, aristocratic classes or groups of landowners—might carry sufficient power to influence government policies, outlook and regulation. How might these relevant institutions and political constituencies hinder or assist the success of your business? How can you minimize the risk and secure the advantage?

Build into your plan a means of handling the probable inefficiencies and costly government decisions that often arise from the workings of a country's bureaucracy. Very likely, you will need to gain an understanding of the interests and goals of the respective institutions and their leaders, knowledge which will then be useful in negotiating trade advantages and in anticipating events.

A key step to success is to establish solid relations with local government officials. You will need to identify the various actors who may have authority over the company's business activities at the national, regional and local levels. For example, a company may need to seek the favor of national cabinet ministers to gain approval of investment in a new manufacturing facility, and then must deal with local customs officials to ensure the efficient import of required parts and materials for the manufacturing activity to proceed.

ADVISORY: One of the best sources of information about how the politics operate in a new and unfamiliar market is the community of "expats" (resident foreigners) who have either done business or lived in the country for an extended period. They will not only know how business is treated by government but they will have a better take on how foreign firms are regarded by local politicians and bureaucrats. They are usually more than happy to hold forth on this topic—but always corroborate their information.

In developing an effective governmental relations strategy, management must carefully identify the relevant actors. This process is best undertaken at two levels:

1. LOOK OUTSIDE YOUR COMPANY. Analyze the key governmental policy areas that might impact your company's activities, such as foreign investment, credit and financing and import and export. Next, identify the main political departments responsible for reviewing and deciding those policies. Finally, work with local consultants and advisors to identify specific departments or units involved in each type of review and decision.

2. LOOK INSIDE YOUR COMPANY. The most difficult and time-consuming governmental and regulatory problems often arise in the course of daily operations. Accordingly, you should poll managers in your company to identify the governmental officials who handle designated functional tasks. This process serves several purposes. First, it adds officials to the company's own "political

map" of who needs to be consulted. Second, it reinforces the significance of governmental relations to all managers in the company. Third, it allows senior managers to identify connections between the national policy makers and lower level officials who carry out those mandates.

The end product of your analysis will be a list of various types of political actors that are relevant to the development of a governmental relations strategy for your company. Each country has its own institutions, which may include any of the following:

- **NATIONAL LEVEL OFFICIALS AND REGULATORY BODIES** Seek out ministries and other governmental units with influence over any required approval for the company's investments or operations. Try to anticipate problems and form strategic alliances to ease the bureaucratic process. Look for unofficial connections. For example, a foreign investment may be reviewed by a central board or department, which in turn may elicit comments from another ministry that has authority over operations involving valuable raw materials or technology that the country desires to import for use by local firms.

- **BUREAUCRATS AND CIVIL SERVANTS** National policy makers may be ousted in elections or other political processes, eliminating useful relationships that your company may have formed. For this reason, nurture the good favor of bureaucrats and civil servants who are likely to remain employed through election turnover. These regional and local officials can wield significant authority, such as in the issuance of building permits, approval and utilization of governmental services or interpretation and application of operational regulations.

- **STATE-OWNED ENTERPRISES** A state-owned enterprise might become either a significant purchaser of the company's products, a supplier of the company's raw materials, a competitor or strategic partner. Often, these enterprises have monopolistic or dominant positions in the local market, making it important to understand how such enterprises interact with the mainstream political and bureaucratic system.

- **POLITICAL PARTY OFFICIALS** Regardless of a country's size or state of development, political party officials will generally exercise significant power. Unelected party leaders can influence the selection of nominees for elections and can be strong lobbyists for the company's interests. If possible, seek friends in the country's large political parties, particularly if a change in power is likely to occur while the company is doing business there. However, a bipartisan strategy could be problematic in countries where transitions occur outside the election process.

- **LABOR LEADERS** Labor leaders can be important actors, particularly if they exercise significant political influence. Labor unions may represent large blocks of voters and can create economic chaos when the government is unwilling to maintain an ongoing dialogue relating to working conditions. Even if a strike does not directly impact the local operations of your company, civil unrest could cripple the domestic economy and adversely impact demand and buying power.

- **SPECIAL INTERESTS** Special interest groups—such as industry associations, consumer activists or environmental activists—may be significant players with respect to various industries and business issues. Although these groups are not officially part of the government structure, they often exercise substantial influence with elected leaders.

ADVISORY: When selecting local consultants or middle-men, be wary of those that claim to have excellent political connections. There are four possibilities: they may, as they state, actually have friends in high places, they may have friends in low places, they may have friends in the wrong places or they may have no friends at all. Trust is good, verification is better.

■ GEOPOLITICAL RELATIONSHIPS Cross-border relationships between countries can have an adverse affect upon trade with one or all of the country members. Therefore, be aware of these connections and plan for opportunities as well as problems. A review of a country's historical development will often disclose its geopolitical relationships, such as vestiges of colonial heritage, war alliances, economic trading pacts, unions and religious and cultural links. Successful entry into one country could easily lead to expansion into another country with close geopolitical ties. On the negative side, rivalry between neighboring countries (e.g., Taiwan and China, Greece and Turkey) could cause unforeseen and dramatic disruptions in business and economic conditions confronting foreign investors.

CULTURAL AND SOCIAL VALUES

Culture is the set of shared values, attitudes and behaviors that characterize and guide a group of people. Of environmental factors, cultural ones are usually the most difficult to evaluate because they vary significantly from country-to-country and changes may occur as countries develop economically. Moreover, although managers can acquire expectations about a country's culture, generalizations are unwise because specific individuals frequently have their own views and habits. Nevertheless, the following factors could be important to your business plan strategy:

■ SOCIAL STRUCTURE AND DYNAMICS An understanding of prevailing norms relating to social structure is important for predicting how local managers and workers will respond to various directives and incentives. It is also essential to know what ties might bind workers to each other and how those bonds might affect company loyalty. In many countries, businesses are built on strong family ties, making it tough for an outsider to gain a foothold.

Social structure and dynamics are typically analyzed in terms of the following three continuums:

▪ *Individualism vs. Collectivism* A population's most common attitudes analyzed in terms of a range from individualism (characterized by independence and self-reliance, such as in the U.S.) on one end to collectivism (featuring responsibilities to a group, such as in Japan) on the opposite end.

▪ *The Individual* The structure and nature of individual relationships, which can range from hierarchical (authority concentrated in a few people or one person) on one side to egalitarian (authority distributed horizontally throughout a group or organization) on the other side.

▪ *Society* The interactions within the society, which may range from autocratic (all decisions made unilaterally without formal consultation of others) at one extreme to participative (a number of parties take part in the deliberative process) at the other extreme.

■ TIME CONCEPTION Differences in conceptions of time between members of different cultures can have significant, if unexpected, effects on a business relationship. For example, managers in the United Kingdom are extremely time-conscious and view time as a limited resource that must be managed with care. In contrast, managers in Thailand consider time to be an abundant resource and tend to place less emphasis on punctuality and strict contract deadlines. These different attitudes could greatly complicate agreements regarding scheduling; and they can be especially problematic for managers who are obligated to deliver goods produced in one foreign market to other parts of the company's organization for consumption or distribution.

■ HUMAN NATURE Societies tend to view the basic nature of human beings differently, including the changeability of their nature. These beliefs often flow from religious values and can have significant importance to managers. For example, if the dominant societal belief is that humans are basically good and trustworthy, management can probably use looser controls and a relatively low level of supervision. On the other hand, in a society where people are viewed as untrustworthy, a company's structure will usually be based on autocratic procedures, tight supervision and rigid control mechanisms. In a society where human nature is thought to be modifiable, management is more likely to be successful when implementing educational and personal development programs.

■ RELIGION In most developing countries and many industrialized nations, religion is a predominant factor, influencing all aspects of political, social and economic life. Religion can be an important determinant of a population's values regarding social structures and human nature, and its impact can be felt throughout the workplace and local markets. Holiday schedules, notions of ethical behavior, conduct in the workplace and business-related entertainment can all be affected by the dominant religious practices of employees. Always account for religion in gauging consumer preferences and creating promotional campaigns. Certain markets might have minimal demand for some products, such as alcohol or pork, because of the population's religious practices. There may also be opportunities for companies that supply products utilized for specific religious practices, such as specially prepared foods or gifts.

■ GENDER ROLES The role of women in society, the workplace and the marketplace is a changing phenomenon. Educate yourself about the practices and trends in each target market with respect to the acceptance of women in education and in employment outside of the home. Women might be a significant market for home products or they might be a potential labor force. It is essential, however, to understand gender-based divisions of responsibilities that apply in a country.

■ LANGUAGE One of the most obvious areas of cultural differences among and within countries is the use of language. Language diversity is a particularly difficult challenge for managers entering a new foreign market. As the cultural medium of communication, language includes the spoken and written word, as well as the style of expression, the use of context and the accompanying nonverbal signals (i.e., "body language"). A single country could even have multiple languages. India, for example, has more than a dozen major languages and hundreds of dialects. Africa has hundreds of tribal languages, at least fifty of which are used by groups exceeding one million people. In addition to ensuring the accuracy and inoffensiveness of internal communications within a company, managers must have a plan to create, translate, transliterate, review and recheck names, slogans and advertising strategies to account for local understanding.

PLAN NOTE: Some countries, such as France, have very strict laws about language that impact everything from packaging, to advertising, to radio and TV content. Other countries, like Vietnam or Malaysia, often target foreign firms and their advertisements as "cultural evils." These considerations must be taken into account in advance to avoid legal and financial troubles in the future.

DEMOGRAPHIC FACTORS

In constructing your business plan, always understand the demographics of each targeted country and periodically review those factors for trends and changes that might signal the need for a corresponding change in your plan. Demographic factors include population growth, age structure, health factors and migratory trends. Each factor can influence the pool of available labor and marketing strategies. Studies have uncovered clear relationships between demographic factors and the overall level of economic development in a country. For example, demographic factors can indicate the following:

- GROWTH RATES Decreasing population growth rates tend to indicate a mature economy whereas relatively high population growth suggests a developing country, which can create opportunities for companies in saturated markets to tap into a new group of customers.

- YOUNG POPULATIONS High percentage of a younger population suggests a less developed country and shorter life expectancy, with an inexperienced, but trainable, labor force. It also suggests the need for health benefits to ensure stability in the workforce.

- PERCAPITA INCOME A rapidly growing population does not necessarily correlate with increasing per capita income, which tends to grow less quickly than the number of consumers; therefore, the demand for basic consumer goods will be healthier in a high population growth environment than the demand for luxury goods.

- UNREST High population growth may be a harbinger of social and political unrest if the country lacks the infrastructure and financial resources to house and educate its new citizens.

- MIGRATION Migration to urban areas can cause infrastructure problems for government planners because developing countries generally lack financial, human and institutional resources required to support a metropolitan area, which will in turn increase the cost of doing business for a firm looking to locate in urban areas.

- URBAN Urban migration may offer increased market demand in a smaller geographic area, which may prove valuable when entering the market, provided advertising, transport, storage and sales infrastructure are adequate.

- IMMIGRATION Immigration trends and policies can indicate whether well-educated workers are leaving the country to seek opportunities in other economies (the so-called "brain drain"), which may affect the quality of local managerial and scientific talent.

Issue 2: Foreign Market Entry Strategies

In preparing an international business plan, you need to be aware of the various strategic tools available for entering a new foreign market. Entry strategies range from merely making direct export sales to investing in business operations in the other country. A different strategy may be used in each country, and two or more strategies may even be employed in one country. Part of this strategy may include selection of a site for the company facilities, if any.

KEY MARKET ENTRY STRATEGIES

Among the available entry strategies, the most common are the following:

- DIRECT EXPORT SALE The simplest method of entry is by direct export sales managed from locations outside the country, often from a preexisting regional or home country headquarters. This approach avoids the expense of establishing a branch office or acquiring a local firm. Promotion and sales can begin without delay. With minimal investment, a company can gauge whether a larger investment is warranted. However, the company will have no local operations. It must therefore develop strategies to locate, understand and meet the demands of a distant market, to deliver products timely and to provide adequate customer service. A local representative may be needed, but keep in mind that national laws may complicate the employment and also termination of the employment.

- STRATEGIC ALLIANCES A strategic alliance is an agreement between two or more companies that share common interest of engaging in activities to achieve a common goal or objective. In pursuing a strategic alliance, each partner shares the risk of the project by contributing specific financial, technological, process and managerial resources. A strategic alliance may be pursued by two or more companies with complimentary skills and resources or may be entered into by two or more competitors seeking to combine similar resources to achieve economies of scale.

  Strategic alliances may be either non-equity or equity arrangements. Nonequity strategic alliances are merely contractual in nature. Examples include development projects (by which all partners pool their capital to design a new product that each partner then has a right to exploit), licensing agreements and distribution and marketing agreements. In contrast, an equity arrangement involves a more formal relationship, often including the formation of a business entity and substantial contributions of capital, technology and managerial resources. The most common form of an equity-based strategic alliance is a joint venture involving the formation of a separate business entity (e.g., corporation or partnership) to pursue an agreed upon business plan. In developing countries, joint ventures are often the preferred form of foreign investment. In still others, it is the only option available in certain commercial sectors.

- NEW FOREIGN ENTITY When no viable strategic partners exist in a targeted foreign market, a company may decide to enter that market by forming a new entity, such as a branch or a wholly-owned local subsidiary. The formation of a new entity may require investment of substantial funds and can be extremely risky unless the company already has considerable familiarity with the market or is able to recruit qualified personnel to assist in the venture. In some countries, a company will face restrictions on foreign ownership of local business operations.

■ FOREIGN INVESTMENTS AND ACQUISITIONS A company may enter a new foreign market by purchasing an equity interest in an existing foreign entity or by purchasing the entity outright, at least where foreign ownership participation is not limited. An ownership interest creates a tighter bond than a strategic alliance, allowing a company more control over the business operations and goals than some of the other entry strategies. However, this strategy also involves a significant cash outlay and other resources. Success may ultimately depend on the company's ability to retain key local employees and to continue to capitalize on the reputation and local contacts that the local firm had developed prior to the acquisition. A company may seek an investment or acquisition transaction after it first enters the market through a strategic alliance with the targeted firm.

PLAN NOTE: The entry strategy, including the reasons for the selection, any anticipated problems and proposed resolutions, constitutes a significant part of the international business plan. Investors, financial advisors and loan officers will all review the chosen entry strategy and evaluate the extent to which your company appears familiar with the best means of doing business in targeted countries. The plan must provide for the procedures required to set up operations, preferable means of protecting and encouraging the company's investment, entry goals and checkpoints for measuring entry progress.

REASON FOR SELECTING THE STRATEGY

You will need to satisfy readers of your plan that the entry strategy you have chosen is likely to achieve the desired goals. Accordingly, answer the following key questions that typically arise when evaluating potential entry strategies:

■ HOW MUCH CONTROL DOES YOUR COMPANY NEED TO EXERCISE OVER BUSINESS ACTIVITIES IN THE FOREIGN COUNTRY?

A company can achieve the greatest level of control over business activities in a foreign country by establishing its own branch office or subsidiary there or by acquiring control of an existing local entity, eliminating the need to negotiate authority with a local partner. In contrast, a licensing or distribution agreement offers more limited control because the company must rely on the strength of its contract provisions and the local party's willingness and ability to fulfill its obligations. A joint venture creates a middle ground, permitting the company to place its own managers in positions of authority in the local entity while at the same time requiring a consensus of the partners on major operational decisions.

■ WHAT KIND OF INVESTMENT COMMITMENT IS YOUR COMPANY GOING TO MAKE?

If your company is willing and able to make a significant investment to enter a new foreign market it should also seriously consider either establishing a new foreign branch or acquiring a controlling interest in an existing local entity. In either case, the company will be purchasing business assets that its own personnel can control and manage. This type of investment is especially appropriate if the market response to the company's products offered through prior licensing or distribution arrangements has been positive and local demand is likely to stay strong in the foreseeable future.

■ CAN YOUR COMPANY RELY ON THE LOYALTY AND ABILITY OF FOREIGN PERSONNEL IN THE SUBJECT COUNTRY?

Reliance on third party personnel, particularly over a distance and across a national border, is a great concern in any form of strategic alliance. Distribution and manufacturing agreements, as well as joint ventures, necessarily create substantial dependence on the foreign party's personnel to perform the tasks negotiated at the outset of the relationship. Since primary allegiance of foreign personnel is likely to be given to their own employer, you may find that foreign employees spend more time on other projects and are subject to organizational issues in the foreign firm completely unrelated to the job at hand. In contrast, a direct sales effort or establishment of a wholly-owned subsidiary can minimize reliance on foreign personnel.

■ CAN YOUR COMPANY HANDLE THE POLITICS ALONE?

A "go it alone" strategy may expose your company to political risks that might be avoided if you involve a local partner in the activity. Foreign investors may find their assets at risk of confiscation in times of civil unrest or political turnover, but they may escape serious harm if they are part of a joint venture previously approved by the government. When a political environment appears unstable, a strategic alliance may be prudent. On the other hand, instability in the government could also mean that today's well-connected strategic alliance partner may fall out of favor tomorrow, and therefore, always back up any arrangements with a local partner with contingency plans for salvaging your company's investment.

■ ARE THE OPPORTUNITIES WORTH THE FINANCIAL RISK?

When writing your entry strategy, compare the opportunities to the risks. The advantages most commonly cited are access to new technologies, cost reduction and learning opportunities. While a company can certainly develop its own proprietary technologies internally—which also allows for better control and protection of patents, trade secrets, processes, technology know-how and other intellectual property rights—this type of entry requires a greater investment. On the other hand, a strategic alliance may be a faster and less costly means of acquiring new technology, complying with local law and obtaining an already established market distribution chain, which in turn can free financial resources for other projects, such as integrating the alliance-generated technology into the company's products.

Have you found a way to lessen the risk of losing your investment—perhaps carefully drafted and enforced licensing arrangements plus special partner economic incentives—while taking advantage of research and cost-saving opportunities offered by a strategic alliance? If you anticipate that expansion into a foreign country will be beneficial in terms of lower wages, cheaper raw materials and shared use of facilities, will you then spend your savings on building a new foreign entity?

Has your company recognized and implemented steps to gain from the learning opportunities likely to be presented when workers of different social and cultural backgrounds meet? Have the risks of miscommunication and misunderstandings been reduced? As part of your plan, you may need to construct training programs and monitoring procedures for assessing development activities, productivity and budgetary issues on all sides.

Ten Tips for a Strong Alliance

When evaluating and selecting a strategic alliance or joint venture partner, compare each candidate against the following list of features. A successful negotiation of the alliance, and also, its continuing strength, is likely to depend on a combination of all of these factors.

1. COMPATIBILITY The potential partners must be compatible in terms of size and structure as well as the underlying corporate cultures. Under the best circumstances, the parties will have had a successful prior relationship with one another.

2. FUNCTIONAL SKILLS AND RESOURCES The functional skills and resources of the potential partner must compliment those of your company. For example, if a primary purpose of the venture is to access the market using the local partner's established contacts, your company should carefully evaluate the partner's ability to distribute products rapidly to the market, not its capability for developing new products.

3. MANAGERIAL RESOURCES The potential partner should have the managerial resources required to provide all needed assistance to the alliance, particularly in those areas where the partner will have primary functional responsibility.

4. FACILITIES AND SUPPORT Although a strategic alliance often is operated as a wholly separate entity, it is useful to have a partner that is willing and able to provide facilities and administrative support for part of the alliance's activities.

5. GOVERNMENTAL AND REGULATORY ACUMEN The potential partner must have skill and experience in dealing with local officials, particularly if the goods or services are subject to regulation. Some governments even control local distribution channels.

6. FINANCIAL RESOURCES The potential partner must have sufficient financial resources to support the completion of the objectives of the alliance, as well as any functional activities that it will be required to undertake for the arrangement.

7. REPUTATION A strategic alliance, particularly a joint venture, can be a very "visible" form of business relationship. Any partner should have a solid reputation in the market for good quality, ethical management and customer satisfaction.

8. COMMITMENT A prospective partner should show good faith commitment to the evaluation and negotiation process and a willingness to implement the alliance. The partner should seek to resolve conflicts and be willing to compromise and should engender feelings of trust and respect.

9. MUTUALITY OF CONTRIBUTION In essence, a strategic alliance is intended to further the business goals of both parties and to create long-term synergies among them. Each should offer incentives to the other aimed at maintaining the relationship. If one party has significant leverage, the other should be given meaningful benefits to keep it interested, loyal and committed to the success of the alliance.

10. CLEAR ROLES The partners should agree to clearly demarcated roles and respect the authority of their respective management teams. Equal control is not necessarily the best practice. Studies have shown that the most successful alliances have one strong leader responsible for ensuring that the business plan is executed and for daily operations, subject to the limitation that major decisions must be made by agreement of both partners. In such an event, the partners should set up a communications network to ensure that essential information, such as regular business and financial reports, flows freely.

IMPLEMENTATION OF ENTRY STRATEGY

A strategy without a plan for implementation generally will not get off the paper. Therefore, individually identify the steps already taken and the actions still required. If your company has decided to form an alliance, has it formed a management team to evaluate and target a partner? Has it negotiated the deal? Has it made an analysis of its own organizational structure aimed at finding internal problems or shortcomings? For example, if there are problems in the supply chain or in customer service, it makes sense to resolve these issues before an alliance becomes fully operational.

The process of implementation should be considered in terms of short- and long-term planning. Immediate needs and actions are important, of course, but entry into a foreign market will have long-lasting effects and can even impact your company's long-term survival and business objectives in other markets. In particular, management should consider how the alliance will affect and support the operational plans of the company overall. If the proposed alliance does not have a strong and direct connection with the core strategies of the company, further consideration should be given to allocating resources to the relationship. In addition, advance planning for contingencies could avoid disastrous consequences in the event that an alliance fails.

Prior planning is essential to maximizing the probability that the objectives of the market entry will be achieved. In fact, it might be wise to have a "pre-" business plan specifically designed for the immediate steps needed to evaluate and implement market entry. Ideally, it will be made before your company commences activities relevant to the market entry; but you can also take preliminary steps with the caveat that one of the first things to be completed will be a definitive plan. Business planning in this context includes the need to consider the impact of divergent social and cultural background on the evaluation and negotiation of the relationships with local partners, government officials, managers or other employees, suppliers and additional parties likely to be involved.

Planning should include systems for monitoring performance and benchmarks for tracking progress. Milestones that are commonly used in business plans include deadlines for completion of product development activities, productivity measures or revenue objectives. Benchmarks may lead to sanctions, however; they are best used as a method for learning about how the relationship is really working and, if necessary, adjusting the expectations of the parties as the alliance matures.

SITE SELECTION

After identifying the strengths and weakness of your company in a global context, consider specific locations for company facilities and other business activities. This analysis must include a review of such factors as the following:

■ OVERHEAD Your company's own overhead costs and requirements and whether your operations can be easily transported and established in the target country.

■ COMPLEMENTARY Whether the foreign location will complement rather than inhibit the flow of production and communications throughout your organization.

■ PURPOSE VS. RISK The purpose for your expansion and whether the opportunity that awaits is greater than the risk. For example, if you are seeking to sell existing products in new markets, focus on those countries with the greatest interest in the products. If low-cost manufacturing is the objective, demand for the finished goods in the chosen country may be only a secondary consideration.

- COMPETITION Industry preferences and the activities of direct competitors.
- LAWS Local laws and regulations affecting your business.
- INFRASTRUCTURE Local infrastructure for supporting productive operations, including availability of utilities, transportation, skilled labor and necessary equipment.

Issue 3: Global Financial Issues

In addition to setting an internal roadmap for development of the business, your business plan is likely to be a key disclosure document provided to prospective financial institutions and investors. For this reason, you may need to consult financial professionals to assist in constructing and analyzing this aspect of your plan. Accountants and other business financial experts can offer invaluable advice on factors to be weighed in evaluating the financial opportunities and risks, the attractiveness of your plan to potential investors, the reasonableness of your projections and the need to comply with local government regulatory requirements, such as securities and disclosure laws.

PLAN NOTE: Advance planning for the financial aspects of global market expansion is essential. At an international level, markets will vary significantly in terms of size, living standards, technologies, infrastructures, education levels, cultural acceptance and similar factors—all of which can be significant measures of financial potential. The business plan should identify these factors and anticipate the actions that your company will need to take and the investment it will need to make to ensure that it can adapt successfully to the global markets targeted.

ASSESSMENT OF PROFITABILITY

Revenues pay the bills and keep the lights burning, but profits build value for a business. In most cases, capital and other resources are limited and should only be dedicated to the pursuit of a new market if the return is justified in light of the associated risks. Investors and managers must carefully assess the profitability of the business plan.

Profitability can often be enhanced by selection of an appropriate strategy for entering the foreign market. Customers can be expensive to acquire, and entry strategies should be chosen with an eye on careful management of costs. The pursuit of profitability often creates trade-offs with other goals, such as autonomous management in the foreign market. Although a company may prefer to set up its own local organization to maintain control, the cost may be excessive compared to establishing a strategic alliance with a local distributor who already has invested in the overhead necessary to launch marketing activities.

Keep in mind that going global could immediately enhance profitability in domestic markets, even if sales elsewhere are left to local resources. By outsourcing otherwise costly manufacturing tasks to a lower-cost market, your company can save money and create a modest competitive advantage in its own country. In fact, for many companies, the primary focus of their first international business plan should be to reduce the costs of production, materials and research and development.

SIZE OF THE MARKET

In the investment context, many financing sources refuse to look at companies unless they are chasing billion Euro (dollar, yen, etc.) market opportunities. Even when money is not the main issue, a trader must decide whether to expend time and effort on entering a small foreign market where there are apparently more risks than solid opportunities. If the market is small, advance planning is crucial.

The focus of your plan should be on profitability and the collateral benefits that might be achieved through participation in a new foreign market. If low-cost local suppliers and distributors are available, you may discover opportunities for excellent profit margins, even in a smaller market. You may find that you can employ an existing local distribution channel to reduce your own investment. The point is, that market size alone should not stop you from taking a hard look at entering a new country that otherwise appears to have a demand for your products. A market with a potential revenue of $10,000,000, solid margins, steady customers and minimal competition can be at least as valuable as a larger market, where you will no doubt encounter numerous competitors and have to make price-cutting promotions.

PLAN TIP: Believe it or not, market size is a deceiving measure of profitability. Indeed, some investors will insist on seeing a business plan for a billion dollar market. But they are often driven by factors beyond your control, including pressures from their own investors to achieve a certain rate of return within a tight time frame. In assessing market size, availability of international financiers should be less of a concern, especially if they are setting an impossible timetable for your expansion. Most likely, there are local funding sources willing to invest smaller amounts and work with you on a business expansion schedule that makes sense.

REALISTIC PROJECTIONS

Just as market size is often touted in the business plan process, managers often feel the need to predict a huge market share in a very short period of time. However, this is a bad choice because readers of the plan may sense that predictions of large market share are simply unrealistic, possibly leading them to doubt other aspects of the entire plan. The skeptical reader of a business plan will say: "Even if you have a strong competitive advantage, it doesn't mean that 80% of the market will actually buy the product." Accordingly, your plan should contain well-considered support for the financial projections that you make, including the following:

- ATTAINABLE It should set modest growth targets that can be reasonably attained and maintained during the first few years.

- PROJECTIONS It should break sales projections apart for each product or service, showing the cost, sales price and profit margin for each.

- PERIOD It should show the projected sales month-by-month for the first year.

- CHANGES It should take into account anticipated trends, seasons and cycles, and also changes in competitive factors present in the country, many of which will almost certainly impact market share figures for at least 12 to 18 months into the future.

PLAN TIP: If you repeat month after month the same number of sales, your plan will be suspect. Don't merely plug some numbers, even if you make a few adjustments up and down during the year and allow for gradual growth each year. Do your research. Explain the reasons that you anticipate changes.

- MARKET It should identify and define the market, competitive products and available technologies in order to make an accurate assessment of the financial opportunities.

PLAN NOTE: Assume your company sells an accounting software program for consumers. The number of households that <u>could</u> use the software is enormous, but the market for this product is not equal to the number of households. It is much smaller because you need to exclude persons who keep records manually because they lack computer hardware or accounting skills. You could further eliminate those whose finances are so simple that they have no incentive to invest in computer equipment for tracking and categorizing a small number of transactions.

- AUDIENCE It should provide the detail required for the specific audience. For investors, it is common to give a summary of projected revenues and expenses. For company managers, it is best to provide detailed projections and historical financial information so that they can monitor the company's progress.

- ACCURATE It must be honest. Even if you get financing based on poorly researched or inflated numbers, trouble will emerge soon enough when your company cannot meet the unrealistic goals it had set at the time the investment was made.

ASSESSMENT OF THE INVESTMENT

For presentation to an investor, a business plan needs to explain the size of the offering. Even if not being prepared to raise money, the plan must address how much capital will be required to execute the strategy and, of course, must identify likely non-investment sources (e.g., existing reserves, government funding for export activities, commercial lenders and/or working capital from current operations). The business plan should contain a separate section that breaks out projected capital disbursements needed to achieve the company's objectives, including payments for facilities, equipment, salaries, license fees and professional expenses.

The stated capital requirements should reflect the financial projections, showing when cash will be needed. If the projections show a $1 million shortfall, then you should be looking for capital in that same range—not $100,000 or $10 million. The projected use of funds should be as specific as possible. The more detailed you are, the more comfortable investors and other managers will feel that the money will be spent effectively. You don't need to specify down to the dollar, but down to the nearest $10,000 is expected.

ADVISORY: When asking for funding, managers walk a "too much or too little" tightrope. Once realistic needs are projected, it is usually best to err on the side of "too much" funding. This prevents managers from having to "return to the well" once the business is up and running. Besides supplying a good lesson in humility, the seeking of additional funds at this stage also distracts management from their core business at a critical point. It is better to have funding and not need it than to need it and not have it. Even so, be realistic.

What a Venture Capitalist Looks for in a Business Plan

As an investment banker, I see roughly one thousand investment opportunities each year. In reviewing them, I ask myself five questions, and only a few have the correct answers.

1. HOW MUCH CAN I MAKE?
- What is the opportunity?
- How big is the market?
- What is the fundamental business model?
- What is the sustainable "unfair" competitive advantage?
- How big can the company become?
- What percentage of market penetration is required for the projections?
- How much will I own?

2. HOW MUCH CAN I LOSE?
- What if the projections aren't met?
- How much more money could I be required to invest?
- How can the burn rate (rate of expenditure on pre-opening overhead) be controlled?
- What is the structure of the investment?
- Will I control enough voting power or board positions to influence my investment?
- Is there a 'liquid' market for the company?

3. HOW DO I GET MY MONEY OUT?
- What is the time horizon of the investment?
- Can the company realistically carry out an IPO (initial public offering)? If so, when?
- Are there obvious strategic buyers?

4. WHO ELSE IS IN THE DEAL?
- How much money does the entrepreneur have in the deal?
- Are there other venture capitalists?
- Are there strategic investors?
- What are the relationships with the banks?
- Who are the advisors to the company? Consultants? Attorneys? Accountants?

5. WHO SAYS YOU ARE GOOD?
- Is there a management team in place?
- Does the team have experience in building successful companies?
- Can the management team build this company?
- Are there unrealistic founder issues?
- What is the marketing strength of the organization?
- Where are the management staffing "needs" and how can they be filled?
- How easy will it be to change management members if necessary?

Gary L. Shields, CFA, Partner
Avtech Ventures

Issue 4: Legal and Regulatory Issues

Business operations are subject to government regulation. They also create legal obligations and liabilities. Local laws and regulations often have the most immediate impact on the way a company conducts business. When your company goes global, it will become subject to a whole new set of laws and rules for each country. Although there are some international treaties that will help you along the way, most laws remain national in scope. Once you cross a country border, you become subject to that country's laws governing imports, exports, labor, immigration, investment, securities, business operation, contracts, sales, product labeling, intellectual property, environment, transportation and so forth.

Seek legal advice in the early stages of preparing your plan. Choose a lawyer in your own country, perhaps your company's own in-house counsel, who is familiar with international transactions, laws and cultures. A lawyer in your own country usually is unable to advise you on the laws of a foreign country, but he or she can assist you in getting the answers you need from local counsel in each country. Initially, request an advisory opinion on the legal issues, regulations and obligations that you are likely to encounter, together with an explanation of the process, approximate time and estimated cost required for overcoming the identified hurdles.

Although you want prospective investors to see the most inviting aspects of your plan, you also need to have made full and adequate disclosure of the legal hurdles that will need to be addressed and overcome. For example, you may need to obtain government approvals, comply with stringent labor and union laws, protect transfers of the company's technology and make provisions for consumer disclosures to reduce legal liabilities. The plan should address the costs associated with compliance, the extent to which compliance might delay the timetable for setting up the operation and the available options in the event that government approval is not granted immediately or at all.

ADVISORY: International commercial law is in a constant state of flux. In international business, the laws set up by individual governments are usually designed to either encourage foreign investment or to protect local industry. Consequently, the regulations must respond to the needs of the marketplace which makes the regulations flexible. Experienced global business operators know that the law is flexible in direct proportion to the size of the investment. Big players get bigger results. It may be best for small operators to align themselves with a firm that can bring its size to bear.

AREAS OF LEGAL REGULATION

The following aspects of your business operation in foreign countries are likely to be subject to local laws:

- **COMMERCIAL** Regulation of licensing, distribution, production and sales arrangements, joint ventures, general contractual relationships, contracts for sales of goods, bankruptcy, collections and debtor-creditor rights.

- **COMPANIES** Formation of companies, associations, corporations, partnerships, limited companies, acquisitions, sales of companies and dissolutions.

- CONSUMER RIGHTS Regulation of product quality, customer service, defective products, liability warranties, guarantees of product performance, deceptive product labeling or advertising, deceptive trade practices, unfair trade or competition and protection.

- ENVIRONMENT Regulation of waste disposal, environmental packaging, water, noise, soil, quality standards and exploitation of natural resources.

- IMPORT/EXPORT Regulation of cross-border transport.

- INVESTMENTS AND BANKING Regulation of securities offerings, capital markets, investment participation of foreign companies, banking, loans, credit facilities and currency and foreign exchange risk.

- LABOR AND EMPLOYMENT Regulation of hiring and firing practices, sales practices, union participation, independent sales representatives, workplace safety and health.

- PRODUCTION AND MANUFACTURING Regulation of product standards, machine and production standards, safety and hygiene standards, research and development incentives and government testing.

- PROPERTY Regulation of ownership, sale and license of real estate, tangible assets and intellectual property (trademarks, patents, formulas, trade secrets, etc.).

- TAXATION Regulation of taxation on income, sales, pensions, benefit plans and import/export fees and duties.

NEGOTIATION STRATEGIES

Companies may need to follow one of several different strategic approaches when dealing with government agencies in a new foreign market. When developing a business plan for entering the new market, the company should clearly identify the preferred strategies and organize its resources accordingly. Possible approaches include the following:

- EXEMPTIONS AND WAIVERS Companies may seek to alter or adjust governmental policies by requesting a short-term exemption or waiver. For example, if the company believes that compliance with a country's domestic content requirements will materially and adversely impact the quality of the manufactured goods, it may seek to extend the deadline for compliance.

- CHANGE OPERATING OR BUSINESS PROCEDURES Companies may decide to avoid governmental controls altogether by changing operating procedures and/or business activities. For example, if one of the company's products is made subject to domestic price controls in the foreign market, the company may shift production to goods that are not regulated. Similarly, restrictions on direct foreign investment might be circumvented through the use of management contracts.

- CHANGE BUSINESS PLAN TO MEET REQUIREMENTS A company that is anxious to enter a promising foreign market or that lacks the resources to bargain effectively for an adjustment or exemption may simply alter its business plan to meet the relevant government requirements. For example, a company may agree to rigorous foreign exchange restrictions in order to gain access to local markets. As another example, a company may elect to dilute its control by entering into a joint venture with a local partner to obtain the benefits of government incentives available only to companies with significant local ownership.

- FORM STRATEGIC ALLIANCES Companies may form strategic alliances. For example, protection from government interference might be obtained through a business relationship with a powerful local company. Such an alliance might be in the form of a joint venture or a contractual arrangement that makes the local company a significant customer or supplier. Another strategy might be to recruit influential local leaders to sit on the board of directors or to provide consulting services.

OPERATING ISSUES

Managers must recognize that maintaining good relations with government officials and related political figures in each foreign market is a key issue that requires a communications strategy and possible modifications of the company's organizational structure. Time and attention must be devoted to the development of specific objectives for dealing with government authorities and for identifying and nourishing appropriate communications channels and procedures through which information gained from these contacts can be effectively disseminated throughout the organization.

- COMMUNICATIONS CHANNELS The company should establish multiple formal and informal communications channels with local political figures. Management should take a proactive approach in such communications. In doing so, be certain to satisfy all formal reporting and meeting requirements with ministry officials and bureaucrats.

In addition, relationships should be formed with persons outside of official government circles. Often, they can serve as conduits to and from key officials within the government, and such arrangements can serve as an "early warning" system to avoid disastrous effects of unexpected policy changes.

The main goal of any communications strategy is to collect relevant information from the government and other political actors, but the company should also view these channels as a part of its public relations strategy. For example, as appropriate, meetings with government officials should be used to educate them about the company's plans and anticipated problems that might have a negative impact on local business activities. If the government is interested in ensuring that the company maintains and expands its presence in the country, it may well be disposed to tackle the problems before they reach a formal review and application stage. Also, sharing of information by the company can increase the trust between company and government officers and provide substantial foundations for government officials to gain support for their own positions.

ADVISORY: When setting up in foreign markets, avoid any close associations with particular political parties or factions. The party that is in power today may be gone tomorrow—along with your investment.

- ORGANIZATIONAL ISSUES As a company grows and enters multiple foreign markets, it should create an efficient organizational structure for handling governmental relations. Information about local government conditions is extremely important to all of the functions within the company. Accordingly, a premium must be placed on collection and distribution of data.

Major issues, such as market entry strategies, must be decided at the highest levels of the company organization. Once these have been determined, each manager and department head should be responsible for establishing and maintaining communications with the appropriate political figures necessary for the implementation of the company's overall strategy. In other words, each manager should be made responsible for taking care of one piece of the government relations puzzle. Although the company might establish a central group to assist managers in the collection and analysis of relevant data and in the development of specific strategies for communicating with local political actors, this department should be limited to a support role. Local managers, who are involved on a day-to-day basis in running the company's activities, are ultimately in the best position to handle company-to-government relations.

Several alternatives to the diffused "local market" organizational approach to government relations are available. For example, a company may take a more centralized approach and establish uniform bargaining positions that must be followed by local managers in all countries. This approach might be appropriate for companies possessing highly valued technological resources because they will presumably have sufficient leverage to force government officials to accede to requests to alter established regulatory requirements. A variation of this approach is for the company headquarters to establish general guidelines on the positions that the company is willing to take with foreign governments but to allow local managers some latitude in discussions with relevant officials. Finally, responsibility for government relations may be placed with local company managers, but with the proviso that they must actively and regularly share the results of their negotiations with counterparts in other countries in order to develop and maintain a set of coordinated bargaining positions. This strategy can actually be very effective for companies involved in truly global industries because it facilitates the sharing of current information from other markets that might impact competitive conditions in other markets.

■ CORRUPTION Although strategy and communications are important, managers must always consider the potential hazards of corruption in foreign markets. Government officials, many of whom are underpaid and overworked, might happily accept your gifts for expediting your matter, ensuring approvals or obtaining requested services. However, these transactions are usually prohibited by laws in both your country and the foreign country. Thus, your company is likely to be subject to two sets of corrupt practices laws. Even if enforcement in one country might be minimal or nonexistent, your company officials who cross over this legal line could well create a liability for your company within your own country. Accordingly, managers must be prepared to deal with corruption issues to ensure that government-business relations do not become muddled. For this reason, the company is advised to prepare a company code of ethical behavior and to train all of its management and other representatives in these policies. Refusing to participate in bribery does not necessarily put a stop to your project. The usual result is that the progress will slow a bit until the inquiring official finds that bribes are not forthcoming. However, a company must be prepared for the total derailment of their project if the official holds fast.

ADVISORY: Lawyers provide a valuable service to companies pursuing international expansion. As more and more countries sign onto the WTO, we conduct business on similar legal playing fields. However, we are not quite at the stage where the playing field is exactly the same everywhere. This is especially true in cultures where business is conducted on a "relationship" basis rather than by the strictures of a written contract. In relationship cultures, the presence of lawyers at the negotiating table can be seen as a sign of mistrust. Your lawyers can be on hand to advise in such situations, but their "legal" profile should be kept to a minimum. Bear in mind that in some developing countries, foreign lawyers are forbidden to even advise on local law. A little pre-market entry research goes a long way here.

CHAPTER 5

Assembling the Working Group

THE WORK OF THE INDIVIDUAL STILL REMAINS THE SPARK THAT MOVES MANKIND AHEAD EVEN MORE THAN TEAMWORK. – IGOR SIKORSKI

TO PREPARE YOUR INTERNATIONAL BUSINESS PLAN, you will need to draw on the experience and talents of many people. In this chapter, we take a brief look at all the parties that might be part of the working group for your company's international business plan. Central to the working group is the person who is tasked with preparing the plan—perhaps you, your department or someone within your chain of command. The plan preparer will need to draw on the expertise of various professionals to assess the proposed technologies and to support the practical feasibility of the plan. A financial expert is an essential member of the working group, as are the senior managers on whom depends the successful implementation of the plan. Presentation of the plan, including objective review, can be just as important as the content, and therefore, the working group should include those who have a gift for clarifying the communications of others: good editors and analysts.

You

Presumably you opened this book because you've been asked to prepare an international business plan, review the work of another or are the owner of a small business enterprise. Business planning should be a priority in every business organization and command the attention of senior managers. The actual drafting might, however, be done by different people depending on the size of the company and available resources. Consider the following examples:

- In a small- to medium-sized business, which may have anywhere from one to 100 employees, the CEO may draft the plan. In turn, the CEO may ask the managers from one or more of the functional areas described below to provide additional information.
- In larger organizations, responsibility for drafting the international business plan may be turned over to a group of middle-level managers from different areas of the company, perhaps even including overseas subsidiaries. The end product will then be routed up to senior management for comment and action.
- An entrepreneur looking to start up a new business with an international focus may not have staff resources to help with research, nor a track record of domestic activity. Special care will need to be given in identifying actual market opportunities and potential risks.

Regardless of who you are, let's start with the basic point. If you are going to be preparing the first draft of the plan, be realistic about your skills, knowledge and expertise. If you are not mathematically inclined, don't focus on financial projections. Start thinking about whom you are going to bring in to help. Similarly, if you try a first stab at the numbers, don't get frustrated, give up and stop working on implementation. Instead, simply move on to another part of the plan and revisit the numbers later.

Another important thing to remember is that information in the plan and the data collected for research purposes (even if it does not actually appear in the plan) is generally sensitive and proprietary to the company. As such, you have to take steps to safeguard that information and the distribution of the draft within your working group. If you aren't familiar with security procedures, including the use of appropriate legends and markings on drafts and confidentiality agreements as described in Chapter 3, be sure to consult legal counsel. Also, make sure the plan cannot be accessed by unauthorized personnel on your company's computer system.

Engineering, Design & Manufacturing

If your firm plans to sell technology, machinery or products with substantial design elements, it is important that someone with a technical background be involved in drafting the business plan. The technologist must be able to explain the technical aspects of your product. Such a person will also be involved in describing the technical aspects of the business and industry. One of the hardest parts of writing this section is making technical subjects easy to understand. To get it to that level may require more rewrites than any other section of the plan.

The analysis and discussion of technology in an international business plan must account for the state of knowledge and level of practice in each of the foreign countries that will be impacted by the plan. For example, the company's ability to take advantage of the benefits of low-cost manufacturing in a foreign country will be dependent on how the company's technology is absorbed and understood in that country. If the technology is too advanced, local laborers may have difficulty achieving the necessary standards of quality and performance. Similarly, the demand for a technology-based product in a new foreign market depends on existing industry standards in the country and the actual needs of potential end-users. High performance automobiles have limited appeal in a country that has few paved roads.

In addition, the engineering and technology analysis must assess the level of intellectual property protection available in the foreign country and the risks associated with competition from substitute technologies or solutions. The ability to attain a competitive advantage through the use of intellectual property rights, particularly patents, varies substantially around the world. Also, consumers in many developing countries are often reluctant to abandon traditional shopping methods and products, thereby increasing the risks associated with introducing innovations.

For goods-based businesses, the plan must carefully describe how you will manufacture the product. If you are not already a manufacturing specialist, you will need to consult someone with a background in manufacturing, production or project management. You may have designed and built the prototype, but full-scale manufacturing is different.

Management

A business plan should include more than just the CVs of the company's senior managers and other key employees. It should fully analyze the appropriate managerial and organizational structure for the company in relation to its stated objectives. This is particularly important for an internationally focused company because of the need to deal with logistical issues caused by distance and differences in time zones.

You may be the company's senior manager, in which case you should have the appropriate vision to determine the type of organizational structure that is necessary. If not, you need to secure information about current reporting channels in order to make recommendations to senior management regarding organizational changes and the types of resources that might be required in order to implement a global strategy. In many cases, a company may turn to one or more outside consultants on human resources and management issues to assist in this process. Moreover, recruiting agencies may be asked to assist the company in locating appropriate candidates for new positions, particularly posts in foreign countries that require personnel with local background and experience.

PLAN NOTE: Venture capital firms and some private "angel" investors insist on management positions and input into the operation. If the requisite expertise is there, this presents no problem. However, business planners will need to resist placing people in management simply because they have invested funds.

Financial

This is where you need a numbers person. Get someone who can "run" the numbers, preferably someone with experience in preparing financial projections. The best choice would be someone with experience in doing projections for business plans. There is a certain art in being able to look at expense items, revenue sources and cost of funds. While an accounting background coupled with an understanding of reporting practices in key target markets is helpful, the finance person should also have management savvy and a good feel for the actual operational requirements of the business. Investors, senior managers and independent directors always appreciate the value of an experienced chief financial officer, regardless of the size of the business.

Legal

While the ultimate responsibility for the preparation and content of the business plan lies with you, attorneys will sometimes play a role in the drafting process. When the business plan is prepared for external use, such as fund-raising from outside investors, one of the attorney's most important jobs is to ensure that the document complies with the disclosure requirements of applicable securities laws. If the plan is being presented to prospective joint venture partners, legal advice should be sought to as to how much must be disclosed in the plan and how to protect the company's proprietary information.

As to the specific content of the plan, legal counsel should be the first resource for discussions of legal and regulatory hurdles confronting the company in trying to enter new foreign markets. In many cases, the company must overcome the requirements of foreign investment and/or technology transfer laws, a process that could delay the start of a new investment project or impact the costs associated with the investment. Also, your legal counsel should become familiar with your entire business, including existing contractual relationships, and should have access to all parts of the plan to ensure that it accurately describes current operations. An experienced business lawyer can often answer basic questions that fall outside of strictly legal issues.

Marketing

Having a well-designed product that can be produced is only the first stage of the battle. You have to get it to the market and get people to buy it—that is where the real work begins. You will need someone with experience in marketing, distribution and sales in each of the target markets. Do not make the mistake common to entrepreneurs of assuming that marketing is easy or that "anybody" can do marketing. Everything—literally, everything—a company does affects and is affected by the marketing process. Marketing should receive your constant attention as it will make the difference between success and failure. Everyone involved in the project must pursue their goals with marketing in mind. The marketing plan section of the business plan is the central nervous system of the project. Be aware that every year hundreds of perfectly good products fall by the wayside because firms let their focus deviate from marketing. Don't let it happen to you.

Securities-Offering Advisors

If the business plan is tied to an offering of securities (equity stock), the company may have engaged an investment banker or finder to assist in locating investors. In those cases, the offering advisor will work to make sure that the plan is an effective selling document. They will also have an interest in making sure that the plan does not expose them to securities law liability. Responsibility for preparation and content of the offering documents will be laid out in any agreement between the company and its professional selling agent.

Professional Editor/Writer

Having finished your first draft, see if you can find a professional editor/writer to rewrite the plan. Business writers can smooth out the rough spots, fill in missing items and create a more professional look. Their work will raise your plan to another level.

Remember that the plan is, in and of itself, a marketing tool, and therefore needs professional treatment. A good editor will make the document functional and, most importantly, readable. Proper editing will be just as valuable to your project as professional legal or financial advice so don't skimp on the budget. As with all such services, you get what you pay for.

Group of Experts

Okay, the plan is finished and has been rewritten several times. Now you should take it for a test spin before you open it up to the critique of the target reader group (e.g., investors). You need to be as careful as possible to ensure that the draft reflects your best efforts and capabilities to complete the task successfully. Seek out businesspeople whom you respect and ask them to read and comment on the plan. When confidentiality is a concern, look for resources within the company who can not only informally review the style of the document but also provide input on the information that may need to be included on their specific functional areas. If the plan is being prepared for presentation to outside investors, consider first presenting it to an external focus group that can provide feedback on the plan and the pitch associated with the plan.

PLAN NOTE: Many municipalities and large consulting firms offer "incubator" services for entrepreneurs looking for professional input. The municipalities provide the services in the hope that a successful firm will bring jobs and taxes to the city or region. Consultancies are hoping to get accountancy or consulting business in the future. Either way, they offer low (or no) cost assistance in business development. They can also act as a conduit for investment.

Internal Audit Group

Remember that the most important use of the business plan for a "going concern" is for internal guidance. For this to happen, you should have regular meetings to review the plan and measure your company's performance against it. This is particularly true if employee performance and compensation are tied to meeting business plan objectives. The most effective approach is to have a designated group with responsibility for reviewing actual company performance versus projections under the plan. As disparities develop, they should have authority to change the plan.

CHAPTER 6

Plan Section 1: Introduction

IT IS BETTER TO KNOW SOME OF THE QUESTIONS THAN ALL OF THE ANSWERS. — JAMES THURBER

YOUR INTERNATIONAL BUSINESS PLAN will begin with an introduction or executive summary. This introduction is composed of three parts: cover page, table of contents and executive summary. In addition, many plans begin with a mission and vision statement.

The specific contents of the introduction will depend on the intended audience for the plan. For example, in the case of a business plan that is to be circulated extensively to outsiders, such as prospective investors, the introduction will include various warnings and disclaimers to protect the confidentiality of the information and satisfy the requirements of applicable securities laws. Obviously, when the plan is intended solely for the internal use of the company, securities law legends are not necessary although it is still appropriate to include notices pertaining to safeguarding the confidentiality of the plan. As noted earlier, however, some cultures may take these disclaimers as warnings or as a representation of a lack of good faith. Plan and format accordingly.

Cover Page

The cover page should, when appropriate, address the confidentiality of the information included in the business plan. The plan should include a statement or legend that provides:

- Information in the plan is your property
- Information in the plan is confidential and proprietary to you
- No copies can be made
- No disclosure of the plan or its contents may be made, except with your written approval
- The plan must be returned to you on request

Each plan should be numbered on the cover page and a space left for inserting the name of the recipient. A distribution log should be maintained and the legends on the cover page should refer to the named recipient as having a duty and obligation to maintain the secrecy of the plan and limit copying and distribution.

In addition, the cover page should include the full name and address of the company, as well as telephone, facsimile and e-mail addresses. The reference should be to the main executive offices of the company. Addresses of other offices, including foreign offices, can be included in the body of the plan.

When the plan is being used in connection with the offering of securities of the company, the cover page will also include various legends (legal statements) that may be required by securities law administrators. If the offering occurs in multiple jurisdictions, each jurisdiction may have its own legend requirements. Additional pages should be inserted behind the initial cover page to include these legends, which generally should be in bold type and capitalized. Counsel can advise on the content and placement of the legends.

PLAN NOTE: When the plan is circulated internationally, confidentiality information and disclaimers may only be binding when (and as) presented in the local language.

Table of Contents

Each reader of a business plan has certain sections of particular interest and not all will read the same parts. In addition, some readers will want to read the plan in a different order than what you have prepared. For example, Lance Parish, a VC analyst, in his insight at the end of Chapter 3, reads the executive summary and then the management description. Only if the plan meets his criteria in these two areas does he read the rest of the plan. A reader who cannot find a particular section of interest is likely to lose interest.

Readers need a "road map" to your plan. This means they need a table of contents. The table of contents should not be limited to section or chapter titles. Most readers are seeking specific issues, such as pricing, competitors or intellectual property. Be sure to list the key topics appearing as subsections in the plan parts. This will make it easier for them to find what they want. On the other hand, the table of contents should not be so voluminous that it is difficult to find key topics. Keep it on one page.

The reader should be able to scan the table and immediately understand the organization of the plan. This means the wording should be kept to a minimum, with indentations to set off different topics and subtopics. This page should be presented as an easily read outline and not be overburdened with text.

Errors in the table of contents give readers the impression that you are inefficient, disorganized or lacking in quality control. Alignment, spelling and title or page errors do not reflect well on your commitment. When too many people get involved in writing the plan, the table of contents can get put together without double checking the information. Often they forget to make adjustments for last minute changes in the plan body that affect titles or pagination. A careful presentation from the beginning will leave the right impression with your reader.

Some business plan writers prefer to place the table of contents after the executive summary, thinking that the most important part of the plan is the executive summary, which the readers will want to see first. Only after reading the executive summary will they care about seeing other parts of the plan and need the table of contents. There is no hard and fast rule, so the choice is yours.

Executive Summary

The executive summary is the most important section of your plan. It is where readers start. If the summary is poorly written and unclear, it probably will be the place where readers stop.

It SHOULD be a marketing tool designed to get readers to look at the rest of your plan and to take it seriously. It should NOT be merely an introduction, a preface, a collection of highlights, a condensation, an abstract or a summary.

PREPARATION OF THE SUMMARY

In many ways, the executive summary is the most difficult part of the plan to prepare. Why? Because in writing it, you must come to grips with shortcomings in the rest of the plan and bring together the key messages regarding the company's plans in a short and concise manner. It is written as a marketing device and must summarize everything your company represents.

There is a difference of opinion on when to write the executive summary. You need your most persuasive arguments in the summary but may not have developed them until you are well into drafting the business plan. Therefore, some leave the drafting of the summary until after all or most of the plan has been completed. It is also possible to outline and roughly write the summary, which will give you an overview of the issues that you need to better research and define. You can then revisit the summary after writing the rest of the plan.

CONTENTS OF SUMMARY

Begin by briefly telling readers why you prepared the plan. Emphasize the significance of the plan to the readers. In other words, is your purpose to attract investors or to provide internal company guidelines? Are you asking readers to study, analyze and comment on the plan, implement the plan or recall the company objectives and policies for purposes of comparing performance? Let the readers know your purpose so they can adjust their reading for the intended use.

Remember, the executive summary is written for specific readers. You must know who your readers are, what they want and what they will do with your plan after reading it. In the span of 90 to 120 seconds, the reader should have all the basic information needed to understand the issues or problems and to move forward with further reading or questions for the drafter. Therefore, the executive summary must be adjusted to your audience. For example:

- *For investors*, highlight characteristics considered important for investment decisions, such as a perceived need in the targeted market, how your business plans to meet that need and what the expected return might be.

- *For members of the board of directors*, describe why the company should decide to invest in a given project, whether it is a new product or service, a new market or an arrangement with a new foreign partner.

- *For a foreign joint venture*, quickly and succinctly define the target market and opportunities for exploitation of the company's current goods, services or resources, the advantages associated with the proposed partnership, the investment required and the anticipated return.

In terms of style, the summary should meet the 3-Cs test: Clear, Concise and Compelling. At the same time, it should convey your enthusiasm and why you are working so hard to create your company or champion the new project. Don't be wordy. Try to say it in two pages, or even one page, if you can effectively convey your message.

Always listen carefully to feedback you get from readers of the plan. Observe what questions they ask after reading it, and in particular, take note of questions that are the same or similar. These questions will indicate areas needing improvement.

ADVISORY: When the readership of the plan is outside your domestic culture, customize the summary for different cultures. While the main body of the plan may remain in your native language (or the language of international commerce, English), translating the summary shows that you are willing to go the "extra mile" (or kilometer) to communicate.

Mission and Vision Statements

Business plans for start-ups or radical departures from an ongoing business may include mission and vision statements. These statements constitute a one- or two-sentence summary of what the company is all about–what it stands for, what it believes in and what its goals are. The two statements are distinctly different.

VISION STATEMENT

Your vision is a long-term goal. It is your dream of what you want the company to be when it grows up. It should be a concise philosophical statement about the future of the firm. It is such a distant goal that you may never achieve it, but you will never stop trying.

MISSION STATEMENT

Your mission is more immediate and achievable. It addresses what you intend to accomplish in the foreseeable future (the next several years). Because the statement is only a few sentences long, each word must be carefully chosen. They must be succinct and powerful, yet convey a clear message. The statements become motivation tools, so they should have passion and be inspirational. Pepsi's "Beat Coke" was both.

Considered on a per-word basis, these two statements are the most time consuming part of your plan. To get them right, involve as many people as possible. In this way, you will develop statements that reflect your company's employees and culture, not just your own views.

Both statements should be based on the company's unique competitive advantages. By doing so, they demonstrate to readers that you understand the market, your company, your goods or services and your competitors.

Don't confine your carefully drafted vision and mission statements to the business plan. Make them part of your corporate culture. Post them in the halls and add them to your company brochures and reports. Review them periodically. Most of all, frequently discuss them and consider whether you are still achieving them.

CHAPTER 7

Plan Section 2:
Company Background and Description

LEARNING WITHOUT THOUGHT IS LABOR LOST.

THOUGHT WITHOUT LEARNING IS PERILOUS.

— CONFUCIUS

THE FIRST SUBSTANTIVE SECTION OF THE BUSINESS PLAN sets the stage so that the reader can gain insight into the background and operation of your company. This section gives context to the mission and vision presented in the Introduction (see Chapter 6), allowing the reader to understand more thoroughly the industry or trade sector of your company and how your company fits into it. Section 2 should provide a comprehensive description of the company, including such things as:

- The historical development of the company
- The current and projected business activities of the company
- The products offered by the company
- The industry segments and markets in which the company is involved

Major customers, competitors, alliances and company management may also be referred to in this section, although these topics will generally be covered in much greater detail later in the business plan.

Historical Development of the Company

Generalizations are difficult to make with regard to the contents of the business plan section that describes the development of the company. At a minimum, however, it is useful to explain how the company was originally formed. For example, in a number of cases involving companies active in the high technology area, the business began when the founders left their previous employers to develop a new technical or product concept that did not fit into the strategic plans of the former employers. Beyond formation, other milestones that might be mentioned, as appropriate, include the following:

- Receipt of initial financing from investors
- Recruitment of experienced management personnel
- Expansion of human resource capabilities in research, manufacturing, sales and finance
- Product testing and initial sales of goods and services

- Formalization of supply and distribution arrangements
- Additional rounds of financing
- Sales milestones

Current and Projected Business Activities

Obviously, a primary reason for preparing the business plan is to analyze the current and projected business activities of the company. At the outset, you should put together a brief summary of the company's development and marketing of its products, including information on revenues, expenses, profits, losses and market share for a recent period. In addition, you should list some of the ongoing projects within the company, such as development of new goods or services, upgrades to information technology systems, new plants and sales offices and strategic partnerships under discussion. The idea is to provide the reader with some notion of the company's current stage of development so that you can explain the next steps in its evolution.

Projected business activities build on the current situation and should hopefully jump out as natural extensions of achieving historical milestones. For example, solid acceptance of one of the company's products in one market may signal an opportunity to introduce the product into a new market with similar demographics. Similarly, the need to reduce the costs of manufacturing to maintain market share and competitive advantage may dictate a need to look to foreign markets for low-cost labor. Arguments for investing in the projected business activities will be made in other parts of the plan.

Products (Goods & Services)

The business plan should include an extensive description of the principal products of the company in each of the industry segments in which the company is active. The form and content of this description, including the required portfolio analysis of the company's products and the issues to be considered when adapting products for foreign markets, is considered in detail later in the book. The discussion of products in the general company description should be limited to providing the reader with a good sense of the types of products developed or sold by the company.

PRODUCT DEFINITION: In most of the developed world, services have overtaken goods as the mainstays of the economy. Because of that, in the remainder of this book, goods and services will be referred to simply as "products" and only separated into tangible or intangible (goods or services) categories when specifically required. For most of us, the "product" of our labor nowadays is a service!

Customers

The business plan should provide the reader with an understanding of the historical and existing markets for the company's products. It might summarize the company's major customer relationships, as well as describe any major outlets for the company's products. Major customers generally include all customers from which the company has derived a significant amount of revenues in recent years, as well as any other customers that the company considers to be "material" to its future prospects. The description of the company's customer base will be expanded in that portion of the business plan that deals with marketing strategies. For a start-up company, this section also would include customers who have signed a memorandum-of-understanding (MOU) and companies that have expressed an interest in the products.

Competitive Advantages and Distinctive Competencies

The business plan must describe the competitive advantages and distinctive competencies that the company believes will allow it to achieve its business and financial objectives. This information is especially important when the plan is being circulated to investors presented with multiple business plan opportunities.

Some plans identify advantages and competencies by means of a series of questions designed to show the manner in which the company completes the tasks necessary for it to develop, produce and distribute its products. This exercise, sometimes referred to as "value-chain analysis," is designed to establish the basis on which the company will compete in the future and, to some extent, to identify areas in which the company's skills fail to match the expertise of competitors.

In any event, the following questions should be considered and answered as relevant to the particular business:

- Is the company able to compete based on its strengths in procurement, processing or manufacturing?
- Is the company able to compete based on its practices with respect to inventories, packaging or production flexibility?
- Is the company able to compete based on its strengths with respect to sales, distribution, customer service, delivery, promotion, maintenance or field engineering?
- Is the company able to compete based on the characteristics and capabilities of its products?
- Is the company able to compete on the basis that its operations are sufficiently flexible as to adapt its products to meet the needs of different customer niches?
- Is the company able to compete based on its human resources strategies?
- Is the company able to compete based on its strengths in research and development?
- Is the company able to compete based on a unique technological advantage, which is either embodied in its product line or is utilized in the course of its manufacturing?
- Is the company able to compete based on its financial assets or strategic business relationships?
- Is the company able to compete based on its managerial skills, internal controls or innovative business goals and philosophies?

Once the key components of the relevant value chain for the company's products are identified, a similar series of questions should be asked for each of its major competitors. Thereafter, the company can choose the basis on which it will compete by reference to the important competitive factors in the industry and specific customer "needs."

PLAN NOTE: Although a given product may be technically "inferior," it may flourish because of the exceptional distribution capabilities of the manufacturer. Some companies may be able to attain the lowest cost entry in the marketplace by using low-cost production facilities in an offshore location. In other cases, the company's unique technology can be utilized to develop new tools or applications for customers to solve their own engineering or development problems.

Industry Sector Analysis

Although the company may have a significant competitive advantage and distinctive competencies, success will be achieved only if the company can adequately assess the potential markets for its products and develop and execute a marketing plan that allows the company to penetrate the market successfully. The process should begin with an analysis of the industries in which the company will be competing.

INDUSTRY STRUCTURE

The business plan should provide the reader with the company's own perception of its industry, its historical evolution and future trends, as well as the role that the company is expected to play within the industry in the next few years. Accordingly, the company should provide a general overview of each of its industry segments and the various business, commercial and social problems that the industry generally, and the company in particular, are seeking to address in conducting business. With respect to each market-based "problem," reference should be made to the "solutions" offered by existing products. Any shortcomings should be noted of other solutions that have created opportunities for the company in light of its competitive advantages.

PLAN TIP: A health care company might attempt to describe the breadth and severity of particular health problems the company feels will support a market for its products. It should further explain why the company's products solve the identified problems as opposed to products available from competitors.

Industry analysis becomes more complex when the company is contemplating expansion into foreign markets. Although a number of industries already have become global, unique factors must be recognized in each country. One important distinction is the role that local government might play in industry activities, particularly when the government offers financial support and other benefits to domestic firms confronted with the possibility of competition from multinational businesses.

MARKET ANALYSIS

The business plan should thoroughly describe each potential market for the company's products. This analysis should cover the following:

- A summary of current size of the market.
- A forecast of the anticipated growth of the market over the next five to ten years.
- The chief characteristics of the market.
- The major types of customers in the market (e.g., large Fortune 500 companies, small firms, individuals, manufacturers, etc.).
- The nature of each anticipated application of the products.
- A review of significant industry trends.
- A breakdown of each target market by size and volume, the products used, the sophistication of the customers, the amount of innovation (e.g., any further research and development) required to meet the needs of the customers, the degree of customization required to penetrate the market and the importance of producing a "standardized" product.

Specific issues that might arise in analyzing a new foreign market are discussed in Chapter 4.

Competitive Analysis

Although the company may have a significant strategic advantage in its chosen market, such as innovative and proprietary technology, a properly chosen market niche that is likely to expand in the future also can be expected to attract competition from other companies. Accordingly, the business plan should describe the following:

- The forces that drive competition in the industry
- The skills and resources of actual and potential competitors
- Any barriers to entry that might be faced by new competitors, including restrictions placed on foreign participation in the local economy
- Potential "substitutes" in the form of products that may provide either a better answer for the needs of the customer or change their requirements altogether
- The potential actions of parties already involved in the relevant value chain that might materially impact the market

COMPETITIVE ENVIRONMENT

The business plan should cover the specific competitive environment in which the company operates, including:

- Identification of the company's major competitors
- Description of the nature and area of their competition, whether direct or indirect
- A candid assessment of the company's standing within the industry, both in terms of sales volume and with respect to the characteristics on which the needs of the customers are satisfied
- Identification of noncompetitive firms that are willing to support the company's products

---

PLAN TIP: One means of entering a foreign market is by gaining access through other firms and distributors that sell competing products. In this case, widespread acceptance and support of your products could hinge on extra features, such as warranty, liability, image or reputation. If your company relies on this approach to introduce its products into a new foreign market, remember that it is often not economical in the entry stage to provide direct warranty or local customer services following the sale. Your company may instead need to rely on local partners to supply the required support. An accurate assessment of the capabilities of local noncompetitive firms could make the difference to fast acceptance and growing market share in a foreign country.

BASIS FOR COMPETITION AND COMPETITIVE FACTORS

A business plan is most useful if it identifies the "basis for competition" within the industry and the various factors (e.g., cost, manufacturing efficiencies, product reliability, technology, breadth of products, capacity, capital, distribution or service) that the company believes may influence future competition within the industry. If the company's products fall into more than one market segment or applications field, the plan should address each one.

SKILLS AND RESOURCES OF COMPETITORS

A mere listing of competitive factors is not very comprehensive. The business plan discussion should extend beyond the listing to an analysis of the following points:

- The features that distinguish the company's products from those offered by competitors
- The strength of the company's resources and assets in relation to competitors
- The competitive strategies of other firms
- The anticipated response of competitors to the company's products, especially when the company is new to the market

BARRIERS TO ENTRY

When formulating an international business plan, you should remember to look into the future as far as reasonably possible. This means that you should consider not only the current competitors in the market, but also the possibility that other firms will enter the market in the future. The risks presented by new competition are particularly high in new and innovative industries, especially if significant profit margins are anticipated and the market is expected to expand within a few years.

As part of your business plan, you would be wise to identify "barriers to entry," which might make it difficult for new competitors to enter the market, including:

- The amount of capital required to achieve required economies of scale
- The proprietary nature of products or technology
- The importance of brand identification
- "Switching costs" for the customer base
- The availability of adequate distribution channels
- The existence of absolute cost advantages
- Regulatory requirements, such as foreign investment laws, that might delay or reduce new competition

When a company is a pioneer in a new market, the business plan should describe the efforts that the company might be able to undertake to create barriers against new competitors. If applicable, reference might be made to the company's strategies for developing a broad product line, a large installed base of satisfied and loyal customers or the establishment and maintenance of a strong technology rights position.

If the company is itself attempting to enter a new market dominated by established firms, the plan must carefully address how the company proposes to overcome any existing advantages held by current market participants. These might include rapidly achieving manufacturing competence through a strategic alliance with another firm or capitalizing on relationships that have been established with potential customers in other business areas. In these situations, it might be best for the company to pursue a strategic alliance with one of the local firms to gain access to manufacturing facilities and existing distribution channels.

CHAPTER 8

Plan Section 3: Products and Services

EVERYONE LIVES BY SELLING SOMETHING.

– ROBERT LOUIS STEVENSON

THE GENERAL DISCUSSION OF YOUR COMPANY'S BACKGROUND and strategic focus described in Chapter 7 should flow nicely into the detailed description and analysis of the products (goods and/or services) of your company. If drafted properly, the portfolio of products will include "solutions" to the competitive opportunities previously identified in the beginning sections of the plan. An international business plan also should address key issues such as adaptation of domestic products to new foreign markets and building a product portfolio for foreign markets that suits the specific characteristics of those countries. Related issues also need to be discussed, particularly the company's new product development efforts and intellectual property rights.

Description of Products

The business plan should include an extensive description of your company's principal products in each industry sector where you are active. In addition, you should describe the status of any major new product or industry segment (e.g., whether such products are in the design or planning stage, whether prototypes exist or whether further engineering is necessary). From a formatting perspective, the discussion of existing and new products is usually broken into separate sections, particularly if development work on new products will be financed with funds from investors reviewing the business plan.

The discussion of products in the business plan should extend beyond mere description. It should include an analysis of your company's key strengths that will make the development, production and sale of products a profitable venture for prospective investors. For example, the discussion should identify any innovative features, potential applications and technological characteristics that may serve as a basis for a particular strategic advantage. This may require an examination of:

- Revenue, cost and potential markets for the products
- Distribution channels for the products
- Assets and resources of the company that are, and will be, needed to support the products in the future

If any weaknesses exist in your company's products portfolio, such as difficulties in product development for exploitation in a particular market, you should include a description as part of the "risk factors" in the business plan. If a strategy has been developed to remedy such weaknesses, explain it.

The business plan should carefully review your company's key product development activities, including related milestones and risks. The business plan should take a forward-looking approach, with an emphasis on:

- New products that the company anticipates developing in response to changing market needs
- Strategies that the company intends to adopt to meet competitive challenges created by new technologies or scientific approaches that may become practical over the next few years

The current status of each product that your company has under development should be described as part of the business plan. For example, a projected new product may simply be an idea that is still in the conceptual stage, meaning some time will pass before preliminary market testing. In other cases, the company may have developed a prototype, may have commenced small manufacturing runs or have tested the services in a small market release. In such situations, it is appropriate for investors to know about the timetable for completing the development of these more mature products, including the amount of additional cash necessary to achieve full production or provision. Moreover, if a product has been developed to the point of its imminent release into the marketplace, your company probably has already generated at least a marketing plan, and that plan also should be discussed in the business plan.

Product Portfolio

Selection of the optimal portfolio of a product offering is the fundamental strategic factor in marketing. Often, companies introduce their existing products into a market where no comparable product exists. Alternatively, companies might have to determine whether adjustments and modifications are needed for existing products to be successful in the country. Finally, a company might launch a product development effort to create new products that are geared to the local market but not replicated elsewhere in the company's global product mix. In any case, as discussed in Chapter 4, marketing managers must evaluate all of the relevant demographic, economic, political, regulatory and cultural factors in each new country's market.

DEMOGRAPHIC FACTORS

Although a good deal of emphasis is placed on economic and cultural factors in the preliminary marketing analysis for a new country, demographic factors are just as important. Managers should not simply assume that foreign markets will have the same demographic profile as the company's home market or neighboring countries. In fact, growth, age and geographic characteristics of each country vary substantially.

The impact of demographics is particularly significant in developing countries. In general, these markets are expanding rapidly, usually youthful and characterized by rapid migration from rural to urban areas. These trends have several consequences for marketing managers. First, higher birth rates mean that average family size is higher and households will more likely have a larger number of persons from several generations. These trends impact how decisions are made for consumer purchases as well as the size of the typical product package unit. Second, developing countries may have a greater appetite for baby- and child-oriented products. Third, rapid urbanization creates opportunities for new products suited to lifestyles in crowded cities and promotional campaigns in large urban markets where they can receive the highest exposure.

ECONOMIC FACTORS

Once the demographic characteristics of a new foreign market are understood, consideration must be given to "effective demand" in the country. Demand is influenced by income levels and the allocation of income among the population. For example, merely because a population is large and growing rapidly does not necessarily mean that the demand for luxury goods will be robust. In fact, most of the population might be struggling to meet the basic needs of life. On the other hand, producers of higher-end goods and services should be mindful of situations in which national income distribution is highly stratified because that country may not have an affluent segment with significant purchasing power. Countries with lower population levels may present more limited market opportunities but potentially greater "disposable" income. Foreign entrants should anticipate faster saturation for export and make preparations for a continuous stream of new complimentary products.

POLITICAL AND REGULATORY FACTORS

Political and regulatory factors are important when defining a product portfolio for a new foreign market. Management must review local trade restrictions and foreign exchange requirements. For example, the company may find that it is unable to import certain products or even raw materials, thereby eliminating the product from its offerings or significantly impacting the economics of attempting to produce locally for domestic distribution. Similarly, certain services may be heavily regulated or prohibited. Some manufacturing may be limited to state-owned enterprises or locally controlled companies. In addition, price controls and fluctuating taxation may damage anticipated profit margins.

CULTURAL FACTORS

Cultural factors definitely influence consumer values and preferences. Areas most often impacted by cultural factors include those consumer products that must conform to local dietary needs, health practices and religious guidelines. Management must always be mindful of the restrictions or taboos that might require adjustment in the packaging, advertising or content of a particular product.

STANDARDIZATION VERSUS ADAPTATION

Environmental factors aside, companies generally have strong reasons for attempting to standardize their product offerings across multiple foreign markets. For one thing, standardization creates opportunities for manufacturing economies of scale and competitive pricing. In addition, a standardized product reduces promotional costs in that a similar message can be delivered across the globe (although care must still be taken to be sure that language and cultural differences are factored into the messaging). Finally, use of a preexisting product minimizes the need for certain pre-launch testing and allows the company to enter a market more quickly.

A standardization policy is more likely to be appropriate as foreign markets become more homogenized and income and educational levels increase. For example, companies that distribute higher-end consumer goods, such as televisions, radios and computers, find that purchasers in more developed countries prefer similar goods despite local technical conditions that may impact the utility of the goods. Pharmaceutical companies also have found that standardizing basic products, such as syringes, is the best way to proceed and usually overcomes all local governmental quality requirements.

However, the lessons from developing countries are very different. Studies indicate that consumer products produced by companies in developed countries often need to be modified to succeed in developing countries. The reason is that many new products for these markets are basic items, such as food and clothing, which necessarily must be tailored to local cultural expectations. Service offerings also need to be adjusted to meet local expectations regarding support and information, particularly if the purchaser in the developing country is unlikely to have had the opportunity to obtain the technical education and skills available to purchasers in more industrialized countries.

ADVISORY: Failure to adapt a product early enough can have disastrous results for the company. In more than one case, companies have begun selling their standardized product into a new foreign market only to discover that local consumers did not like the product. At that point, no amount of local testing and adjustments can overcome the initial bad impression in the minds of consumers. The company may have to withdraw from the market; it may re-enter at a later date with a localized product and new marketing pitch that masks the identity of the seller and its relationship to the earlier failed product.

Research and Development

At some point in the evolution of an organization, the operators must consider research and development strategies and procedures. In general, research and development is the process of developing new products. But it also includes improving and enhancing existing products, creating or adopting methods for enhancing the efficiency and cost-effectiveness of internal production and business systems. So-called R&D activities includes applied research designed to solve specific problems and achieve agreed upon commercial results, adaptation of basic research (i.e., advanced knowledge and technology not originally created for commercial purposes) and acquisition and adaptation of technologies and ideas from third parties through licensing and other technology transfer methods.

There are a number of key issues that must be addressed when describing the company's development processes. For example, it is important to identify the sources for the company's products. The company might rely on its internal engineers and researchers for development of new products. Alternatively, it may license or acquire all or part of its products from third parties. Manufacturing capabilities also present an interesting question, particularly when the company is relatively small and lacks the financial resources necessary to build its own plants or facilities for production. Finally, the company's distribution strategy may rely on its own sales force, sales representative and distribution agreements with third parties, or a combination of both.

Historically, global organizations adopted a centralized structure for R&D management with a central office or department responsible for deciding the type of research that would be performed and how innovations would be shared throughout the organization. Since all geographic divisions within the organization were dependent on the development of new ideas, it was thought to be essential that one central point within the company would serve as the clearinghouse. However, several recent trends have challenged the notion of centralized R&D, including the view that innovation can be found throughout the world and not just in two or three countries. There is also a need to develop localized solutions to production problems and customer requirements. Governments offer incentives to foreign companies that are willing to set up R&D departments that utilize local scientists and collaborate with educational institutions in neighboring communities.

GLOBAL INNOVATION MANAGEMENT

Although the R&D activities of global organization may be dispersed over a number of locations in different foreign countries, long-term strategic R&D goals of the company must still be established by senior executives at the top of the organizational hierarchy. At that level, the company can best determine if its main interest is the development of a large portfolio of new products or the generation of new technologies that can be licensed to third parties. The latter can be used to improve the quality of the company's own production processes. Initiatives to enhance and improve existing products to extend their life cycle should also be launched at the top in conjunction with the pursuit of new foreign markets for such products. In any event, once these decisions have been made, the challenge for strategic managers in each region and country is to assign projects and priorities to their respective R&D departments.

ORGANIZATIONAL R&D GUIDELINES

When planning for global R&D activities, managers must follow certain overriding guidelines that apply to each project and to the structure and operation of the entire R&D function. These guidelines should cover the scope and goals of R&D projects, the speed of the development cycle and procedures for benchmarking R&D activities.

PLAN TIP: It is common for companies to actively seek breakthrough products that can alter competitive conditions and generate significant returns on investment. However, the easier way to achieve positive results from R&D is to concentrate on smaller R&D projects that have foreseeable objectives and are more easily managed. In selecting such projects, pay attention to the requirements of all segments of the global organization. A good R&D project for a global organization is one that results in new products or applications that can be quickly diffused to all parts of the company and applied in multiple markets, thereby effectively spreading out the cost of R&D.

Efforts should be made to streamline the decision-making process with respect to R&D projects. Companies should first define general standards of performance that would apply to all R&D projects. These might include projected return on investment, time for completion of the development cycle and the optimal size of the development team. Once those standards are established, they should be applied in a way that minimizes the decision-making hierarchy so that designers and scientists can get rapid feedback from top managers in the event that new ideas arise during the actual research activities.

GLOBAL R&D ORGANIZATIONAL PROCEDURES

Although a global organization will generally have at least some small, centralized R&D office, the primary focus will usually be on the activities being carried out in the various foreign R&D departments and how the results of those activities can be applied in other parts of the organization. Each R&D department should have a clear and concise goal and direction that can be supported by appropriate budgets and monitored through agreed upon standards and benchmarks. In most cases, these departments will have relatively short-term projects, such as modification of products to suit local needs and customs and technical service. If appropriate, funds can also be allocated for the development of completely new products (i.e., different from those otherwise offered globally) to meet the needs of the local market and compliment the company's product line.

Planning and budgeting, which are important functions in strictly domestic R&D activities, become even more significant for global organizations. The key question is to determine how R&D activities can be best allocated among the various foreign R&D departments. The general solution is that comparative advantages can be created from a global R&D organization and should be exploited by companies whenever possible. For example, a company may be able to access a pool of specialized scientists and engineers in one part of the world who are positioned to uncover technological solutions more quickly than colleagues in other parts of the world. The overhead costs associated with R&D may be lower in a particular country, either due to lower overall cost of living or the availability of local government incentives.

Communication is another important element in conducting global R&D. In many cases, effective R&D, even for discrete foreign markets, requires collaboration among personnel spread throughout the world. Product development teams will often include scientists and engineers from several different locations, thereby allowing work on a project to proceed on a round-the-clock basis. For this approach to be effective, management must create a comprehensive global communication system that will support all of the required interaction. This may include use of the Internet and intranets as well as project management strategies that create the proper sequence of activities and tasks.

Intellectual Property

In large part, your company's competitive value depends on its R&D activities and ability to protect the products that embody that technology. Accordingly, the business plan must identify and secure the company's intellectual property (IP) rights, including patents, copyrights, trademarks and trade secrets. Although it is not necessary to include full legal descriptions of each IP right, the reader should gain a sense of the efforts that have been made to protect the company's core IP in all key geographic markets.

Obviously, the significance of IP to any business enterprise will depend on its purpose, mode of operations and the environment and markets in which it operates. For example, the growth and development of a high-tech firm clearly depends on its ability to build and maintain a strong portfolio of technology "assets." On the other hand, the strength of other firms may not be in technology or research but in their skills in production, marketing and distribution. Even in those cases, technical assets such as production "know how," trade secrets (e.g., customer lists and informational databases) and trademarks may play an important role in the success of the firm. For this reason, the business plan should describe the company's policies and viewpoint regarding the overall importance of IP rights in the particular industries and markets where it is active.

CHAPTER 9

Plan Section 4:
Manufacturing or Methodology

I HAVEN'T FAILED. I HAVE JUST FOUND 10,000 WAYS

THAT DON'T WORK. – EDISON

MANUFACTURING INVOLVES A WIDE VARIETY OF ACTIVITIES dedicated to the commercial production of the company's physical goods in quantities and at rates consistent with market demand for the products. Although research and development can be quite expensive, manufacturing also represents a significant cost to the company, and every effort should be made to reduce manufacturing costs so that the company can obtain a pricing advantage over competitors. Some of the activities during the manufacturing and production stage include:

- The construction of manufacturing facilities and related equipment
- The design and implementation of quality control procedures
- The development of a distribution system (i.e., shipment and warehousing processes)
- The creation of customer assistance schemes
- Contracting for procurement of parts, raw materials and other production items

A service provider will be faced with many of the same issues as a manufacturer. The primary distinction will be the focus on the methodology of services instead of the manufacture of products. A service provider may need training facilities, educational procedures, continuing support for improvement of services and quality control, a distribution system, customer assistance program and a means for procuring the materials necessary to support the provision of the services. Often, a service provider also sells goods in connection with the services, in which case, manufacturing issues also will come into play.

Business Plan Disclosure Issues

The business plan should describe how the company intends to manufacture its goods or establish its service methodology, and how it will distribute its products to customers or into appropriate distribution channels. The following issues should be addressed:

- Will the company retain its manufacturing of goods or methodology of services internally or subcontract with others for all or part of the process? If the company will be subcontracting, does it plan to develop internal capacity in the future?

- Does the company or its subcontractor have manufacturing or methodology advantages in relation to the company's competitors? If so, how long can those advantages be exploited and how are they protected?
- What is the company's current manufacturing or methodology capacity? Is it sufficient to meet the requirements of the company in the future? If not, what plans does the company have for expanding such capacity and what costs and risks are associated with such plans?
- What are the critical parts or components in the manufacturing or methodology? How are these parts or components acquired or derived? Are any of them "single-sourced," or does the company have several suppliers or resources? What lead times are required to obtain the parts or components or to train service providers? How does this delay impact the ability of the company to meet increases in demand?
- What are the standard costs for manufacturing products at various volumes or of establishing the methodology of services at various amounts?

Internal Manufacturing or Methodology

Many companies prefer to rely on their own internal facilities for production. A company may establish its facilities in a single location or may set up facilities in multiple places to take advantage of reduced costs and to provide products in close proximity to the actual markets. For example, if the company develops a large market for its products in a foreign country, it may decide to manufacture or train local residents to provide services there to satisfy local demand as opposed to importing products or employees from remote locations.

A company's internal manufacturing or methodology strategy must address the following key issues:

- Can an internal process achieve costs that enhance the profitability of the product? Management must consider on a per unit or sale basis the initial investment required to establish the facility, the overhead costs associated with operating and maintaining it and additional operational costs. In many cases, it may be cheaper to outsource.

ADVISORY: Both manufacturers and service providers should consider implementation of Activity Based Costing (ABC) techniques as early as possible in the processes. This form of cost accounting provides "true" per unit cost figures since it traces overhead usage to individual products rather than assigning overhead on a production volume basis.

- Can the company develop proprietary processes? Processes that can be patented create significant competitive and cost advantages as well as revenue opportunities through licensing. In this regard, an added advantage in the service sector is the availability of business method patents in some countries.
- Can automated equipment be used to reduce and/or control production costs (e.g., manufacturers use assembly line robotics, services use interface technology such as ATMs)? Can a methodology be largely learned by self-instruction? Companies may achieve significant cost economies by automating these processes, particularly if the automation process is also proprietary.

▓ Can the company take advantage of low cost materials and/or labor? A primary attraction of establishing a wholly-owned foreign production facility is the ability to access lower cost inputs to the production process, including raw materials (e.g., petroleum refineries) and workers (e.g., Bangalore's computer programmers). The downside is that training costs may be significantly higher.

The business plan should contemplate the development and use of productivity programs focusing on ongoing strategies for reduction of manufacturing and methodology costs and increased productivity in future planning periods. In addition, if the company elects to adopt a global strategy for its manufacturing or methodology, systems must be established to monitor the quality of the goods produced or services provided throughout the organization. Otherwise, the apparent cost savings will be worthless if the products are sub par, have significant defects or require extensive post-sale support.

Third Party Production Arrangements

Some companies invest in their own facilities (sometimes to take advantage of lower costs of foreign labor and materials), but another common arrangement is to enter into various production and supply arrangements with third parties. These arrangements are ongoing contracts pursuant to which a firm agrees to manufacture or otherwise procure specified goods or services for sale to the buyer to be resold by the buying firm in its own business operations.

The basic form of production and supply arrangement requires that the buyer deliver orders for the products over the term of the agreement. Those orders will be accepted and filled by the third party producer in much the same way as a long-term sales contract. The contractual terms of these arrangements can be quite complex, with variations triggered by the term of the agreement and the company's volume and delivery requirements. For example, a production and supply agreement should always include the following items:

▓ Description of the products
▓ The manner in which the products are to be priced
▓ The manner of delivery of products and any requirements with respect to shipping and insurance
▓ The specific requirements of the buying firm with respect to performance and content of the products
▓ The form and timing of payment and related credit arrangements
▓ Any warranties and limitations that might be imposed on the respective liabilities of the parties to the agreement

TYPES OF PRODUCTION AGREEMENTS

Several variations on the basic form of a production agreement are described here.

■ CUSTOMIZED

Production and supply agreements often cover products that are already in commercial production, although such arrangements may also be appropriate when the product has just been created and the developer is seeking assistance to produce in sufficient quantity to begin marketing activities. Such an agreement to produce will focus on the specifications of the products and will generally provide for the seller to produce a prototype acceptable to both parties before large-scale production begins. The parties will typically limit the projected production levels for an initial period, pending feedback of market acceptance. A somewhat looser form of customized production arrangement is a long-term contract under which the seller is limited in its choice of vendors for supplies necessary for the production covered by the contract. Such an arrangement may not include unique specifications, but the purchaser is looking for mechanisms to assure the consistency of products purchased over the term of the contract.

■ REQUIREMENTS CONTRACT

A requirements contract is an agreement on the part of the seller to provide all products that the buyer may request during a specified period of time and at a predetermined price, whether fixed or periodically adjusted. The essence of a requirements contract is that the buyer agrees not to purchase similar products from any other party, although the seller may be free to sell the products to other customers. However, if the seller is unable to meet all of the buyer's requirements, the buyer has the right to purchase elsewhere or terminate the contract. Pricing of products sold under a requirements contract will vary with the volume of purchases, and the buyer usually has a right of termination in the event of price increases by the seller.

■ OUTPUT AGREEMENT

An output agreement involves an undertaking by the producer to sell its entire production to the buyer in return for the buyer's commitment to take all the output. Each party's obligation under an output agreement will continue only for a specified period of time. In general, the law imposes a good faith obligation on the parties to such an agreement. This obliges the seller to sell what it produces in good faith and, thus, cannot tender a quantity either far greater, far less or unreasonably disproportionate to a stated estimate. If there is no stated estimate, the law generally fills in by assuming the parties would have intended the output to be in an amount that is "normal" or comparable to prior output (for example, based on output during the prior years of the agreement).

■ ORIGINAL EQUIPMENT MANUFACTURER AGREEMENT (GOODS ONLY)

Another common form of manufacturing relationship, and one that is especially popular in global markets, involves a seller and a buyer who is an original equipment manufacturer (OEM). An OEM relationship combines elements of manufacturing and distribution functions. The seller will agree to sell goods to the OEM which, in turn, will add some "value" to the goods, such as enhancements or new applications, and then sell the "value-added" products to its own customers. An OEM agreement usually involves detailed negotiations over the specific requirements of the OEM with regard to the products as well as the terms on which the products will be sold to the OEM. If properly structured, an OEM relationship can provide a smaller firm with a significant customer for its products at a time when it may be struggling to develop its own distribution network and stable of customer accounts.

In OEM arrangements, the seller may agree to provide additional service and maintenance on the products delivered to the OEM, and the scope of these services may be included in a separate form of service and maintenance agreement. An OEM relying on products that are to be furnished by the seller over an extended period of time may require that the seller deposit certain technical information and source codes in escrow. This will protect the OEM in the event that the seller should default under its obligations to continue to supply the specified products to the OEM. If there is a default, the OEM would have the right to access the escrowed materials and commence manufacturing the goods covered by the agreement without the need for further consent from the seller.

LICENSE TO PRODUCE AND DISTRIBUTE

A developer or owner of a product line (goods or services) may grant a license to another party to produce and distribute them as finished products to customers. In return, the licensor would receive a royalty based on some measure of the producer-distributor's performance, such as the quantity sold or the net proceeds it receives from the sale of the products.

This type of relationship, which will include contractual provisions typically found as part of a distributorship arrangement, may be attractive if the producer-distributor can produce at or below the costs that would be incurred by the licensor. Similar benefits would be derived if the products needed to be adapted to conform with specific local requirements of the country or region where they are sold by the producer. A license for the conduct of both activities can be cost-effective, but the licensor may be rightly concerned about losing control of the licensed technology or methodology.

LICENSE AND PRODUCT PURCHASE AGREEMENT

An interesting hybrid form of production arrangement is a license and product purchase agreement. This arrangement involves the grant of a license for the production and sale of goods or services developed by the licensor, coupled with an agreement for the sale of a specified number of the licensed products by the licensee back to the licensor at the best prices offered by the licensee to its OEMs and/or resellers. The licensor obtains revenues from the sale of the products by the licensee, and also obtains a guaranteed source of the licensed products that it can resell to its own customers. In turn, the licensee effectively receives a guaranteed purchase order to help defer some of the initial costs of "ramping up" for large-scale production of the licensed products.

CHAPTER 10

Plan Section 5: Marketing

A MAN SELLING A BLIND HORSE ALWAYS PRAISES ITS

FEET. — GERMAN PROVERB

MARKETING IS CONSIDERED by many to be the most important part of a business plan. Experience has demonstrated that numerous businesses with great products have failed because marketing and distribution were inadequate.

Marketing strategy is integrally connected with topics already covered in other chapters, notably production, environmental analysis and entry strategies. In fact, the threshold issue is to identify markets that are best suited for adaptation of existing products. The relevant factors include demographic indicators, income and education levels, technical capabilities of the marketplace and logistical problems associated with getting the product to the end-users. These factors can be discussed in the marketing section of the business plan or as part of the general analysis of global business opportunities that are available to the company.

After selection of the geographic markets and determination of the appropriate product strategy for those markets, the plan should deal with other marketing issues on a country-by-country or market-by-market basis. Don't make the mistake of assuming that the same strategies will work in different countries. This holds true even when countries are in close proximity and share similar demographic characteristics (e.g., Switzerland, Austria, Germany). Analyze each market separately, even if a decision is ultimately made to combine marketing efforts for several markets (e.g., one distributor for two or more countries in the same region and/or a promotional campaign covering several linguistically comparable countries).

When the business plan is prepared in connection with obtaining financing for the entire business, and not merely for expansion into foreign markets, the marketing section should analyze all existing markets. This would include the primary domestic market for the company.

Customer Analysis

Even if the company's major customer relationships have already been described early in the business plan, the marketing section should contain more detailed information and analysis specifically related to the following:

- The requirements and needs of the customers
- The impact that selection and use of the company's products will have on the customer's business or personal activities
- The company's strategy for customer relationship management
- The methods that the company has used, and proposes to use, for market research and to continuously monitor customer needs

REQUIREMENTS AND NEEDS OF CUSTOMERS

An important aspect of the business plan is to provide the reader with a good sense of how the company interacts with customers to track their changing requirements. The business plan should clearly demonstrate knowledge of the needs and requirements of the customer base. One method commonly used is to describe the mechanisms that may have been established and maintained by the company to motivate employees to understand customer needs. This may involve discussion of the company's customer service procedures, and includes regular contacts between representatives of the company and its customers. Routine inquiries and discussions regarding the terms of purchase and sale, warranties, returns and shipping dates should be part of these discussions.

If possible, the business plan should address how customer needs are defined throughout the industry and how the company is addressing those requirements. For example, it is often said that customers seek "quality" as the most important factor in a vendor relationship. This is becoming a standard part of the vendor-buyer relationship, so you should make an effort to describe the quality dimensions in your particular industry. Emphasis should be placed on the manner in which "quality" is measured, customer perceptions of the quality component of different firms and development and evolution of those perceptions over time. Quality is defined by the expectations of the customer, not by the producers. As such, the company will need to be cognizant of such things as durability, lack of defects, reliability and serviceability. Special features or an overall "quality name," which is a function of historical customer satisfaction and promotional activities, should be placed at the forefront.

IMPACT OF PRODUCTS ON CUSTOMERS

Customer analysis requires an assessment of the effect that use of the company's products might have on the business activities of potential customers. In conducting this customer analysis, the company might ask the following questions:

- What economic factors are faced by the "decision-makers" at each of the company's major customers?
- What incentives might be present to persuade them to switch or to use substitute products?
- How important is the company's product in developing the customer's own product, both technically and in terms of cost?
- What amount of savings will a customer realize from using the company's products?
- What investment return will the customer realize from purchasing the products?
- Will use of the company's products necessitate any material changes in the manner in which the customer conducts its business activities (e.g., required purchase of other equipment, change in work habits or modifications in organizational structure)?
- How sophisticated is the customer's information about the product offered by the company and the marketplace for such products?
- How will expected changes in the customer's business activities affect the customer's purchasing of and reliance upon your firm's products?

CUSTOMER RELATIONSHIP MANAGEMENT

One of the key components in the marketing area is "customer relationship management" (CRM). Business planners must appreciate that it is often easier to grow sales through existing customers than to attract new customers. Technological changes, including the Internet, have created new opportunities for companies to communicate with customers, survey their needs and handle their problems.

The quality and stability of each of the company's major customer relationships should be examined in the business plan. The key issue is whether the company has, through contractual arrangements or otherwise, established a good relationship with each of its major customers. This relationship prevents customers from switching to either another vendor or to self-production. In addition to regular contacts between the company's representatives and its customers, the company should establish functional incentives for employees with respect to retention of existing customers. In addition, the company should create and describe in the business plan, a list of advertising information that is sent to the company's customers, including:

- Brochures
- Catalogs
- Mailers
- Publicity releases
- Newspaper or magazine articles
- Other promotional literature concerning the company, its products or personnel

MARKET RESEARCH

Smart decisions about customer relations and promotional strategies begin with solid market research. The details of market research activities are not usually part of the actual business plan, but at a minimum the reader should be made aware of the time and effort you have expended in collecting and analyzing the necessary information. Actual details of the research can be provided in appendices.

- **SURVEY THE CONSUMERS** The company should survey potential customers regarding its proposed products to determine whether a sufficient need exists in the marketplace to support the company's new business activities. If potential customers have been able to see or test a prototype of the product, the business plan should discuss their reactions, as well as any actions the company proposes to take to respond to issues, questions or problems raised by test groups. If the company has actually been able to solicit serious indications of interest or even orders from prospective customers, this should be highlighted in the business plan—particularly, if the product is relatively new and actual sales activities have been limited.

- **COLLECT THE DATA** Market research is especially important to a company newly entering a foreign country. The launch of sales operations in unknown territories is extremely difficult, particularly if the company has little or no experience in international activities. Data usually can be found from sources in the company's home country, including university libraries and government publications; but that information cannot replace facts collected on site—right inside the foreign country—and interpreted by managers and consultants familiar with the local market. In addition, even when resources are available for local information collection, companies may quickly discover that infrastructure deficiencies make the process quite difficult and the results much more unreliable.

■ RECOGNIZE AND RESOLVE RESEARCH HURDLES Data collection in new foreign markets must overcome survey problems. Language differences, local attitudes regarding disclosure of preferences and other information, a lack of trained local market researchers and inconsistencies of trade figures are all common problems. For example, in some lesser developed markets, mail and telephone surveys are not likely to yield representative results. This is often due to problems in postal deliveries and telephone services, as well as literacy shortcomings and the lack of widespread phone installation. Consumers may be unfamiliar with product preference surveys and great care must be taken in developing questions that are sensitive to cultural norms. Another disconcerting hurdle is that government-prepared statistics are often significantly biased, particularly for import figures of specific products, thereby making it extremely difficult to judge local demand.

Pricing

Pricing is the second most important element of the company's marketing strategy. Some companies may be able to seize a competitive advantage in a new foreign market by introducing products not previously distributed in the country. Most companies, however, are likely to be confronted with comparable or substitute products marketed by domestic firms or other global competitors. Accordingly, it is not surprising that marketing managers in global enterprises often focus primarily on pricing strategies in the initial entry stages.

In the absence of government price controls or other artificial pricing limitations, companies must determine the price for their products based on such traditional factors as competitive prices, required return on investment, margins and near-term strategic objectives (e.g., building market share). Many developing countries still impose some form of price controls on specified goods, making it necessary to start negotiating with the government to set prices at a level that provides some margin of protection. Alternatively, the company may diversify its product offerings into other areas to make up for losses on controlled products.

Pricing issues are not limited to direct sales activities. In fact, they can be a very important consideration when the company seeks to export goods or services that it might be producing in the local market. For example, if the host country's exchange rate is strengthening or is overvalued, the foreign producer's effective price for its exports is increased and sales levels may suffer. On the other hand, a devalued currency might make the company's exported products more attractive. The availability of export subsidies also can have a dramatic impact on pricing strategies.

Promotion

Promotional strategies for a new foreign market include selection of the appropriate media for disseminating messages and information about the company's products, formulation of the marketing message and provision of customer service and support.

MEDIA CHOICE

In developing promotional strategies, managers may choose from among a wide range of media, but the effectiveness of each strategy will vary significantly depending on the level of consumer income and development in the chosen country. Alternatives include newspapers and magazines, radio, television, motion pictures, billboards and posters, direct mail and telemarketing, personal presentations by sales representatives, Internet advertisements and informal communications channels. The efficacy of each strategy will depend on the local communications infrastructure. The income available to purchase and use various communications tools (e.g., televisions), the literacy rates and the location of the target purchasing groups in the local market also come into play. In general, the level of advertising expenditures as a percentage of GDP increases significantly as income begins to rise in the country.

■ NEWSPAPERS AND MAGAZINES Newspapers and magazines are traditional avenues for advertising communications in many countries. Unfortunately, print media will not be as effective in countries having lower literacy rates among those persons that make the primary purchasing decisions. To develop an effective print media strategy, marketing managers need to analyze who the primary purchasers are in the foreign market.

PLAN NOTE: In country A, literacy rates are rising because of recent improvements in education. However, middle-aged adults, traditionally the primary buyers of print media in most societies, have not been educated and are thus less likely to buy print media. In country B, a wide gap remains in literacy levels between men and women. Men often make the purchasing decisions for the entire family, including products for women. Therefore, print advertising messages need to focus on the buyers (men) as opposed to the consumers of the product (women).

Distribution patterns for newspapers and magazines should also be analyzed. In many countries, newspapers are mainly distributed in the urban areas where the literacy rates tend to be high and delivery costs low. The number of newspapers and magazines published is often severely limited, requiring readers to share copies, with the result that advertisements may take much longer to reach a large pool of prospective buyers. Magazine coverage tends to be even more limited and circulation is often restricted to a specific socioeconomic group. However, this media format presents interesting opportunities for market segmentation.

Managers should further review available domestic print media as opposed to the international print media that is sold or distributed within the country. If domestic print media is primarily government owned or produced, managers will need to determine whether their advertising can and should be printed in such newspapers or magazines. In addition to government restrictions on advertising and content, placement of advertising in such media can suggest a political alignment with the current authorities, which may or may not be advisable depending on the preferences of the targeted purchasers. While available international print media may be glitzy, glossy and allow for coverage of multiple country markets at one time, remember that it often remains on store shelves; consumers favor local print media which caters to their language, cultural tastes and individual concerns.

PLAN NOTE: Several local firms in a particular country were asked to provide the names of international newspapers and magazines that were locally available so that a multinational company could determine whether its advertising had appeared there (as evidence of its reputation among consumers). Not only did the local firms not know the 100-year-old multinational company, but they also were unable to supply more than five names of international print media. The multinational company then sent its own representatives into the market where they found magazine and newspaper racks in numerous bookstores and newsstands throughout the capital city. Many shops were stacked with more than 20 international magazines, including four to six months of back issues. Had the local firms been deceptive, unaware or merely disinterested?

Whether you choose domestic or international media, in some countries you will face content restrictions requiring modification of your advertising. For example, some countries prohibit the advertising of all alcohol products. Many countries have agencies that review and ban advertisements with content that the officials determine undermines religious precepts (India), moral principles (Iran) or political figures or policies (Vietnam). In such countries, you will need to find creative ways to adjust your promotions to reach potential consumers.

■ RADIO AND TELEVISION Radio is a very popular and powerful communications tool in many developing countries. In fact, radio ownership is generally much higher than television ownership in some countries and offers opportunities to communicate promotional messages in rural areas not easily reached through print media. Television ownership depends highly on consumer income levels and available infrastructure. Oddly enough, in emerging markets a television is usually one of the earliest purchases when income rises and basic needs have been covered. In general, urban middle and upper classes have the highest concentration of television ownership and the company should target its promotional campaigns accordingly. Given the affluence of television owners in lower middle-income countries, the fact that a majority of the advertising expenditures in those countries are aimed toward television is not surprising. The percentage decreases as countries develop and a greater percentage of the advertising budget is allocated to print media and direct advertising.

Marketing managers should bear a few other things in mind when planning for radio and television advertising. First, government controls on radio and television promotions are imposed in many countries. In fact, some countries prohibit commercial advertising on radio channels. Second, radio and television stations are often state-owned, which means the government may restrict the timing and length of promotional messages. Third, the number of television sets per capita can be a deceiving measure of the utility of this form of communication because a television set in one household in a densely populated urban area may be viewed by a number of families.

■ OTHER PROMOTIONAL MEDIA The use and effectiveness of other promotional media will vary substantially from country to country. For example, movie theaters are a novel and popular form of recreational activity in developing countries and motion pictures are often accompanied by commercial advertisements. Billboards and posters are generally a low-cost advertising method. However, it is difficult to measure their effectiveness. Direct mail and telemarketing are used mostly in industrialized countries where reliable postal and phone systems are established and market research has been completed to identify appropriate purchaser target groups. Some E.U. nations, such as Germany, have tight restrictions on direct marketing, especially telemarketing (so check local regulations carefully). Finally, informal communications, so-called "word of mouth," may be effective in a particular region. For example, it may be useful to convene a series of meetings with community and business leaders to discuss the opening of new sales outlets in the area, thereby generating enthusiasm for the products and related employment opportunities.

Advertising on the Internet is another alternative. A few years ago, as the popularity of the Internet grew in industrialized countries, many companies seized online advertising as a dynamic promotional strategy. Optimists saw Internet advertising as a way to reach consumers around the globe without the expense associated with developing local market campaigns in each foreign country where the advertiser's products were sold. Unfortunately, the Internet is not necessarily the final answer to the global marketer's problems. For one thing, the level of Internet use in many countries is insignificant. For another, companies still must contend with language differences, cultural issues and local preferences to ensure consumer understanding of the marketing messages. Additionally, the making of payments and delivery of goods and services remain dependent on traditional infrastructure. Nonetheless, a Web site that describes a company's products and that provides information on how to contact local sales representatives for the particular country can be an effective investment. This is particularly so if a company is selling directly to other businesses in the foreign market (the "B2B"—business-to-business—market).

MARKETING MESSAGES

Developing an effective and appealing marketing message is truly a challenge for any global business. Language and cultural differences create opportunities for major misunderstandings. It is important to involve people familiar with the local market when developing messages and analyzing advertising copy that the company wishes to "import" into a new country.

The first thing to consider is the possibility of a wide number of distinct dialects within the foreign market. For example, substantial linguistic diversity exists within countries in the sub-Saharan and Asian regions, although each government is attempting to promote a single dialect as the official national language to further unity. In any event, if there is a large target group that uses a different dialect, consideration should be given to the use of special marketing messages that take these differences into account (e.g., India has 18 "official" languages and 1,600 dialects for marketers to overcome).

Another potential source of marketing blunders lies in the direct translation of words and phrases used in other countries. A classic example was the attempt to translate the "Come Alive with Pepsi" slogan for Taiwan. The result ran something along the lines of "Pepsi will bring your ancestors back from the dead"—a very interesting product claim. Needless to say, this was not the desired marketing message.

Finally, an understanding of cultural norms is essential in developing an appropriate local marketing message. In many cases, gestures, colors and clothing in commercials that may be popular in one country will be considered insulting in another market. Care should be taken when injecting sexual tension into advertisements. For example, consumers in one country may enjoy a perfume maker's inference that its product will generate interest from numerous men; but such an approach would be inappropriate in Muslim countries where overt flirtation with women is taboo. Another example would be the avoidance of the number "4" in advertising in China because in Mandarin it sounds like the word for "death."

(See *A Short Course in International Marketing Blunders*, also by World Trade Press.)

CUSTOMER SERVICE AND SUPPORT

Support and service focus on activities occurring after the production and sale of the product. They are part of both the company's engineering and marketing strategies. From an engineering perspective, support and service include the ability of a company to provide technical instructions, warranty services and other repairs, spare parts and, in some cases, improvements and enhancements. As a marketing tool, support and service is a means for maintaining customer satisfaction, building loyalty and developing ongoing relationships. These allow the company to further understand the changing needs of its customer base. In fact, post-sale contacts with customers serve as the basis for identifying new product spin-offs or design changes that can become part of the company's product portfolio.

The issue of customer service is particularly important in developing countries where it is difficult to obtain information about the products from other sources and customers are likely to be less familiar with the products and the underlying technology. Solid service and support develop trust and allows the company to begin working with local customers to design new products suited to the needs of the marketplace.

As with production and distribution, the key choice for the company with respect to support and service is whether it should conduct such activities directly using its own personnel or subcontract with third parties. The business plan should describe the company's plans in this area. The company should be mindful of the risks associated with using third party support and service providers. Obviously, any failure by such parties to perform their duties may lead to substantial customer dissatisfaction and harm the company's "goodwill," at least locally, if not beyond the country's borders. Also, the company may be deprived of the opportunity to maintain regular contact with end-users of its products. Finally, companies should be wary of transferring a good deal of their proprietary technical information to a third party who will carry out the company's sales duties. Investors may be concerned that the third party will misappropriate the technical information, thus reducing its competitive advantage.

Distribution

Even the best products, though reasonably priced, may find it difficult to overcome distribution problems. When entering a new foreign market, companies need to plan for movement of products into and around the country. Distribution must be speedy, reliable and cost-effective. Otherwise, consumers will turn to other sources for their product requirements and the company will quickly learn that it has excess inventory sitting in facilities far away from the potential end-users.

Distribution is a particularly difficult issue in developing countries, which often lack the requisite infrastructure. Companies often balk at entering new markets where the transport infrastructure is weak, telecommunications services are poor and storage facilities are scarce and/or poorly maintained. Distribution channels also may be clogged by an excess number of intermediaries. It is not uncommon for products to go through four to eight sets of "middle-men" from the time they are first produced to the point where they are purchased by consumers. In addition, research has shown that distribution channels in many developing countries often will be dominated by a single ethnic group or political elite. This places a premium on creating strategies for forging good connections. Finally, the lack of effective information communication creates market imperfections because prices may vary substantially within the country.

Companies often elect to form strategic alliances with local companies to distribute products in new foreign markets. Such a decision should be based on weighing the costs of establishing a proprietary distribution system (and the accompanying benefits from greater control of distribution channels) against the anticipated efficiencies of simply building on the existing systems and relationships of the alliance partner. Factors to consider might be the number of outlets controlled by the local distributor, the existing product line of the distributor and the profit margins available on specific sales transactions. This should include the risk that the distributor might become a competitor. Use of a local distributor might be merely a first step in entering the market. The company may want to reserve the right to assume control of distribution on its own, perhaps by acquiring the distributor at some later date. Even if the alliance strategy is used, the company should establish mechanisms for having its own representative involved in the launch of the product. This is the best way for the company to gather its own intelligence on the local market and customer needs.

ADVISORY: In nations where technical acumen is low and locally produced consumer goods are few, foreign producers are usually excluded from any direct control of distribution. Local firms are given exclusive right to "add value" at this point.

If the company decides to mount its own distribution system, a number of factors and potential problems must be considered. First of all, the cost of acquiring or building the necessary distribution outlets and storage facilities must be carefully calculated. In some cases, companies may be surprisingly successful in launching non-traditional distribution outlets, including enclosed stores that operate alongside open markets and street vendors. In any event, location is important and the company must go through the process described earlier in the book to make sure that it places outlets in the proper areas. Second, the company must consider the need to engage in distribution-related activities that differ significantly from those in its home country. For example, deficiencies in local transport may require that the company create its own systems for moving goods around the country. Similarly, the company may need to extend credit to retailers due to the fact that the local banking system is unable or unwilling to offer commercial credit plans.

An effective, yet challenging, middle ground strategy is to seek synergistic combinations of home country and local market distribution strategies.

PLAN NOTE: A Canadian company produced snack foods that it normally distributed through direct store drops to major supermarkets in the US and domestically. When the company looked to expand distribution into Mexico, it discovered a system that was heavily reliant on small family-run outlets that catered to consumers with limited mobility and a tendency to buy in small quantities and visit the stores frequently. These consumer buying patterns created cash flow problems for retailers, limiting their ability to make big orders. In addition, the small size of the stores made large inventories impossible. The solution for the Canadian company was to create its own armada of local salesman-drivers who would make frequent visits to these small outlets. As a result, the company could penetrate the Mexican market by leveraging on the traditional distribution system.

The above-described situation in Mexico, which is repeated in other less developed markets around the globe, illustrates opportunities for using existing distribution systems as the basis for creating new types of outlets. For example, fast food companies have been successful in launching new franchises in major urban areas around the developing world by positioning them as natural extensions of existing outdoor vendors or quick lunch stops. Of course, these outlets have adapted their menus to local tastes but have maintained their quick service and tight cost control methods from their original operations. Some have spawned dynamic imitators like the Belgian hamburger chain *Quick* in its response to the *McDonald's* and *Burger King* franchises.

CHAPTER 11

Plan Section 6: Management and Organizational Structure

IF EVERYONE IS THINKING ALIKE, THEN SOMEBODY ISN'T

THINKING. — GEN. GEORGE PATTON

EVEN THE BEST PRODUCT or the most talented group of product developers cannot succeed without good company management and an appropriate organizational structure. In reality, wise investors will not take a serious look at any business plan that does not include participation by an experienced team of professional managers. Even if the plan is strictly internal to the company, describing team and management players is important. Each should have a proven track record in the specific industry or functional activity. Management and organization issues are particularly demanding for global companies and should always be analyzed in great detail in the business plan. Sadly, this area is often ignored while the plan drafter spends most of the time discussing new products. Good ideas are easier to find than good managers.

Senior Managers and Owners

If your plan is being written in part for outside investors it should include an extensive description of the company's senior managers and owners, including:

- Management team's names, skills and experiences
- Recruitment and compensation of senior managers
- Directors' names and experience
- Owners' names and ownership structure

MANAGEMENT TEAM'S NAMES, SKILLS AND EXPERIENCES

The business plan should list the names of the managers in such a way that surname and given name are easily distinguished. This can have serious consequences when working with transnational/multicultural teams. Gender indicators should also be used to avoid confusion and embarrassment. Next, describe the skills, experience and performance record of the senior managers, and then relate these background items to the company's needs. Do not merely list education and job titles, but also describe how they are related to their position and duties at the company.

Investors want to know if managers' experiences are applicable to the company's purposes. To evaluate, they must understand the person's previous career history. In addition, they want to see if the skills of the managers will carry the company through its takeoff. They do not want to worry about replacing managers soon after funding.

If the business plan is simply being prepared for internal use in connection with the launch of global operations, it should still include an inventory of the skills and experiences of senior managers. You may find that one or more members of the existing management team have prior experience in a particular foreign market or that they have worked with companies with an active global marketing or manufacturing strategy. These connections can be a valuable resource for recruiting new talent or understanding the problems that may confront the company as it goes global.

In many cases, some of the required managerial positions will be unfilled at the time the plan is being prepared. Therefore, your business plan should identify all the anticipated managerial staffing requirements, the anticipated timing for recruiting candidates to fill additional positions and the specific qualifications for such positions. For example, in the case of a start-up business, the company may delay bringing on an experienced chief financial officer until funding has been obtained. However, investors will want assurances that their money will be well protected once the investment is closed. For your global plan, key management positions in each of the target countries must be identified in advance.

PLAN NOTE: Individual managers can be quite sensitive about how their work experience is presented in the business plan. Plan writers/editors should get each manager to write their own "mini-CV" based on guidelines (e.g., word count, applicable experience, etc.). Often "embellishments" have to be deleted, but this saves time and avoids bruised egos. It is also a good indicator of what each manager "brings to the table" for the new business. Often it is a matter of interpretation.

RECRUITMENT AND COMPENSATION

The business plan should describe how the company intends to recruit and compensate its key managers. Compensation practices may vary substantially from country to country and no single answer will always apply across the board in any global organization. The business plan should describe base salaries, cash bonuses, equity incentive plans, profit sharing plans and other benefits that might be included in the overall compensation package. Remember that retirement and health benefits commonly offered to employees in one country may be a completely new concept in another country. Where such services are provided and highly regulated by the government, they may even be taxable.

PLAN NOTE: Accordingly, you will have to determine what benefits can be provided on a company-wide basis. Whenever possible, compensation should be tied to specific business milestones. This is a particularly important strategy for entering a new foreign market. The formula should be fair to the manager and recognize the risks associated with the venture. Such compensation should also foster goal congruence.

DIRECTORS' NAMES AND EXPERIENCE

Assuming the business is organized as a corporate or limited liability entity, which is the predominant form of business organization throughout the world, responsibility for management oversight will be vested with a board of directors or similar body. Accordingly, the members of the company's board of directors should be identified in the business plan, along with a description of their background, experience and how they became involved with the company. Directorships should not be handed out carelessly and each director should be able to provide tangible value, experience and contacts to the business.

ADVISORY: When the company is entering a new geographic area, it would be useful to have at least one board member with significant business experience in the area as well as contacts with local businesses and government agencies.

OWNERS' NAMES AND OWNERSHIP STRUCTURE

Certainly when the business plan is being prepared for prospective investors, it should include information on the current owners of the company and the ownership structure, including the economic and voting rights of the owners. For a corporation, this information would include the shareholders of the corporation and a description of the respective rights, preferences and privileges of their shares. If there are a number of shareholders, it is probably sufficient to simply list the major shareholders unless a small shareholder has significant voting rights under a separate agreement.

Obviously, the ownership structure of the company is important in negotiating the terms of any new investment. If the company has already received outside financing, new investors will look to the shareholder summary as a means for understanding the investment history of the company. For example, investors will look at the timing and pricing of the most recent round of equity financing and compare it to price per share (i.e., valuation) that the company is seeking in the current financing round. Investors will also be interested in the background and experience of prior investors, including their track record in backing successful companies in the same industry.

Another thing to keep in mind is the possibility that one or more of the existing owners might have rights that impact the company's entry strategies in a particular geographic area. For example, a company might receive investment funding from an Asian company in exchange for a right of first refusal in favor of the investor's affiliates to distribute the company's products in specified countries within Asia.

ADVISORY: If the planners are considering using stock options as a form of compensation for employees it should be noted that this is not universally considered a legitimate form of compensation. Many countries have laws forbidding "deferred payroll" while others have complex rules for taxing the options. Planners need to seek out both accounting and legal counsel on this matter before proposing compensation and ownership structures.

Organizational Structure

Organizational structure can be a complex subject. This means there is no single best method that should be used to organize a company's various functions and activities. Moreover, it is likely that the optimal organizational structure for the firm will change over time, as the company evolves, develops new products and moves into different areas and as changes begin to occur at the senior management level. Nonetheless, the business plan should describe how the company's employees are organized and how the chain of responsibility for particular functions has been laid out.

A software development company, for instance, may organize itself "horizontally" based on distinct business activities, such as research, product development, systems integration, production, marketing and sales, system management, service and support. Another company might organize itself around a particular product, drawing on functional specialists in each of the required areas (e.g., engineering, marketing, production, etc.).

Whatever structure you chose, it is important that the business plan:

- Describe reporting responsibilities
- Demonstrate how goals and objectives will be set
- Indicate how performance will be monitored
- Give guidance on how customers, suppliers and distributors will interface with the company
- Explain how the company's financial and budget planning systems will be connected so that senior managers can track allocation and utilization of funds for a particular project or activity

EVOLUTIONARY ORGANIZATIONAL ISSUES

New and small companies will likely have a very simple organizational structure. Most of their resources will be devoted to new product development, perhaps supervised by persons serving in other management positions. In such cases, a focus on product development means less attention is paid to the details of day-to-day operations and distribution.

As a result, the business plan must be evolutionary. It must set out the company's plans for fully developing its organizational structure, first by bringing in experienced senior managers, and then recruiting the necessary human resources. If the company's future depends on hiring talent in high demand (e.g., software engineers), the plan should also describe why the company believes it will be able to recruit whomever it needs.

The inevitable evolution of the organization means that the roles of various persons may change substantially over time. For example, the general manager of administration who additionally handles accounting, finance and human resources may have his or her duties split among three or four people. Similarly, the scientist who founded and managed the company in its earliest stages may ultimately return to the role of researcher and "technological guru" as new people are brought in to handle management tasks.

GLOBAL ORGANIZATIONAL ISSUES

In developing the business plan for launching global operations, crucial decisions must be made regarding the overall organization of the company. Similarly, the procedures that need to be implemented to facilitate the circulation of information within the company must be formulated. The organization structure for a global business must be strong enough to ensure that managerial authority is vested in those persons with the requisite skills and information to make the required strategic decisions. At the same time, the structure should be flexible enough to deal with unique problems that might arise in a specific region or country. This will make it necessary to allow for the assembly of functional teams to deal with new products and projects.

■ THE GEOGRAPHICAL STRUCTURE Although any one of a variety of organizational forms might be adopted by an organization as it builds global operations, one common choice is a hierarchical structure marked at the highest levels by segmentation based on geographic regions. For example, the chief executive officer of the company may designate a separate senior manager to head up each division for operations in the Americas (North and South), Europe and Asia. The main reason for such a structure is the need for decisions to be made during the business day of the region in which they are applicable. In addition, of course, regional differentiation is the most reliable way to bundle markets with similar cultures, languages and environmental problems and solutions.

Each of the "top level" regions might be further divided into smaller and more natural geographic areas based on country boundaries, geopolitical links, language, social and cultural background or infrastructure. For example, the operations in the Americas might be divided into North and South (or English, Spanish, Portuguese), each of which would have its own general manager with reporting responsibility to the senior manager of the Americas. In some cases, further layers of management might be added to the mix (e.g., United States, Canada, Mexico, etc.). Too many levels of management, however, involve too many decision makers and slow the decision-making process.

Wherever geographic lines are finally drawn, the next step is for the manager of that region to select managers and staff who will have primary responsibility for the direction of specific products. The number of teams should approximate the major global product and service offerings of the company, thereby allowing communication among managers of the same product operating in different regions. Of course, it may be necessary to appoint additional managers to handle region-specific products that are not offered globally. In any event, each of the teams should have representatives from each of the functional areas relevant to the product, including accounting, finance, operations and marketing. Once the product is discontinued, members of the team can be reassigned to new projects within the same geographic area.

■ GLOBAL ROLE OF THE CEO Another organizational issue to consider is the changing role of the chief executive officer of the company as business expands into foreign markets and the structure of the company changes along the lines outlined above. The role of the chief executive officer will change significantly as authority and responsibility are passed to the senior managers in each of the geographic regions. As the organization grows, the chief executive officer will be spending more time allocating resources among the geographic regions and making sure that any decisions regarding global products are made and communicated in an efficient manner. Among other things, this means constructing a solid communications network that links product managers in different countries. Another key role for the chief executive officer is making sure that the board of directors is informed about the recommendations of senior management relating to the long-term strategy of the company. A well selected and highly informed board can provide the support necessary to manage the required resources.

CHAPTER 12

Plan Section 7: Human Resources

MANKIND ARE ANIMALS THAT MAKE BARGAINS, NO

OTHER ANIMAL DOES THIS. — ADAM SMITH

ALL COMPANIES ENGAGE IN HUMAN RESOURCE MANAGEMENT. Human resource (commonly referred to as HR) management includes such tasks as employee recruitment and selection, training, compensation, review and promotion and termination of the employment relationship. Management of human resources is a key function at any business level. Global human resource management has been cited as one of the critical planning and success factors for companies embarking on any strategy of foreign expansion. Given the cultural and legal differences that exist among countries, this is an area where conflicts can easily arise. In fact, poorly managed global human resources have often contributed to the failure of international operations. This issue should be addressed well before a company launches its overseas expansion activities and is seen as a critical factor in an international business plan.

General Information

The business plan should give the reader a good understanding of the human resources of the company, including:

- The number of employees involved in major functional areas
- Compensation methodology
- Job descriptions
- Terms of key employment contracts or agreements
- Structure of the work force, including union relationships and relative level of employee skills and morale
- Employee benefit plans

In many international business plans, the discussion of human resources is little more than a recital of statistics, including the number of employees in each functional area. A better practice is to describe how the company intends to recruit, assess and reward a strong team of dedicated and talented managers and employees. This is particularly important if the company is in an industry experiencing tremendous competitive pressures or fast growth. Employees with specialized talents in such companies will be targets for other companies' recruitment efforts. If possible, an attempt should be made to compare the personnel practices of the company to those of its competitors.

If the company has only a few employees, the business plan should generally focus on how it intends to find and employ qualified personnel as the company continues to grow. One of the key considerations in this area is a compensation and incentive program that the company is offering or intends to offer to its employees. This includes:

- Opportunities to purchase stock in the company (where applicable)
- Benefits, including health care insurance
- Incentive bonus programs

As the work force expands, however, the company must take a much broader view of personnel matters. In such situations, the plan additionally should cover the company's policies on:

- Training and education
- Employee communications
- Performance measurement
- Morale
- Managing employee turnover

Problems in Developing a Global Human Resources Strategy

Human resources are a significant aspect of any business that hires and trains employees, builds and relies on employee loyalty and demands job efficiency. In the global arena, the provision for, and an understanding of, human resources becomes even more imperative. Now, relations between managers and staff stretch across significant distances, time zones and a cultural, moral, religious and educational morass. Unfortunately, companies often neglect or give minimum treatment to human resources in their global business plans, when in fact development of a human resource strategy could mean the difference between success and failure. Accordingly, as you construct your plan, be certain to address the following concerns:

■ HUMAN RESOURCE MANAGER AS PART OF THE TEAM

Unfortunately, most people with the title of "manager" believe themselves to be proficient at managing human resources. Actually, only a small percentage of managers handle this key issue properly. What existing human resource expertise does your company currently have? Have you consulted them as part of the planning process? Have you made them part of your global operations team? If the answer to the last two questions is "No," you had better make amends quickly.

■ SELECTION AND REVIEW OF PERSONNEL

Have you determined appropriate criteria for the selection and review of the personnel who are to be involved in the management and operation of international activities? From what employment pool will you seek personnel— local residents of the foreign country, nationals of your own home country or nationals of an independent third country? Is nationality or residency going to be a factor in your selection, and if so, why? Have you selected managers to handle operations in foreign markets who are particularly sensitive to the specific environmental factors in the marketplace? If such managers are not available, have you made provision to hire managers with the necessary expertise or to train managers? Does your plan provide procedures for ensuring that your chosen personnel have the necessary market-specific knowledge and skills (e.g., language)?

Finding the right people to work in a global-oriented organization can be a challenge, particularly when recruiting must take place around the world. Before making a final decision about entering a new foreign market, consideration must be given to how local employees will be found and retained. Also, determine whether and how employees from other parts of the organization will be relocated to the new market.

The selection criterion to be applied in hiring employees for foreign markets will most likely be somewhat different than in the case of domestic employees. For example, the requisite social and cultural skills places a premium on finding employees that have the necessary maturity and stability to deal with strange environments, large amounts of travel and the stress of launching a new business operation. Technical skills, including familiarity with the company's technology and communications systems, are also very important. Employees must be willing to go through the required training necessary for effectiveness in the foreign market, including the acquisition of new language skills. Finally, employees must have the social skills to get along with local workers as well as with managers and colleagues elsewhere in the organization. In the case of managers, this includes the diplomacy and tact needed to mediate misunderstandings that may arise in the foreign country and communication glitches within the global organization. Advance planning can help to ease workplace tensions and uncertainties in the face of employee relocation and company reorganization. This will be an even more sensitive issue if family members are to accompany the staff members assigned to the foreign venture.

- ONGOING TRAINING

Does your plan cover ongoing training for employees in the foreign operations and for new employees? Have you provided a methodology for educating new employees by which they will become fully versed in the company's products, in activities in the home market, as well as operations in the foreign markets?

Training is important in any organization and the need to budget for educational programs in global businesses is particularly important. By way of example, a company may choose to rely on a recruiting strategy where employees for the project are chosen primarily from the existing home country staff. Consequently, significant amounts will need to be spent on language classes and intercultural training. The latter focuses on the skills required for home country staff to understand and appreciate the cultural norms, expectations and communication styles that apply in the host country. This may require training from consultants and educators with specific experience in the new country.

- LOCAL CUSTOMS AND PRACTICES

Have you carefully analyzed local customs and practices relating to compensation and performance reviews? Does your plan allow for compensation arrangements that are acceptable in the foreign country as compared to your home market? Will the benefit packages and company standards and policies have meaning to employees in new foreign markets? Does your plan include a means of presenting new benefit concepts to employees in foreign countries where labor and cultural practices differ from your home country? Have you considered whether your own company may need to modify its own compensation policies to allow for common practices overseas?

Compensation issues can be quite complex and challenging for a global organization. Management needs to take into account local conditions as well the relative parity of compensation arrangements for similar jobs in different countries throughout the entire company. Main areas to consider include base salaries, benefits and tax laws.

BASE SALARIES

Parity and competitiveness are two key factors in setting the base salaries for employees in a global organization. Management should always attempt to be fair and consistent in the treatment of employees throughout the organization and make a special effort to be sure that employees performing like activities are dealt with equitably. In addition, the salary system should be flexible enough to avoid disincentives to movement to other locations within the global organization based solely on compensation. Finally, the base salary in each country should be competitive with comparable firms in the area.

BENEFITS

Compensation includes not only salaries, but also various financial and non-financial benefits. For example, employees in the United States are used to receiving medical and dental insurance and opportunities to receive an ownership interest in the company through the issuance of stock options. In other countries, benefits can take the form of extended vacations and holiday periods. Employees relocating from one country to another country may receive an allowance for moving expenses and adjustments in their base salaries specifically tied to changes in the cost-of-living between the two countries.

While benefits and expense allowances are fairly common around the world, their content and importance will vary from country to country. In developing a human resources plan for operations in a new country, management should consider the following questions and issues:

- What benefits are typically provided to employees in the country and how might they differ from benefits offered elsewhere in the organization?
- What legal restrictions and requirements are imposed on benefits in the new country?
- What benefits already offered to employees elsewhere in the organization might be attractive to employees in the new country?
- Should differences in the benefits available in various countries be offset by adjustments in base salaries?

While reviewing benefits-related issues, consideration should also be given to pension plans and other retirement benefits. The company's role in post-employment support of its workers varies among countries and will depend on local custom and the scope of any national social security programs. In any event, management must carefully review the local practices and regulations in each country and consider how the requirements of a specific country might fit into the overall plans of the organization.

TAXATION

Each jurisdiction has its own set of tax laws and regulations, and countries often have numerous tax treaties with other nations that attempt to reconcile potential issues that might arise concerning dual jurisdiction over a taxpayer. For example, a Japanese citizen who is posted to work at a subsidiary in Germany may, in theory, be subject to tax on any wages earned in both Japan and Germany. However, the tax treaty between the two nations, and specific country laws, will determine the amount of tax owed and the country to which the tax will be paid. Otherwise, workers would never agree to any foreign posting out of fear of double taxation.

Countries also may have different rules regarding taxation of various types of employee compensation. For example, while the United States has created special tax-driven incentives for companies to provide stock options to their employees to allow them to share in growth of the value of the business, other countries may have no preferences in that area and/or may treat options less favorably than other types of payments (see ADVISORY on this topic in previous chapter). As such, research is required before any attempt can be made to adopt any type of integrated compensation scheme for a global organization.

ADVISORY: Managers and staff sent on overseas projects need to be well looked after during their expatriate assignments. They will not only have the day-to-day stress of work but the additional worry of operating in a strange culture. Problems experienced by their spouses and children will add to stress. Budgetary and support needs should be considered during the planning phase. Many a worthwhile international project has been scuttled by "expat" burnout or family-related issues that could have been avoided. Regular communication and easily accessed support act as the perfect preventative measure.

CHAPTER 13

Plan Section 8: Special Topics

I INVENT NOTHING. I REDISCOVER.

– RODIN

DEPENDING ON THE CIRCUMSTANCES, the basic business plan topics may need to be supplemented by details covered by one or more special topics. In this chapter, we take a brief look at some of the more common issues that might arise in a specific context, including financing strategies, facilities and equipment, operations, information management, risk management strategies and regulatory matters.

Financing

Even the best product requires working capital to finance development of appropriate opportunities. In the case of a domestic company, financing requirements will cover facilities, raw materials, marketing and sales, salaries and reserves to keep the company going as inventories are sold and collections are made from customers. Cash is also required to fund new product development initiatives that will not generate a return for several months or years in the future. The transition to global activities will require cash to develop the infrastructure for exporting products, as well as funds for the establishment of new facilities and sales offices in foreign countries.

The international business plan will generally include extensive financial information, including historical results of operations and projections for future receipts and disbursements of cash. These projections must be tied directly to the identified sources of funds described elsewhere in the business plan. In describing the sources of funding, the plan must include projections or estimates regarding the timing of receipts, the sources of funds and the terms of repayment in the case of debt financing.

A variety of funding sources may be available to your company for expansion into new foreign markets. Of course, the company may fund internal operations out of cash that is generated from current domestic activities. Each bit of income collected from the business should be allocated either toward distribution to the owners of the business or to some form of reinvestment in the business in worthwhile projects. As noted elsewhere in this book, there will come a time in the evolution of the business when the highest expected return on investment may be in a new foreign market as opposed to a local market that is already mature.

Investors may be brought in specifically to fund a business plan that is focused on international operations and expansion. The funds may be paid directly to the company with the understanding that an agreed portion will be allocated to foreign activities that have been identified in the business plan. Such projects as the construction of a new production facility in Asia or the establishment of a joint venture in South America can have cash set aside for development.

Small- and medium-sized businesses may qualify for special government financing programs in their home countries, including incentives for developing export businesses that generate foreign exchange funds that can be recycled in the local economy. These programs range from outright grants to loan programs at attractive rates to guarantees of loans that come directly from commercial lenders.

In any event, the key issue in this area is making sure that the company has a clear and coherent plan for raising the funds necessary to complete execution of the entire business plan on a timely basis. Also, given the uncertainties associated with developments in a global economy, as well as in a specific foreign country, the plan should always include appropriate reserves that can be tapped when economic conditions deteriorate.

Facilities and Equipment

The business plan should include a description of the company's physical assets, including real property and equipment. The scope of the company's physical plant and facilities will, of course, depend on the type of business and the geographic range of the company's operations. At a minimum, the company will generally have a main office that serves as a home for all of its business records, senior management and appropriate support staff. In addition, the company may have its own production facilities and sales offices. In each case, the facility may be owned outright by the company or leased from a third party.

The business plan should describe the main facilities of the company, including a list of locations, size (e.g., square footage), the amount of monthly payments in the case of leased facilities and a summary of management's view regarding the adequacy of the listed properties for the conduct of the company's business. Facilities analysis can be particularly important in the case of a pending global expansion. Each of the managers, as well as prospective investors, need to determine if the company has a reasonable plan in place to position itself to successfully enter a new foreign market.

A threshold question that must be answered in developing an international business plan is how to identify the best locations for facilities in each new foreign market. This analysis must take into account proximity to potential customers and the infrastructure needed to move the required goods, raw materials and equipment around the country.

Equipment, including office furnishings, computers, fabrication machines and other physical assets necessary for the conduct of the business, should also be described in the business plan. The level of detail required in this area is not as great as the information relating to facilities. The company's ability to acquire the right to use key assets should also be verified in the plan. As with facilities, there are a variety of strategies that can be used with respect to equipment, including purchase and leasing options. Availability of equipment in foreign countries is an important logistical question. This is particularly true if there is a need for specialized equipment to adequately exploit the technology embedded in the company's production processes.

Operations

In addition to detailed information regarding the company's management structure and human resources, the business plan should consider the key operational areas of the business. In this case, the term "operations" refers to the nuts and bolts of keeping the company going on a day-to-day basis, including functions such as payroll, procurement, accounting, bookkeeping and tax compliance.

Responsibility for operational activities will vary depending on the size and structure of the company. In some cases, a company may have a chief executive officer (CEO) who has primary responsibility for the overall strategic direction of the company as determined by the board of directors. The firm may also have a person who serves as chief operating officer (COO) who generally implements the strategy and keeps the business running smoothly. In a small business, strategy and operations are handled by one person. In larger businesses, the CEO and COO are joined by other senior executives, including the chief financial officer (CFO).

The challenge of operations expands exponentially when the business goes global. Information management challenges are discussed separately below. In addition, the COO must handle a variety of tasks, including the following:

- Establishing record keeping and accounting procedures in foreign offices, including recruitment of personnel, training in local customs, accounting and tax laws. Outside tax and accounting experts will also need to be located in order to assist with preparation and filing of required reports and documents.

- Facilities management, including the purchase or lease of real properties required for the anticipated foreign operations.

- Contract management, including the development of standard form contracts for use in the company's business and management of internal contract managers and outside counsel.

- Collection, analysis and distribution of information, including output and quality reports on the company's manufacturing processes.

Information Management

One of the most important features of a successful business, yet often overlooked in connection with global operations is an effective global information and communications system. Factors that should always be taken into account include regional differences in time zones and work schedules and development of computer standards for the entire organization. Due to this, large firms appoint a CIO (chief information officer).

TIME ZONES AND WORK SCHEDULES

The computer systems for a global organization must automatically take into account differences in time zones when compiling and distributing scheduling and production information across multiple countries. In addition, work schedules may differ in various parts of the world. For example, some branches may begin and end work earlier in the day due to climatic conditions or local customs. Another consideration is different local practices regarding celebration of holidays and official vacation periods. Either of these factors may cause delays in creation of information and/or production and other inputs that might be transferred to other regions.

DEVELOPMENT OF COMPUTER STANDARDS

In an ideal world, a global business organization will be able to develop and implement common standards for computer equipment used throughout the company. This would also include common software programs and configuration as well as access to local vendors with equivalent skills and experience throughout the organization. Unfortunately, this is usually a difficult goal to achieve due to limitations on the type of equipment and support services that might be available in specific locations. Accordingly, a global organization will often need to adapt to these shortcomings and make appropriate allowances as it develops organizational information management and communications requirements.

Risk Management Strategies

Every business confronts various risks regardless of the scope of its activities. The business plan should identify both the opportunities and risks relating to the company's business. Ordinary day-to-day business risks of product liability claims, theft, destruction of property need not be given special emphasis, but larger challenges such as expropriation of foreign assets and suspension of raw material supplies due to political unrest in foreign countries should be dealt with in some detail. There are a variety of strategies that might be used with respect to risk management, including insurance policies and internal procedures to ensure that receivables are kept up-to-date and that vendors perform their obligations under contracts.

Regulatory Matters

Depending on the circumstances, the business plan may need to include a detailed discussion of specific regulatory hurdles that must be overcome in order for the company's products to be distributed and promoted in various markets. For example, if the company is involved in the development of new pharmaceutical products, the business plan must describe regulatory procedures with respect to testing of the products to confirm their efficacy and safety. In particular, reference should be made to the amount of time required to obtain the necessary approvals and the additional costs that may be incurred in order to complete the review process.

Supplemental Information

There is no standard list of exhibits or appendices that you should include with your international business plan, nor is there any standard format. Various items typically are included with most plans to enhance the reader's understanding of your company and its business. If possible, include an index or table of contents for the exhibits. You could then tab each exhibit for easy reference.

Of the exhibits commonly added, most important are the financial statements as described in the next chapter. In addition, you might include one or more of the following supplemental materials:

- Detailed CVs of key managers and employees
- Professional references
- Photographs or drawings of the product/prototype
- Patent summaries
- Market studies, articles from trade journals and third party evaluations
- List of major customers, suppliers and distributors
- Advertising literature, company brochures and promotional materials
- Summary of major contracts
- Charter documents (i.e., articles or certificate of incorporation, bylaws) and major agreements among the ownership group
- Charts, graphs or tables expanding on information presented in the business plan

CHAPTER 14

Plan Section 9: Financial Information

IN THE STATE OF NATURE PROFIT IS THE MEASURE OF RIGHT. — THOMAS HOBBES

MANY REASONS EXIST for the launch and operation of a business. The most important is making money to provide the owners and investors with a return on their investment. Accordingly, the business plan should include a substantial amount of financial information and analysis. Although the senior managers of the company will be familiar with its financial condition, preparation of this information should be left to those with special expertise. In larger companies, the chief financial officer (CFO) and controller will take the lead in this area. In smaller companies, the chief executive officer (CEO) will have this task, generally accompanied with help from independent accountants.

Key Financial Statements

The key sections to the financials are:

- Historical financial statements
- Proforma financial statements
- Operating budgets

In cases where the business plan is being used in connection with capital raising activities, the plan also should describe the amount of cash that is required. This includes the intended use of proceeds and the strategy for returning the funds to the investors (e.g., public offering, sale of the company, redemption or scheduled repayment of debt securities). This is commonly known as an "exit strategy."

For a going concern looking at an expansion, the historical and projected statements will include the big three—Balance Sheet, Income Statement and Cash Flow Statement. (Start-ups will only have projections of these three documents.) They should cover three to five years—with the most recent two to three years on a month-by-month basis, and the others by quarter. The financial section only contains summaries of the big three. Detailed statements are included at the end of the plan in appendices along with other supplemental materials. The statements do not have to be audited, unless they already are. Nevertheless, they must be prepared in accordance with "generally accepted accounting principles" (GAAP) for the jurisdiction in which the company is located.

Budgets cover start-up and ongoing periods. As with the historical and projected statements, summaries are included in the financials section of your plan, with details in the supplemental materials.

Historical Financial Statements

Historical financial statements serve a number of purposes. First, they indicate the company's current position. Is it still emerging, positioned for a take-off or fully developed? On an operating level, how does its expenses and revenues compare to competitors? Is it spending more on production, marketing or management than others? Are changes necessary in how the company operates? If so, what cost savings (and increased profits) can be expected?

Second, they indicate how the company has been managed in the past. Has the company wisely used its funds or squandered them? Has the company effectively used its opportunities? If not, management changes may be required to induce investors. Also, has the company met its operating budgets? If not, the business plan should explain why and describe what is being done to correct the situation.

Your business plan should also describe your accounting system and, when applicable, the inventory control system. Similarly, indicate the names of any external accountants and auditors, and how long they have represented you.

Proforma Financial Statement

Although each part of the financial section is important, some readers (particularly those with financial backgrounds) devote most of their attention to projections. Therefore, make sure they are accurate, supportable and persuasive.

If they are to be believable, projections must be consistent with past performance. They must also be internally consistent. For example, if you project sales of $1,000,000, the projections must also include provisions for inventory levels and sales costs that are sufficient to support the revenue goals.

DISCLAIMERS

When projections are prepared in connection with capital raising, you must include disclaimers. These disclaimers will state that while management believes the projections and underlying assumptions are reasonable and reliable, the company does not represent that its operations will actually meet or conform to the projections. Disclaimers should be in bold-faced type—not fine print.

RISK FACTORS

When used to raise money, many plans include a list of risk factors that may limit the company's ability to achieve projections. Whether or not you have covered risks elsewhere, it is advisable to recap them in one place—usually the projections section—even if you are only cross-referencing to detailed descriptions.

ASSUMPTIONS

The plan also should include key assumptions you have made in preparing the financials. They will help the reader understand how you arrived at your conclusions and help when you need to make revisions to take into account changes in economic and market conditions. For example, if you assume a 3% inflation rate and inflation rises to 5%, you can determine how much of any variation is due to changes in inflation and how much is attributable to other causes.

The specific financial assumptions that are material to your business will depend on the scope of activities and the particular economic risks associated with the company. In the case of a consumer goods company, for example, some of the financial assumptions would include the following:

- National and local income taxes
- Payroll taxes
- Employee benefits
- Receivables: payment lag, depends on your industry (used for cash flow only)
- Allowance for bad debts
- Inventory: maintained at a set percent above projected sales for the next period and manufactured a set length of time prior to sales (used for cash flow only)
- Sales and marketing expenses: percentage of projected sales price

Your projections should also be adjusted for inflation, interest rates, currency fluctuations, productivity changes and market growth.

Operating Budgets

The business plan is an overview of how you intend to operate your company. For instance, you are going to produce an improved widget, establish distributors throughout the world, fill out your management team and get 10% of the market.

How you accomplish these goals is contained in the specifics of your budget. For instance, how much will you spend on research, development, manufacturing and sales to achieve the goals of your business plan?

If you are launching your business into a new foreign market, you should prepare two types of budgets. The first should cover the start-up phase while the second covers the operating phase after the business is up and running. Another way of clarifying the two is that the start-up budget breaks the inertia and gets the process moving. The operating budget shows how you will keep it rolling.

START-UP

In this budget, you describe what it is going to take for you to get your company organized. During this phase you will encounter a number of non-recurring one-time expenses, such as for equipment and space. There will also be deposits and down payments.

If your business will take a while before it is selling to the market, even after acquiring equipment, space and personnel, you should run the start-up budget through this period. For example, if it will take you six months to acquire equipment and another three months to conduct test runs, the budget should cover all nine months.

Some of the items that you should include in your start-up budget are:

- Occupancy
- Licenses and permits
- Equipment
- Raw materials and supplies
- Inventory
- Depreciation

- Personnel, including salaries, wages, benefits, training and education
- Legal, accounting and other professional fees
- Insurance
- Marketing, advertising and promotions
- Commissions
- Utilities
- Taxes

PLAN NOTE: Be sure to include any income the business generates during this period. And, consider starting small. Many firms "test the water" with small projects before starting full-scale operations.

OPERATING

An operating budget will cover the period from when your company opens for business. It indicates how you will spend your money, when you will receive revenue and how you will cover any shortfalls between the two. Particularly, if you will be operating in a deficit during the first several months or quarters, you should indicate where the money will come from during this period.

Some categories will be the same as with the start-up budget, but the coverage will differ. Your focus changes from getting started to running the business. Many numbers will be lower than in the start-up budget. For instance, new equipment and advertising are likely to be greater in the start-up period as the company builds infrastructure and gains name recognition. Some of the main items are:

- Occupancy
- Licenses and permits
- Equipment
- Raw materials and supplies
- Inventory
- Depreciation
- Repairs and maintenance
- Personnel, including salaries, wages, benefits and training
- Legal, accounting and other professional fees
- Insurance
- Marketing, advertising and promotions
- Commissions
- Utilities
- Debt service
- Taxes

Of course, you will also need to include sales projections. Various methods can be used for projecting sales, including:

- Average sales per call
- Average sales per salesperson
- Average sales of competitors
- Industry standards

Next, compute your cost of goods sold. These are the same as those identified in the income statement. When calculating variable and fixed costs, allow for changes over time. Also adjust for inflation, interest rates, productivity changes and market growth.

SAMPLE
BALANCE SHEET
YOUR COMPANY NAME
AS OF (DATE)

ASSETS

CURRENT ASSETS
CASH .... $___.00
PETTY CASH .... $___.00
ACCOUNTS RECEIVABLE .... $___.00
INVENTORY .... $___.00
SHORT-TERM INVESTMENTS .... $___.00
PREPAID EXPENSES .... $___.00
LONG-TERM INVESTMENTS .... $___.00
FIXED ASSETS
LAND .... $___.00
BUILDINGS .... $___.00
IMPROVEMENTS .... $___.00
EQUIPMENT .... $___.00
FURNITURE .... $___.00
AUTOMOBILE .... $___.00
OTHER ASSETS .... $___.00
TOTAL ASSETS .... $___.00

LIABILITIES

CURRENT LIABILITIES
ACCOUNTS PAYABLE .... $___.00
NOTES PAYABLE .... $___.00
INTEREST PAYABLE .... $___.00
TAXES PAYABLE .... $___.00
FEDERAL INCOME TAX .... $___.00
STATE INCOME TAX .... $___.00
SELF-EMPLOYMENT TAX .... $___.00
SALES TAX .... $___.00
PROPERTY TAX .... $___.00
PAYROLL ACCRUAL .... $___.00
LONG-TERM LIABILITIES
TOTAL LIABILITIES .... $___.00

OWNER'S EQUITY (NET WORTH)

PAID-IN-CAPITAL .... $___.00
SURPLUS PAID IN .... $___.00
RETAINED EARNINGS .... $___.00
TOTAL OWNER'S EQUITY .... $___.00
TOTAL LIABILITIES AND OWNER'S EQUITY .... $___.00

Comments on Balance Sheet

Let's consider each of the line items in the balance sheet shown in the sidebar on the preceding page. Starting with the top, include your business name and the date of the balance sheet.

There are two distinctive characteristics of the balance sheet. First, it is a snap shot as of a certain date. Second, it is always in balance. The assets are equal to the liabilities plus owner's equity. Mathematically, the formula is represented by

ASSETS = LIABILITIES + OWNER'S EQUITY + (REVENUES–EXPENSES)

The (Revenues – Expenses) represents the Income Statement and affects equity either positively (profit) or negatively (loss).

ASSETS

Assets are everything that your business owns. There are four types of assets: 1) current, 2) long-term, 3) fixed and 4) other.

■ CURRENT ASSETS

Current assets are those that can be utilized within 12 months of the balance sheet dates. They include:

▪ CASH: Cash, cash equivalents and resources that can be converted into cash within 12 months (or during one established cycle of your company's operation). Examples are money on hand and demand deposits in the bank, such as checking accounts and regular savings accounts.

▪ PETTY CASH: Any fund for small miscellaneous expenditures.

▪ ACCOUNTS RECEIVABLE: Amounts due from customers as payment for goods and services.

▪ INVENTORY: Raw materials on hand, work in progress and finished goods, either manufactured or purchased for resale.

▪ SHORT-TERM (TEMPORARY OR MARKETABLE) INVESTMENTS: Interest or dividend-yielding certificates that you expect to convert into cash within a year. Examples are stocks and bonds, certificates of deposit and time deposit savings accounts. They should be recorded at the lower level of cost or market value.

▪ PREPAID EXPENSES: Goods and services you bought or rented in advance. Examples are office supplies, insurance and office, factory or warehouse space.

■ LONG-TERM INVESTMENTS

Also called long-term assets, they are holdings you intend to keep for at least a year. Typically, they yield interest or dividends. Examples are stocks, bonds and saving accounts reserved for special purposes.

■ FIXED ASSETS

Also called plant and equipment, fixed assets include all resources you own or rent for use in operations that you do not intend to resell.

▪ LAND: Historical (original) purchase price, not current market value.

▪ BUILDINGS, IMPROVEMENTS, EQUIPMENT, FURNITURE AND AUTOMOBILE: Such items as used in your business.

▪ INTANGIBLES: Patents, formulas, copyrights, goodwill other intellectual property.

▪ DEPRECIATION: Deductions from the book value of specific tangible long-term assets.

▪ AMORTIZATION: Deductions from the book value of specific intangible assets.

LIABILITIES

Liabilities are everything that your business owes. There are two types of liabilities – current and long-term.

■ CURRENT LIABILITIES

Current liabilities are all debts, monetary obligations and claims payable within 12 months of the balance sheet date or within one established cycle of operation of your business. Typically they include:

▨ ACCOUNTS PAYABLE: Amounts owed to suppliers for goods and services purchased for your business.

▨ NOTES PAYABLE: Principal owing on short-term debt for borrowed funds. Includes current amount due on notes with terms in excess of 12 months.

▨ INTEREST PAYABLE: Accrued fees due on short- and long-term borrowed capital and credit.

▨ TAXES PAYABLE: Estimated amounts incurred during the current period. Usually calculated by an accountant or bookkeeper. Includes taxes on national income, local income, self-employment, sales and property taxes.

▨ PAYROLL ACCRUAL: Salaries and wages currently owed.

■ LONG-TERM LIABILITIES

▨ NOTES PAYABLE: Notes, contract payments or mortgage payments due over a period exceeding 12 months or one cycle of operation of your business. They are listed by outstanding balance less current amount due.

OWNER'S EQUITY

Also called net worth, owner's equity is how the balance sheet gets balanced. The difference between assets and liabilities is owner's equity. If positive, it represents the claim of the owners to the business' assets. If negative, it represents obligations of the owners.

In a proprietorship or partnership, equity is each owner's original investment plus any earnings after withdrawals. In corporations, it is the value of the capital stock plus retained earnings.

TOTAL LIABILITIES AND OWNER'S EQUITY

As noted, total liabilities plus owner's equity equals total assets.

SAMPLE
INCOME STATEMENT

YOUR COMPANY NAME
AS OF (DATE)

REVENUE

TOTAL NET SALES OR REVENUES .... $___.00
COSTS OF SALES .... $___.00
GROSS PROFIT .... $___.00
GROSS PROFIT MARGIN .... ___ %

VARIABLE EXPENSES

SALARIES .... $___.00
PAYROLL EXPENSES .... $___.00
OUTSIDE SERVICES .... $___.00
ACCOUNTING AND LEGAL .... $___.00
ADVERTISING .... $___.00
AUTOMOBILE .... $___.00
OFFICE SUPPLIES .... $___.00
REPAIRS AND MAINTENANCE .... $___.00
UTILITIES .... $___.00
MISCELLANEOUS .... $___.00
TOTAL VARIABLE EXPENSES .... $___.00

FIXED EXPENSES

RENT .... $___.00
DEPRECIATION .... $___.00
INSURANCE .... $___.00
LICENSES/PERMITS .... $___.00
LOAN PAYMENTS .... $___.00
MISCELLANEOUS .... $___.00
TOTAL FIXED EXPENSES .... $___.00
TOTAL EXPENSES .... $___.00

PROFIT

NET PROFIT (LOSS) BEFORE TAXES .... $___.00
TAXES .... $___.00
NET PROFIT (LOSS) AFTER TAXES .... $___.00

Comments on Income Statement

The income statement (or Profit and Loss Statement—P&L) differs from the balance sheet in two ways. First, it is not in balance. Rather, it is designed to show what is *out of balance*, meaning which is greater – revenues or expenses. In that way, you can tell if you are making or losing money (i.e., profitable or not). This statement must be prepared *before* a balance sheet is formulated. Profit or loss will then be applied to the equity portion of the balance sheet.

Second, it takes a look at your company not on a given day or single point in time, but over a period–for instance, one month, three months, six months or a year.

Income statements are particularly effective when comparisons are made. By preparing the income statement on a monthly, quarterly and annual basis, and then comparing results to previous years, you can see how you are doing, where problems exist and what you need to improve. Actual results on a monthly, quarterly and annual basis should be compared with projections. Differences should be noted and addressed. This makes it possible for you to compare your company to competitors. Particularly important are industry comparisons of:

- Cost of sales as a percentage of total net sales
- Gross profit margin

You can obtain industry averages from your trade association, chamber of commerce or bank.

To facilitate such comparisons, many companies add columns showing prior periods, period a year ago, year-to-date, percentage of year-to-date and industry averages.

Let's consider each of the line items in the income statement. As with the balance sheet, starting at the top of the statement, include your business name and time period covered.

TOTAL NET SALES OR REVENUES

Simply stated, this line shows what you received for the goods or services you sold. You should reduce the total by any returns, allowances or markdowns. Exclude any revenue not directly related to your business.

COST OF SALES (DIRECT COSTS)

Include any costs for the goods or products you sold. Be sure to add transportation and distribution costs.

GROSS PROFIT

Subtract total cost of sales from total net sales to obtain gross profit.

GROSS PROFIT MARGIN

Gross profit is often measured as percentage of total sales or revenues. It is calculated by dividing gross profit by total net sales.

VARIABLE EXPENSES

Variable or controllable expenses are items that change with the volume of your business. They differ from fixed expenses that do not change. The leading items in this category are:

- ▨ SALARIES & WAGES: Base pay plus overtime.
- ▨ PAYROLL BENEFIT EXPENSES: Paid vacations, sick leave, health insurance, unemployment insurance and social security taxes.
- ▨ EXTERNAL LABOR: Costs of subcontractors, overflow work and special or one-time services.
- ▨ EXTERNAL PROFESSIONAL SERVICES: Includes accounting, legal, consulting.
- ▨ ADVERTISING: Advertising and public relations expenses.
- ▨ TRANSPORTATION & TRAVEL: Charges for personal cars used in business, including parking, tools, buying trips, hotels, etc.
- ▨ OFFICE SUPPLIES: Services and items purchased for use in administering the business.
- ▨ REPAIRS AND MAINTENANCE: Regular maintenance and repair, including major expenditures.
- ▨ UTILITIES: Telephone, electricity, natural gas, water and similar items.
- ▨ MISCELLANEOUS: Unspecified, small expenditures without separate accounts.

FIXED EXPENSES

These expenses are fixed and do not change as the volume of your business increases or decreases. Examples are:

- ▨ RENT: Real estate used in business.
- ▨ MANAGEMENT SALARIES (fixed portion non-bonus).
- ▨ DEPRECIATION & AMORTIZATION of tangible and intangible capital assets.
- ▨ INSURANCE: Fire or liability policies on property or products and workers' compensation.
- ▨ LICENSES/PERMITS: Fees for governmental permissions.
- ▨ LOAN PAYMENTS: Interest on outstanding loans.
- ▨ MISCELLANEOUS: Unspecified, small expenditures without separate accounts.

TOTAL EXPENSES

Total of variable and fixed expenses.

NET PROFIT (LOSS) BEFORE TAXES

Difference between Total Net Sales and Total Expenses (variable + fixed).

TAXES

National and local income taxes payable based on your net profits before taxes.

NET PROFIT (LOSS) AFTER TAXES

Subtract Taxes from Net Profit before Taxes.

SAMPLE
CASH FLOW STATEMENT

YOUR COMPANY NAME
AS OF (DATE)

CASH ON HAND (BEGINNING OF PERIOD) .... $___.00
CASH RECEIPTS .... $___.00
    CASH SALES .... $___.00
    COLLECTIONS FROM CREDIT ACCOUNTS .... $___.00
    LOANS OR OTHER CASH INFUSIONS .... $___.00
TOTAL CASH RECEIPTS .... $___.00
TOTAL CASH AVAILABLE (BEFORE CASH PAID OUT) .... $___.00
CASH PAID OUT .... $___.00
    PURCHASES (MERCHANDISE) .... $___.00
    SALARIES .... $___.00
    PAYROLL EXPENSES .... $___.00
    OUTSIDE SERVICES .... $___.00
    ACCOUNTING AND LEGAL .... $___.00
    ADVERTISING .... $___.00
    AUTOMOBILE .... $___.00
    OFFICE SUPPLIES .... $___.00
    REPAIRS AND MAINTENANCE .... $___.00
    RENT .... $___.00
    UTILITIES .... $___.00
    INSURANCE .... $___.00
    LICENSES/PERMITS .... $___.00
    LOAN PAYMENTS .... $___.00
    TAXES .... $___.00
    OTHER EXPENSES (SPECIFY) .... $___.00
    MISCELLANEOUS .... $___.00
    SUBTOTAL .... $___.00
RESERVE AND/OR ESCROW .... $___.00
OWNER'S WITHDRAWAL (SOLE PROPRIETORSHIPS AND PARTNERSHIPS ONLY) .... $___.00
DIVIDEND PAYMENTS (CORPORATIONS ONLY) .... $___.00
TOTAL CASH PAID OUT .... $___.00
CASH POSITION (END OF MONTH) .... $___.00
ADDITIONAL OPERATING DATA .... $___.00
    SALES VOLUME (DOLLARS) .... $___.00
    ACCOUNTS RECEIVABLE (END OF PERIOD) .... $___.00
    BAD DEBT (END OF PERIOD) .... $___.00
    INVENTORY ON HAND (END OF PERIOD) .... $___.00
    ACCOUNTS PAYABLE (END OF PERIOD) .... $___.00

Comments on Cash Flow Statement

As with the income statement, the cash flow statement is a picture of your business in motion. Unlike the income statement, however, it focuses on only one aspect of the motion—your use of cash during the period covered.

Let's consider each of the line items in the cash flow statement. As with the others, starting at the top, include your business name and the time period covered.

CASH ON HAND (BEGINNING OF PERIOD)

This shows how much cash you started the period with. It will be the same as your cash on hand at the end of the previous period.

CASH RECEIPTS

This category shows cash coming in during the period covered by the statement. The main items are:

- CASH SALES: Cash from sales. Omit credit sales.
- COLLECTIONS FROM CREDIT ACCOUNTS: When cash is received on credit sales, this is where you enter the cash amount.
- LOANS OR OTHER CASH INJECTION: Borrowed money, money from the sale of stocks or bonds (corporate) or the additional capital paid in by owners (proprietorship/partnership).

TOTAL CASH AVAILABLE (BEFORE CASH PAID OUT)

Total of Cash on Hand and Cash Receipts.

CASH PAID OUT

Under this category list all outflows of cash – what you paid out during the period covered by the cash flow statement. The main types are cash payments for:

- PURCHASES (MERCHANDISE): Purchases for supplies, transportation and distribution costs.
- SALARIES & WAGES: Base pay plus overtime.
- PAYROLL BENEFITS EXPENSES: Paid vacations, sick leave, health insurance, unemployment insurance and social security taxes.
- EXTERNAL LABOR: Costs of subcontractors, overflow work and special or one-time services.
- EXTERNAL PROFESSIONAL SERVICES: Includes legal, accounting and consulting.
- ADVERTISING: Advertising and public relations expenses.
- TRANSPORTATION AND TRAVEL EXPENSES: Charges for personal cars used in business, including parking, tools, buying trips, hotels, etc.
- OFFICE SUPPLIES: Services and items purchased for use in the business.
- REPAIRS AND MAINTENANCE: Regular maintenance and repair, including major expenditures.
- RENT: Real estate or equipment used in business.
- UTILITIES: Telephone, electricity, natural gas, water and similar items.
- INSURANCE: Fire or liability policies on property or products and workers' benefits.

- ▧ LICENSES/PERMITS: Fees for governmental permissions.
- ▧ LOAN PAYMENTS: Debt service.
- ▧ TAXES
- ▧ MISCELLANEOUS: Unspecified, small expenditures without separate accounts.
- ▧ SUBTOTAL: Total of all Cash Paid Out.

RESERVE AND/OR ESCROW

Examples include funds held in escrow for insurance, taxes or equipment to reduce impact of large periodic payments.

OWNER'S WITHDRAWAL / DIVIDEND PAYMENTS

Includes cash withdrawals and payments on behalf of owners, such as income tax, social security, health insurance and executive life insurance premiums along with dividends payments to shareholders of corporate stock.

TOTAL CASH PAID OUT

Total of Cash Paid Out, Reserve and/or Escrow and Owner's Withdrawal.

CASH POSITION (END OF MONTH)

Difference between Total Cash Available less Total Cash Paid Out. This entry will become "Cash on Hand" for the beginning of the next period.

ADDITIONAL OPERATING DATA

In addition to the cash flow information, it is traditional to show some non-cash flow operating data on this statement. The numbers supplement the cash flow information and assist management's planning efforts.

- ▧ SALES VOLUME (dollars): Total number of units of products sold multiplied by the price for each. Reduce for any returns, allowances or markdowns. Exclude revenue not directly related to your business.
- ▧ ACCOUNTS RECEIVABLE (end of current period): Previous unpaid credit sales plus current period's credit sales, less cash received during current period.
- ▧ BAD DEBTS AND DOUBTFUL ACCOUNTS: Amounts receivable that are past due and not likely to be collected.
- ▧ INVENTORY ON HAND (end on period): Last period's inventory plus merchandise received and/or manufactured during current period, minus amount sold during current period.
- ▧ ACCOUNTS PAYABLE (end of period): Last period's payable plus current period's payable, minus amount paid during current period.
- ▧ DEPRECIATION AND AMORTIZATION of tangible and intangible capital assets.

ADVISORY: Almost all of the documents described in this chapter can be generated from modern computer accounting programs. Also available are "template" electronic accounting systems for companies based on industry standard "charts of accounts" for specific sectors. Software can be customized and there are packages for small and large firms alike. International businesses will need to further customize to various local standards. There are hundreds of such packages on the market today. We recommend thorough research and testing before deciding on the "right" software. It is a major investment that can either pay off handsomely or become an expensive burden.

CHAPTER 15

Business Plan Drafting Worksheet

A WISE MAN TURNS CHANCE INTO FORTUNE.

– THOMAS FULLER

BUSINESS PLAN PREPARATION can be a daunting task and it helps to have some solid guidelines to be sure that all the important areas are covered. This business plan drafting worksheet includes an extensive list of questions and information that should be answered and provided in a good business plan. In some cases, the items will overlap and the organizational emphasis will vary depending on the type of business and the purpose of the plan. However, working through these items should provide a good starting point.

The drafter should allow sufficient time to thoughtfully answer each of the questions. In the plan itself, refer to independent research reports, as well as any other credible evidence to support the claims and strategies of the company. Further information on each of the areas is included in the substantive chapters in this book. The business plan exemplars in the ensuing chapters should be consulted for ideas regarding presentation of the responses in the plan. Also, reference should be made to the chapter on financial information for specific issues relating to the presentation of financial statements in the plan.

The International Business Plan

I. INTRODUCTION / EXECUTIVE SUMMARY

1. Briefly describe the company's business.

2. Describe the significant features of the company's products.

3. Describe the market potential for the company's products.

4. Describe the financial goals of the company (e.g., reaching $2 million in sales in the new market in two years, profitability in three years and specified levels of sales and after-tax profits within four years).

5. Describe the purpose of the plan and its relation to the attainment of the company's financial goals.

PLAN NOTE: This section should showcase the highlights of the company's business plan and provide the reader with a snapshot of the information included elsewhere in the plan. After reviewing the executive summary, the reader should have a clear understanding of the company's products, market opportunities and financial objectives. The executive summary should be written <u>after</u> the rest of the plan has been drafted. In most cases, the executive summary should be no more than two pages (one page is best). The global aspects of the plan should be highlighted in the executive summary by focusing on foreign market opportunities and the financial goals of the company in those markets.

II. COMPANY DESCRIPTION

1. Describe the company's principal line(s) of business.

2. For each line of business, describe the company's products.

3. For each line of business and related product, describe the actual or anticipated customer base and their specific needs with respect to the types of products offered by the company.

4. Describe the specific steps taken by the company to identify customer needs, including interviews, market surveys, research or beta testing.

5. For each identified customer base for the company's products, describe the company's distinctive competence or competitive advantage (i.e., why will those customers purchase the products of the company as opposed to those offered by competitors or substitutes).

6. For each product, describe the profitability structure, including anticipated sales price, costs and profit margins.

ADVISORY: This section lists details about each of the company's products. Emphasis should be placed on relating the products to the needs of an identified group of customers. This process will demonstrate how the company will be able to service those needs in a manner that distinguishes it from competitors. Although this section includes several questions regarding the company's anticipated customer base, such issues also may be addressed in "Industry Background and Market Analysis" below.

III. INDUSTRY BACKGROUND AND MARKET ANALYSIS

1. Describe the industry or industries in which the company is active.

2. Describe the size of each industry and anticipated growth patterns over the next five to ten years.

3. Identify the major industry segments that would have an interest in the company's products.

4. Describe the business types that will likely be the major customers for the company's products (e.g., large corporations or small partnerships).

5. Identify and describe any other major demographic or technological trends in the industry.

6. Describe the actual or potential impact of regulatory requirements on the company's products.

PLAN NOTE: The industry and market for the company's products include a variety of variables, many of which are covered in greater detail in other sections. For example, customer needs and buying habits, as well as the strengths and weaknesses of competitors, will impact trends in the industry and marketplace. In this section, the view is more broad-based and looks at general demographic and technological factors, as well as any other changes that might impact the company in the years to come. If the company's products are subject to extensive regulation, or the company's foreign investment plans will be subject to government review in the target countries, additional time will need to be spent on regulatory matters and strategies.

IV. COMPETITION

1. Identify and briefly describe the major actual and potential competitors in each of the company's target markets.

2. Identify and describe the major factors of competition in each target market.

3. Candidly analyze how prospective customers will perceive the way that the company compares with competitors with respect to each of the aforementioned factors of competition.

4. Describe the steps that the company intends to take to exploit competitive advantages and/or reduce or eliminate competitive disadvantages.

5. Describe the anticipated response of major competitors to the steps enumerated in Item 4 above.

ADVISORY: Competitive factors vary in each geographic market. For example, some competitors are global companies active in each market where the customer base is sufficiently large to warrant attention. In other cases, competition will come from local companies content to do business solely within its borders. These firms can often be very competitive and attract strong brand recognition and loyalty. Also, while price may be the significant factor in one market, customer service may be the key in other areas.

V. MARKETING AND SALES

1. Describe the company's overall marketing strategies and objectives (e.g., how is the company to be perceived in the market and what are its goals with respect to developing market share).

2. Describe the company's strategies with respect to distribution of its products (e.g., direct sales, independent sales representatives, distribution agreements with third parties, etc.).

3. Describe the company's promotion strategies.

4. Describe the company's pricing strategies, including anticipated changes as brand acceptance develops.

5. Identify and describe the company's main "sales pitch" (i.e. the main messaging in sales and promotion activities).

6. Describe the company's strategies with respect to service and support of customers and distributors.

7. Describe the company's sales strategies and activities (e.g., customer identification, sales staffing requirements and compensation, sales goals and sales tracking).

PLAN NOTE: These questions cover the main issues in establishing and implementing the company's marketing and sales strategies. Take care to establish the right strategy in each geographic market since the company may need to vary its distribution channels and promotional activities from country to country. While not highlighted in these questions, the plan also should provide the reader with a good sense of the priorities of the company with respect to attacking specific markets and launching a particular marketing activity. In most cases, the company's budget will require that marketing activities proceed in two or more planned stages over a fixed period of time.

VI. TECHNOLOGY AND R&D

1. Describe the key aspects of the technology required for the company to operate its business.

2. Describe the status of each element of the technology enumerated in Item 1 above (e.g., idea, prototype, small production runs, etc.).

3. Describe the company's ownership and/or usage rights with respect to each key element of its technology.

4. Describe the general status of technology in the company's main markets, including companies that have technology that is superior or equal to the company's technology.

5. Describe anticipated trends in relevant technology over the next five years, including specific new technologies that might become commercially viable during that period and factors that might restrict their development or acceptance.

6. Describe the company's key research and development activities, related milestones and risks.

7. Describe how the results of the company's research and development activities will be used in the company's business (e.g., new products, new production methods, updated versions of existing products that meet identified customer needs, etc.).

8. Describe the impact of regulatory approval requirements on the company's research and development activities.

PLAN NOTE: Technology is important for every business, regardless of the type of products distributed by the company. For some companies, the technology is integrated into the products themselves. In other cases, technology allows the company to achieve competitive advantage in the production process. In any event, the plan should describe the company's key technology and strategies for development of new products and process technologies. In some cases, R&D is supplemented or completely replaced by active technology purchase or licensing programs that rely on third party development efforts.

VII. PRODUCTION AND OPERATIONS

1. Describe the company's production and operations activities and strategies.

2. Describe any significant agreements with third parties with respect to production.

3. Describe any competitive advantage or disadvantage of the company with respect to production activities and the steps the company will take to exploit or eliminate such advantages or disadvantages.

PLAN NOTE: Production is often an area where companies will look to foreign markets for low-cost alternatives. In such situations, the plan should carefully analyze the costs and risks associated with offshore production.

VIII. MANAGEMENT AND HUMAN RESOURCES

1. Describe the management and organizational structure of the company, including all key foreign business units.

2. Describe the company's recruitment, training and compensation policies.

3. Describe the company's internal information management structure.

4. In the case of a business plan used to raise capital, describe the skills and track record of the key managers and the company's plans for recruiting additional managers.

ADVISORY: Management skills, human resources and organizational structure are key elements of any business plan. For an international business plan, specific attention should be paid to the organization of the foreign business unit, recruiting qualified local managers and establishing an information and reporting system to monitor operations around the globe.

CHAPTER 16

Sample Plan #1:
Software Company

THE MORE YOU SWEAT THE LUCKIER YOU GET.

— RAY KROC

THIS SAMPLE BUSINESS PLAN relates to an established system integrator looking to expand its home country operations by obtaining the rights to new products developed in foreign markets and adapting them for use in the home country. This strategy can be particularly appealing in situations where the demand for the company's current product offering is softening. It can also be used if changes in the marketplace dictate that new innovations are likely to come from outside the country as opposed to coming from local developers and manufacturers.

The company anticipates that it will be able to obtain local rights from foreign companies based on its experience and familiarity with the local market and its existing customer relationships. This is an attractive combination for foreign manufacturers unwilling to make the large investment necessary to launch its own direct sales efforts. The software products highlighted in this plan are used in the banking industry, which is generally subject to complex regulation. As such, the software will often need to be customized for local rules and practices, another reason to rely on a local firm. This plan was originally written when Japan began its ongoing plunge into economic problems and government regulators began looking to make reforms in the banking and commercial credit areas.

Software Company Adapting Foreign Products to Local Market

SOFTWARE SYSTEMS COMPANY
INTERNATIONAL LOCALIZATION PLAN

Software Systems Company ("SSC" or the "Company") is a leading system integrator in Japan. The Company is principally involved in system integration and system development, and also provides facility management services, consulting services and vending activities. Over the last decade, SSC has been able to establish a distinguished reputation for the quality of its services to a prestigious list of clients in the finance, information systems and industry sectors. In the future, SSC intends to expand both horizontally and vertically through strategic alliances, internal research and development and acquisitions. The primary purpose of this plan is to describe the terms and conditions of the Company's first strategic business relationship for the localization of software products developed by a United Kingdom firm for exploitation in the financial services and credit card management areas.

OVERVIEW OF THE JAPANESE SOFTWARE MARKET

PLAN TIP: Many business plans in technical areas, such as software, include a discussion of the underlying intellectual property. In this case, however, general familiarity with software and its functions is assumed and the plan moves directly into an overview of various trends and conditions in the home country software market (i.e., Japan). This is an important opportunity to highlight local differences that might serve as impediments for foreign firms seeking to enter the market with their products.

The story of the Japanese software market is linked, in large part, to the Japanese economy as a whole. During the many years of economic growth in Japan, many enterprises made large investments in their computer technology for information processing and office automation. These companies considered those investments as assets and utilized them for corporate expansion. The software industry, including SSC, enjoyed rapid growth in the market. However, the recent economic difficulties in Japan have resulted in several key changes in the competitive environment.

First, many of SSC's existing and potential clients, particularly in the financial area, became reluctant to make any further investments in computer technology, including development of new software products and applications. Since SSC historically derived almost half of its revenues from that sector of the economy, it became quite difficult for SSC and other companies in the software industry to pursue long-term planning and marketing efforts.

Second, along with the market crash came a technological innovation, namely an era of smaller computers. Until the beginning of the 1980s, the software market in Japan was focused upon mainframe computer applications. Large main framers developed computer systems that could be used in both the business application and process control engineering area, and FORTRAN, ALGOL and COBOL were the main languages. Since then, however, the market has shifted sharply toward UNIX and LAN based processing networks. While until a few years ago there was a heavy mix of these two business environments, the UNIX/LAN oriented concept now has clearly achieved market dominance.

Finally, it became apparent that software innovation was to play an important factor in the future of the industry. In the past, the Japanese software was bespoke-type products, and there were few application package software products other than operating systems and development tools. Application software had to be customized to the needs of the client. However, SSC perceived that the role of computers in Japanese businesses has changed significantly in the past few years. Computer systems have long been used for automation and speed-up of daily processes. During that period, partial effectiveness has been realized without changing the whole social and corporate structure. Recently, however, the strategic trend has turned to redesigning the total process and structure of the business, a movement that has been accelerated by a new wave of technology. SSC anticipated that the role of the computer will be the subject of serious reevaluation and that software requirements among the Japanese business community will change substantially; new products will have the function of global business processing with multi-language, multi-currency and network capability. These new products can be integrated into a client's business procedures to provide a solution for the client's specific needs.

Structural changes have been accompanied by shifts in the Japanese economic environment. As Japanese industry entered an increasingly global economy with various close relationships, increasing numbers of companies began to expect worldwide functionality and product support. Above all, support for multiple languages, currency, local taxes, payment types, localized documentation and service staff are increasingly expected. In addition, growing macroeconomic concern that huge investments in IT failed to significantly increase "white collar productivity" has led most companies to look for software which will improve the managerial productivity as well as the ability to process transactions. This has become part of the basis for SSC's future strategic plans.

Estimates of the future growth of the Japanese software market have been tempered by recent economic events in Japan. In ____, a MITI survey and analysis by the Fuji Research Institute forecast that the annual market growth rate for the Japanese software development market, including system integration, would be ____% for the period from ____ to ____, a rate which was similar to that experienced in the previous ____-year period. However, in light of the recession which has plagued Japan since 1992, the estimated rate of growth has been decreased substantially, and SMC is now projecting that the software development market will grow at a rate of between _% and _% over the next ____ years, or at least until the level of pessimism among firms diminishes. It can be expected that the government will attempt to stimulate the entire economy along with certain industry sectors through the use of various monetary and fiscal measures, as well as through large-scale public projects in the computer technology area.

In spite of general economic uncertainties, SSC believes that the changing marketing conditions in Japan—particularly those that mandate companies to focus on practices that make them more competitive—have created strong investment opportunities in the software industry. In the past, businesses have streamlined processes while implementing new applications. More recently, the focus is shifting toward new strategies of re-engineering business processes in line with the reshaped organizations and customer focus, and then selecting the software which best supports the new processes. Deregulation will be a trigger to reshape the social structure in every field in Japan—such as banking, retail, medical, manufacturing and other market sectors—and will lead to the re-engineering of social systems. As Japan becomes even more closely linked with other Asian markets, Japanese business systems will drastically change over the next five years. SSC believes that software will be an important factor in the rapid transformation of the economic infrastructure.

THE COMPANY'S STRATEGIC BUSINESS PLAN

PLAN TIP: The industry background section above, when coupled with this general description of the company's strategic business plan, is similar in function to the presentation of problems, opportunities and solutions included in the other exemplar business plans. The business plan should always include, in some form or fashion, a statement of how the company intends to respond to changes and trends in the relevant marketplace. In this case, the company has decided to identify appropriate foreign partners as candidates for obtaining licenses to adapt their software products to the Japanese market. The remainder of the plan focuses on how the licensed software will be exploited.

SSC has traditionally pursued a job-shop style production strategy that has largely focused upon the creation of special varieties of software application products that could be sold to clients at premium prices. However, SSC also has pursued strategies of cost leadership and standardization by modularization of products and composing them into final products. Low cost position has given SSC a defense against rivalry from competitors and high margins that can be reinvested in new technologies and facilities. Cost leadership has required pursuit of cost reductions from experience, tight cost and overhead control.

While some large system integrators may be able to attain relatively greater market shares in the Japanese software industry, SSC believes that the historically fragmented structure of the industry will not change dramatically in the future. While SSC will continue to follow its strategies of cost leadership and standardization, its primary strategic focus in the future will emphasize specialization by product segment and customer type while secondarily concentrating on research and development and other acquisition of products that have advanced technological capabilities. SSC anticipates that a strategy of "technology advantage" will allow it to meet the changing needs of the Japanese business market.

SSC's changing business strategy also will entail changes in regard to its relationships with outside parties. In those cases where a project consisted primarily of system development and facility management, the Company did not require any outside suppliers of software or hardware products. The only significant requirement for completing those projects was the internal programming manpower. However, in order for the Company to pursue its objectives in the system integration area, it will be necessary for it to acquire access to a variety of new suppliers and distributors.

SSC's strategic planning over the next few years will be based upon the assumption that legacy software methodology will be a diminishing factor; the future requirements of the Company's client base will lie with the implementation of pre-fabricated software into the client's procedures to provide them with their own unique business solutions. Since SSC's business is client-oriented, SSC's mission will be to develop and acquire software products that meet the requirements of its customer base so SSC can approach those clients with appropriate solutions.

In order for SSC to execute its strategic plan, it must establish core expertise in both technology and application. The core expertise in the technological area will be pursued not only through internal research and development, but also through the acquisition of suitable strategic products from outside parties that SSC believes can be easily adapted to the requirements of its client base in the Japanese market. While SSC is looking for partners that can provide the Company with strong support and technical assistance, SSC also is looking for one or more products that could be adapted and released to the market on a timely basis.

According to industry sources, slightly more than one-half of the software products sold in Japan are made in the United States or Europe; most Japanese-made products are Japanese word processing software and the application system specified to the domestic business process. SSC believes that the best opportunities for identifying innovative software products that can be adapted to the local market lies with foreign companies. Accordingly, SSC has made a broad search for complimentary firms in the United States and Europe; and it has recently completed its initial efforts by entering into an arrangement with Euro Systems Integration Group ("ESIG").

ESIG, which is based in the United Kingdom, is a large-scale system integrator with operations mainly in Europe. Two years ago, ESIG launched its activities in Asia through ESIG Asia Pacific ("ESIAP"), which is owned by ESIG and is in charge of distributing ESIG's banking network products in the entire Asian market. ESIAP, which has about ____ employees, is headquartered in Singapore, and also has offices in Malaysia and other countries in Southeast Asia. SSC is planning to join with their Singapore office for the exclusive local distribution of its financial products and for joint R&D. In the future, SSC will expand the partnership with ESIG's headquarters in Europe. (See Exhibit ____ for further information regarding ESIG, its products, and its technology.)

While the strategic partnership with ESIG will be an important source of revenue over the next few years, SSC will seek other strategic partnering opportunities that will allow it to acquire a larger share in the Japanese market. Partnerships of this type will include close cooperation in basic research and development, cross-border joint projects and licensing arrangements. SSC may either build a relationship with foreign partners through software products, expertise transfer, joint marketing and new investment, or it may assist established foreign companies in their efforts to localize their products and distribute them through the Company's broad customer base and distribution network.

In addition, SSC hopes to build on its relationship with ESIG to move into other market opportunities. For example, significant opportunities for new development efforts may exist in the public service and energy areas. SSC has several excellent clients in these fields. They are operating well even in the current recession because they are practically government-owned companies. Although they have a big demand for the computer systems, SSC is rather weak in the fields of material logistics and power station systems. SSC will ultimately be requesting that ESIG transfer its technical expertise in these areas to the Company.

THE COMPANY'S BUSINESS ACTIVITIES

PLAN NOTE: This section includes a brief description of the company's business activities. Since this company's primary focus is services, as opposed to manufacture of products, the discussion is divided into groupings of similar customer offerings with the presumption that a customer will engage the company to provide a bundle of related tasks to achieve a specified result. The new products that are to be licensed by the company will be integrated as one of the tools included in the company's service offerings.

SSC's primary business activities can be characterized as system integration and system development. In addition, SSC also is engaged in facility management, consulting services and vending activities. These business activities generally have developed independently, primarily since the Company has not heretofore been active in providing its customers with total solution services. However, in recent years, the Company has become more involved in system integration activities, which call upon it to provide total solutions. As such, these activities have become more closely aligned.

SYSTEM INTEGRATION

System integration (SI) is the ultimate goal of SSC's business. SI encompasses all other business activities of SSC, and makes full utilization of its historical assets. Basically, the SI process starts with consulting services, followed by software development with software/hardware products vending, and sometimes is followed by facility management services. Several typical SI projects the Company has been involved with are described in Exhibit ____.

SSC's prior experience with SI is relevant to its ability to exploit the new products described below, since both emphasize solution-oriented activities. The new projects with the licensed products will be much more oriented to business consulting rather than information technology. The licensed products should be the tools for SSC's consulting services, not just accelerating software development. Once the consulting phase is completed, all subsequent system implementation work will be done by SSC's experienced system engineers.

SYSTEM DEVELOPMENT

System development is defined as all phases of requirement classification, software design, programming, testing and software maintenance, with the specific requirements of the client determining the scope of the project. There are some differences in the process between mainframe and smaller computers like UNIX workstations and PCs. However, the basic processes are generally identical. The licensed products can skip some phases or reduce the labor-oriented portions of the work. SSC has traditionally acted as a software factory creating software on a custom basis particularly for banks, insurance companies and retailers. A detailed description of the Company's system development experience is included as Exhibit ____.

Projects involving information systems pertain to all computer-based information technology that allows a firm to utilize data quickly and efficiently. Management and accounting systems are both application-oriented concepts, with accounting systems being more functionally specified. Projects relating to management systems include accounting, logistics, production, financial and all other management functional systems. Network systems are technological design projects in which more than one computer device at separate locations are connected together through wire. Information and network systems projects are designed to enhance the speed and accuracy of the transaction process, regardless of the size of the system, and clients also seek security, capacity and expandability. As to management and accounting systems, application viewpoint, user interface and flexibility are the first priorities for clients. Some of the Company's current system development projects are described in Exhibit ____.

SSC's experience and skills with respect to system development will be very useful in exploiting the capabilities of the new ESIG products. In the system development phases of the new SI projects, the licensed products will be quite advantageous due to the excellent technical functionality, thereby increasing the rate of productivity of the development phase by as much as 70% over conventional methods. In addition, the sophisticated base of technology available with the new products will assist SSC in training its younger engineers, which will have the effect of producing even greater productivity in the future.

ESIG Products

PLAN NOTE: This section describes the two main banking products that are to be licensed by the company from the foreign partner for localization and distribution in Japan. The level of detail will vary depending on the audience, and the reader will often be referred to more detailed descriptions and specifications included as exhibits to the main plan. In any event, the plan itself should, at a minimum, clearly identify the functional characteristics of the software products.

NetSwitch and CardManage are the two main banking products in ESIG's product line and supply two of the areas of functionality needed by banks in managing their businesses: authorization and credit card management.

NetSwitch

NetSwitch is a non-stop network switching system with the function of authorization. NetSwitch has high reliability and can be used for various communications protocols, including front-end switching between ATMs, POS terminals and CATs (Credit Authorization Terminals) and banking systems. NetSwitch currently focuses on communications with Visa and MasterCard, but will also be applicable to multiple protocol handling. NetSwitch components are structured with functionally separated modules, such as communication, terminal controls (for ATM and POS) and business process applications. Each module consists of more fragmented parts, and replacement of the parts will easily generate a new functional module. In this way, NetSwitch can be applied to various kinds of communication protocols and terminal devices. It also can be easily expanded with additional parts. A full description of the NetSwitch technology appears at Exhibit ____.

CardManage

CardManage is an application software covering the function of credit card management. CardManage is recognized as the leading integrated card management system in the world. CardManage comprises five modules: Cardholder and Merchant Processing, On-line Collections, On-line Authorizations, Memo Tickler System, and Acquisition and Scoring System. These modules can operate in a stand-alone manner and can combine to provide a full management system. CardManage can be implemented on-site or in a service bureau. A full description of the CardManage system and each of aforementioned modules appears at Exhibit ____.

While CardManage is a recognized leader in other markets, it must be enhanced before release to banks and credit card firms in Japan. While CardManage covers all the basic processes of credit card management, the major Japanese banks and credit card companies already have their own capabilities in this area. However, SSC believes that banks and credit card companies would be interested in a new and enhanced version of the product that can be used for strategic purposes, in addition to financial settlement. Such a product would include the ability to create a customer database, an interface to the customers' management information systems, smart card options and multimedia base. ESIG has already begun to enhance the product in other areas to provide smart card functions, and SSC will join the development process in order to introduce a new version of CardManage into the financial sector in Japan. Also, while CardManage will have a limited market in the Japanese banking area, SSC believes it will be accepted by many retailers who are about to enter the credit card business.

MARKET SIZE

PLAN NOTE: The original business plan included extensive detail and statistical information on the financial and non-financial sector markets identified in the text. This has been omitted from the example but a business plan drafter always should include specific information from an independent source on the size of the target markets. The description of market size always should, however, be accompanied by an analysis of the "real buyers" in the market. For example, while a market might be quite large when all sizes of firms are included, the real buyers may be limited to a subset of that market who are willing to invest the funds necessary for the purchase and deployment of the product. This is particularly important with the acquisition of new software as this will often require substantial changes in existing information technology systems and the habits of employees within the buyer's organization. This section includes one of the strongest features of the exemplar plans in that it describes the specific market survey activities that the company has undertaken to determine if the market will be receptive to the new products.

There are two separate markets for the CardManage product: the financial sector market and the non-financial sector market. SSC believes that those institutions that the Japanese Ministry of Finance and the Bank of Japan have approved for participation in the financing business are most likely to consider issuing credit cards. These financial institutions can be categorized as banks, credit companies, insurance firms, agriculture and fishery financing institutions and securities firms. In each case, prospective clients, as well as their system infrastructures, would be under strict government controls. In addition to possible clients in the financial sector, the Company believes there will be card-issuing business applications among entities that have direct and indirect consumers in any of their marketing networks.

The Company believes that NetSwitch is a synergetic product with CardManage, therefore, a portion of the market for NetSwitch will be essentially the same as the total projected market for CardManage. In addition, SSC believes that another potential market for this product will be non-financial institutions with a demand for EDI [Electronic Data Interchange].

SSC has contacted more than 100 organizations that either currently deal with credit card systems or which will be possible customers for these new ESIG Products.

Large Japanese Department Stores. SSC contacted an affiliate of one of the largest department stores in Japan. The store already had a huge card management system on the mainframe computer with over ten million cardholders. The problem in the existing system is that they are suffering from high operating costs. The store indicated that some other card issuers want to shift their facility and operation to outside sources, but their card system is too big to sell to other organizations as a packaged product. They implied that some of their rivals would be re-planning the design of card management systems. Additionally, they forecasted that when the

Japanese financial market was deregulated, all banking networks would be re-organized and non-stop switching systems like NetSwitch would become best-sellers.

Japanese Hotels. Top ranked Japanese hotels are demanding an excellent card management system for strategic marketing and financial settlement. Many high-ranked hotels located in Japan are now experiencing a hard time in their corporate management. Most of their computer facilities are designed for hotel operation rather than marketing. Some hotels have mainframe computers, but most are medium-sized computer users. They advised us that the sales strategy for hotels, including themselves, should be to provide a total consulting service of marketing to them and to convert the products for smaller computers.

Life Insurance Companies. All leading life insurance companies issue their own house-card for customer services. But their own cards are not effectively utilized by the clients. In addition to credit for insurance premiums, they want to provide total services through the cards; for example, claim management, including automated suggestions.

Local Community Membership Groups. Local community membership groups often issue their own credit cards. For example, one group contacted by the Company has issued over 40,000 cards. Some are credit card type and others are non-credit card type house cards. They are planning various kinds of events in which their cardholders use the cards. The main purpose of such events will be the renewal of the customer information database for the group's future marketing strategies. They want proposals for card business because they are not card management experts. There are many other such local groups all over the country that are connected together through networks. The group SSC contacted is in the substantial position in the networked group, and there may be millions of cardholders in all the groups.

Retail Stores. Although most large retailers already have their own card management systems, many medium-sized retail stores are still at entry level. Powerful customer information databases would be the most important factor to prevail in card management products. Also, small retailers or chain stores might have an interest in a product that could be used on PCs, since the movement to small-sized computers will be unavoidable. In addition, retailers of all sizes may have an interest in enhancements to their card management systems to improve direct marketing opportunities to cardholders.

Computer Suppliers. Hardware suppliers may be interested in providing total credit card systems to customers. If so, the Company may be able to forge alliances with the computer suppliers for solutions in total application systems. Computer suppliers would be primarily interested in quick response to maintenance calls, upgrades, troubleshooting and operational instruction.

DEVELOPMENT AND SALES PLANS

SSC has concluded that the Japanese market for the new ESIG products would be quite different from those of Europe and other parts of Asia.

- SSC believes that many potential Japanese customers are looking for a product that will allow for total system integration of credit card and banking strategies. As this is different than the current products, SSC must gain a greater understanding of the detailed technical information of each module of the new products. This will require a transfer of technical expertise to SSC through an exchange of technical personnel.

- Customers may be interested in purchasing not only the whole product, but also the individual modules. Pricing should be a function of data volume and system scale. In addition, it will be important to produce new modules for the Japanese market, such as a powerful database for customer information.

- Customers are interested in the response time and throughput of online network interfaces.

- Customers are concerned about the possibility of interface with Japanese proprietary networks, such as CAFIS and CATNET. The kinds of services or data that would be offered to clients is also an important matter.

- The portability to the UNIX environment should be considered. Given the anticipated movement to smaller machines, it will be important that the products be rewritten for smaller computers, such as IBM AS400 workstations and PC's, for the large and uncultivated Japanese market. Also, the function for local area networks should be considered.

- Customers will be concerned about the continuous involvement of the original supplier for maintenance, upgrades, troubleshooting and operational instruction. Accordingly, provision should be made for ongoing access to ESIG personnel.

Localization of the products will require (1) translation to Japanese language in screen display, report and operation manual, (2) making the network protocol modules and (3) making modules for Japanese proprietary business customs. At the beginning, SSC will organize into two groups for marketing and technical work, both of which will be directly controlled by top management of the Company. Both marketing and technical staff will need to travel to Singapore and the United Kingdom to master how to apply the products to clients' solution. After the localization work, the two groups are integrated into a single team, which means sales engineers will be supporting both sales and technical matters. SSC is preparing to re-organize the internal structure and increase the staff.

The Company estimates that development and customization of CardManage will require approximately ____ months for each project. SSC projects that the average revenue from a single system will be approximately ____ yen. ____ percent of revenue will come from the product and the remaining ____% from the software development and customization work. Development costs for a single system are assumed to be approximately ____ yen, and royalties to ESIG will be __% of the product revenue. The Company's forecasts for the number of installations of CardManage are set forth in Exhibit ____.

The Company estimates that development and customization of NetSwitch will require approximately ____ months for each project. The Company projects that the average revenue from a single system will be approximately ____ yen. Approximately ____% of revenue will come from the product and the remaining ____% from the software development and customization work. The development costs for a single system are assumed to be approximately ____ yen and royalties to ESIG will be ____% of the product revenue. The Company's forecasts for the number of installations of NetSwitch are set forth in Exhibit ____.

See Exhibit ____ for a description of the timetable for the development and commercialization of the new ESIG products.

CUSTOMERS AND MARKETING

CUSTOMERS

One of the significant strategic advantages of SSC is its strong relationships with a broad base of customers in a variety of industries. For example, in the finance area, SSC has successfully completed projects with mainframe computers, various types of UNIX-based platforms and process control, and has worked with a number of leading Japanese banks. In addition, SSC has worked on projects for securities firms, insurance firms and credit card companies, and is now engaged in projects that involve integration between the banking system and retailers. In the process control field, SSC has worked on several projects in the telecommunications area. The Company anticipates that its work in the financing and telecommunications areas will produce a good synergy to cope with new technologies, such as LAN remote control of 24-hour non-stop operations and logistics control.

SSC's customer base for the last three fiscal years was as follows: ____ (____), ____ (____) and ____ (____). Among SSC's current customers, there are approximately __ financial institutions, including credit card companies, and ____ global operating corporations with remote network systems. The Company believes that these customers will be potential clients for the new products. This is because, regardless of the scale of the Japanese financial institutions, they must follow the general direction of globalization and deregulation. From a technical viewpoint, these companies will be forced to participate in the global banking network beyond the internal and domestic networks. This means that, operationally, Japanese banks must adapt to the standards of BIS (Bank of International Settlement) and National Bank Standard's chart of accounts. SSC has already made a number of presentations to its existing clients in the financial area and has gotten a strong response and interest in the new products for the above reasons.

As a general matter, SSC's customary contracts with its customers cover obligations, inspection guarantees, payments, intellectual property rights, non-disclosure, termination, duration, non-transferability and dispute resolution. All specific design elements and contents of the software are part of the sale order documentation and are incorporated into the general contractual agreement. There are two basic types of sales orders. The first type calls for the completion of specific products in accordance with the particular requirements of the customer. The actual sale of the product by SSC is conditioned upon inspection and acceptance of the final product by the customer. The second type of sales order covers consultancy services under which SSC system engineers provide on-site assistance to customers with respect to a wide variety of matters. These consulting services are charged at hourly rates as well as by setting a specific base rate per month.

Historically, SSC's pricing for software development was based largely on the number of labor hours, which was calculated in man-hours. Accordingly, the price for SSC's products has always been heavily dependent on labor cost and expenses. As SSC changes its general marketing strategies to emphasize technology-intensive products rather than labor-intensive products, it can be expected that SSC's pricing reflects the value to the customer from SSC's higher productivity, the technology embodied in SSC's products and the expertise provided by SSC's consultants.

The sales orders for SSC's new products will include both product and consultancy services, and will be divided into two general categories. The first category would itself be broken down into two phases. The first phase will include the work required to adapt the basic software to the requirements of the customer, a process of developing business solutions that is similar to system integration. In this case, the clients are willing to pay a premium to SSC for its business consulting services, and will not be as concerned regarding pricing of the specific products. The second phase will cover the technical support necessary for the customers to operate the products in their own environments, including maintenance, upgrading and troubleshooting. In the second category, contracts will simply cover products, in which case the clients will not be as concerned regarding consulting services.

MARKETING

The Company has sales offices in Tokyo, Osaka and Nagoya. Salespersons in each office are marketing its territory and get the first contact with prospective clients. Consultants respond to client demands for presentation of system proposals. Service system engineers keep in contact with the clients after the Company has completed the projects and hear the new requirements and demands of the customers.

SSC's sales process begins with pre-sales by salespersons. The head office and branches have several salespersons for the first contact to the possible clients. Consultants follow the first contact and make interviews/presentations to them. All terms and conditions of the agreement with clients are discussed by salespersons and consultants. All the projects take at least several months to be completed and SSC has an opportunity to take other orders during that period, thereby allowing the Company to simultaneously perform multiple projects with a single client. For continuous business with existing clients, SSC's service system engineers are in charge of the maintenance phase of each project and remain informed about the new demands or requirements of the clients. Branch offices have the same policy of sales and marketing regardless of their smaller size. In some cases, salespersons and consultants from the Tokyo head office help the branches' sales promotion because the head office outnumbers the branches in sales personnel and consulting capability. Even though research and development activities are only conducted in the Tokyo head office, all technology and business consulting expertise are transferred to and from the branches.

HUMAN RESOURCES AND ORGANIZATIONAL STRUCTURE

As of _____, the Company had a total of ____ employees, of which ____ were technical employees and ____ were non-technical employees. While most of SSC's engineers are relatively young, with an average of ____ years, ____ of them are senior system engineers or analysts with over ten years of experience. ____ system auditors are dedicated to quality control. SSC has a quality first recruitment policy and invests heavily in staff training. The Company believes that its unique combination of commitment, specialist skills and experience has been essential to the successful completion of its various projects for its clients.

DESCRIPTION OF CURRENT BUSINESS ORGANIZATION

The current business organization for the Company's existing businesses is as described on Exhibit ____. The activities of the various organizational groups within the Company can be briefly summarized as follows:

Business Development Group. SSC has a separate group of strategists who make an overall corporate design. The strategists drive the overall marketing and technology of the Company to the ideal direction. This group has primary responsibility for the Company's global partnership strategies (e.g., ESIG), brand-new advanced technology and ISO9OOO consulting services.

Administrative Department. SSC has a rather small administrative organization, which results in low overhead cost. Administrative personnel at SSC's head office in Tokyo handle all of the Company's financial, legal and secretarial functions.

Information System Department. All engineers in this department are specialized in mainframe technology. Regardless of the global trend to downsizing and open architecture, SSC considers that mainframe business will maintain a stable position for large-scale computing. With long years of experience in mainframe technology, SSC has a steady growth projection for this cluster. New technological trends, however, can also be seen in mainframe technology. The new role of mainframe computers is the network server to global networks. Therefore, there will be a need for frequent exchanges of technology with the Advanced Technology Department.

Advanced Technology Department. As all staff in this department face the most advanced technology, they play an important role as a profit center as well as a research and development center. UNIX will be the base technology for the time being and this department is in charge of UNIX technology. At the same time, the future technology base, namely personal computers, is being followed by the staff in this department. Another characteristic of this department is that the duration of a single project is rather short and flexible.

Western District Representative (Nagoya and Osaka Branches). Branch offices are mainly to allow SSC to provide quick services in remote geographic areas. The Nagoya area has many manufacturing firms, such as Toyota Motors and Nippon Denso and SSC is targeting this market through the Nagoya branch. The Osaka branch targets another large geographic market.

ORGANIZATION OF NEW BUSINESS UNIT

ADVISORY: This section is another unique feature of the exemplar plans included in this book. The company has decided to form and organize a new business unit to develop and exploit the licensed products. It is common to form a new business unit, such as a wholly-owned subsidiary, when a company is moving into a new foreign market. In this case, the business unit will be a division within its current organization, but will have an autonomous group of managers with responsibility for various functions, such as strategic planning, technology and marketing. Initial managers will be transferred from within the organization on the basis of their familiarity with the underlying technology and experience with current customers that have been targeted as likely candidates for the new products. In situations where the plan is being used to raise additional funds, it should be supplemented by background information on the key personnel of the new business unit. An investor will want to determine if the managers have the requisite skills and experience to execute the plan.

In connection with the development and exploitation of its new products, the Company will be forming a new business unit that will be structured as described on Exhibit ____. The new business unit for the new project has already started as a project steering team and will be formally organized as a new department. The manager of the department will report directly to SSC's president. The department consists of three functional teams operating in the areas of strategic planning, marketing and technology.

Strategic Planning Team. The strategic planning team is in charge of the overall strategy in this project, including the communication between the Company and ESIG, financial issues in the project, human resources, sub-distributors, market-technology interfaces and management. Currently, _____ has all responsibility for the functions of the team, and another ____ people will be joining the team in the next ____ months.

Marketing Team. The marketing team is in charge of public relations, pre-sales, product demonstration and presentation, business consulting, help desk and other all services to clients. Currently, _____ and _____ have responsibility for the functions of the team. Within the next ____ months, another ____ people will join the team.

Technology Team. The technology team is in charge of all technical matters in the project, including product localization, translation, technical training and consulting, and overall technical services to clients. Currently, _____ has all responsibility for the functions of this team.

Customer Solution Teams. Customer solution teams will be organized every time new orders come in from clients. As more fully discussed elsewhere, a typical project for respective clients requires ____ consultants and application engineers. The core teams (strategy team, marketing team and technology team) will select the required staff from the other departments and flexibly organize the team. A team leader will also be selected among the staff from other department. The solution teams will be disbanded after the project is completed. The core teams will provide all required assistance to the customer solution team during the project. It is anticipated that the composition of the customer solution teams will be rotated in order to build a broad range of expertise among the Company's personnel.

FUTURE HUMAN RESOURCE REQUIREMENTS

In accordance with the Company's expansion program, it is anticipated that additional personnel will be required in the near future. SSC currently has an ongoing recruiting policy that is designed to maintain current levels of employment, but in the case of unexpected changes, it is possible that additional skills will be obtained through professional recruiters and the acquisition of other software development companies. In any case, the Company believes that it will be able to easily recruit excellent system engineers from outside sources in order to meet the requirements of the new products, thereby substantially increasing its production capacity. Since the requirements of SSC's existing businesses are similar to those for the new products, the Company believes that the new personnel can be used for expansion across all of its existing and proposed businesses.

PRODUCTION

SYSTEM DEVELOPMENT AND PRODUCTION PROCESS

In most cases, new systems are produced by project teams consisting of ____ - ____ persons. During the first stage, one or two consultants work ____ weeks with clients in order to classify and define system requirements. Salespersons participate in the discussion with the clients about contractual issues, such as product size, period, project team organization, pricing and payment terms. The second stage involves software design and programming. In mainframe projects, the total system is divided into several modules of functions and each module is implemented by a smaller group. In small computer projects, the work is done by a single team. This stage involves a variety of tests, all of which can be quite time-consuming. Among the tests conducted are module relation tests, system tests and total operation tests; and all test data should cover every possible case. These tests take several trials and errors with feedback method and therefore takes much more labor than any other phase. After the various total operation tests have been completed, the new system is installed on a target computer, and the finished product must be adjusted to the client's operation and must be inspected and approved by the client. Once the inspection is finished, SSC recognizes the product as sold. Maintenance is usually provided under a separate contract and includes a free-of-charge guarantee with respect to specified performance characteristics.

QUALITY CONTROL

With respect to quality control, SSC is now preparing for certification of ISO9000. ISO9000 (more precisely ISO9000-3) is the standard for software quality guarantee, and is similar in function to the guarantees provided for tangible products. While this certification is not yet covered by government regulation, it is anticipated that in several years the government will be requiring every software company to obtain the certificate. In fact, ISO9000 consulting services may well become a new potential market in Japan and SSC is considering entering one or more strategic alliances with accounting and/or consulting firms in order to get into this new business.

SERVICE

One of SSC's strategic advantages is the service capacity it makes available to its customers. There are basically two separate types of service projects: the implementation of products and consultancy services. In the former type of project, there is at least six month of guaranteed "warranty-type" maintenance provided free-of-charge to clients. As a general rule, service and maintenance charges outside of the warranty are approximately ____% of the product price. In the latter type of project, all of SSC's jobs are consultancy services and there is no obligation regarding the completed work. In this case, the services are usually charged on an hourly basis.

COMPETITION

In the major sectors in which SSC operates, competitors include medium-sized software companies that do not have any affiliation with computer manufacturers or major computer users, including _____, _____, _____ and _____. Based on revenues for the most recent calendar year, SSC was ranked _____ by turnover. The industry remains very fragmented, and may actually include several hundred competitors in nominal numbers.

The key competitive factors appear to include pricing, service structure and the ability to use the products on a wide variety of hardware/software platforms. Also, while companies compete on cost leadership and quality, in most cases, customer loyalty to a supplier is quite high and customers generally seek to have stable and familiar relations with a single supplier. SSC believes that, compared to possible competitors, it has an advantage in that it already has a substantial production and service capacity, prestigious list of clients, geographical accessibility to the western Japan area and accumulated expertise of software technology. SSC also has effectively competed through cost reduction, as shown by its high level of profitability per engineer.

SSC's strategic plans for the future include seeking competitive advantages with respect to the · development and/or acquisition of new "leading-edge" technological products. In this area, competition comes from other firms with an established reputation with mainframes that are now seeking to address the open systems market. The Company believes that successful products should be multi-relational database, multi-desktop environment open systems products. In order for SSC to seize a competitive advantage from development of these products, it must be able to introduce the products to the market on a timely basis, as competitors may be able to move quickly with their own development efforts, particularly if they are able to effectively use software produced by third parties as building blocks to accelerate their development efforts.

SSC also expects to be able to enhance its competitiveness through modifications in its pricing policies. As SSC changes its general marketing strategies to emphasize technology-intensive products rather than labor-intensive products, it can be expected that SSC's pricing will no longer be based solely upon labor costs; rather it will reflect the value to the customer from SSC's higher productivity, the technology embodied in SSC's products and the expertise provided by SSC's consultants. In fact, it is anticipated that SSC will actually be able to reduce its labor costs and related expenses with respect to its new software development work, and that such savings can be passed along to its customers.

FINANCING STRATEGY

Initial expenses associated with the localization of the licensed products will include the costs of establishing the new business unit described above, as well as the development expenses for the localization process and marketing and sales costs in approaching target market customers. It is anticipated that the localization process will take several months to complete before the licensed products are suitable for sale and deployment in the local market. Funds for those activities will come from the Company's general working capital. In addition, the Company is considering raising additional funds from private investors to support the activities of the new business unit, including additional strategic alliances covering other software products. Pro-forma results of operations for the next 24 months are included as Exhibit _____, including profit and loss statements, balance sheets, cash flow analysis and a description of material assumptions underlying the pro-forma figures.

CHAPTER 17

Sample Plan #2:
Technology Manufacturer

THE BUYER NEEDS A HUNDRED EYES, THE SELLER BUT

ONE. — ITALIAN PROVERB

THIS SAMPLE BUSINESS PLAN relates to a developer and manufacturer of digital encoding, decoding and multiplexing products (i.e., a technology-based products company). Although the company is relatively young, the innovative power of its proprietary technology has created immediate opportunities for global expansion. The company, formed and operated in Israel, has obtained significant funding for expansion based on achievement of technical milestones and initial customer orders. While the company could continue to operate as a niche player from Israel and deploy sales representatives to various parts of the world, it has decided to establish formal sales operations in three key markets: the United States, Europe and the Asia Pacific region. United States operations will be through a wholly-owned subsidiary, while sales activities in Europe and Asia will be through a distributor network. In addition, the company is looking to outsource customer service and pursue low-cost manufacturing in the Asia-Pacific region. Potential customers include a number of large telecommunications firms, many of which are owned or substantially regulated by national governments. This adds a specific government relations feature to this business plan and strategy.

Technology Product Company Entering Multiple Global Markets

ADM TECHNOLOGIES
INTERNATIONAL BUSINESS PLAN

ADM Technologies ("ADM" or the "Company") is an innovative and emerging leader in the market for digital media products and systems. The Company's best of breed technology, optimal timing of market entry and skilled resources will ensure a very bright future in what is expected to be a global, multi-billion dollar market. ADM has developed advanced technology and system architecture that delivers improved technical performance and operational efficiency at lower cost than existing products. ADM digital encoding, decoding and multiplexing products will meet the requirements of three critical functions that must be performed in digital media broadcasting systems.

The Company launched operations in 1997 in Israel where it began its initial research and product development. In 1998, ADM was awarded its first large contract with a leading company in the digital communications market that required ADM to design and develop an advanced multi-channel decoder for a new digital media platform. This early stage activity provided the impetus and resources for ADM to develop second-generation products during 1999, which has resulted in the ADMX4 and ADMX16 efficient multi-channel digital media decoders. These innovative new products have been exhibited at industry trade shows in the United States and in Europe, receiving wide acclaim and generating a substantial number of qualified opportunities for future business.

Serious sales activities have been launched within the last ____ months from the Company's headquarters in Israel. Sales of the Company's products during that period have been approximately $____ million. Based on the promise of the Company's technology and the initial sale successes, ADM has raised $____ million to continue its product development efforts and develop the sales and manufacturing infrastructure necessary for expansion of its business into the global markets described below. A list of the major events in the development of ADM is included as Exhibit ____.

ADM is looking to take advantage of the mass conversion from analog to digital infrastructure required to modernize tens of thousands of head ends belonging to television broadcasters, cable companies and telecommunication service providers ("Telcos"). The global business of digital media, particularly in multi-channel video, audio, voice and data services is a phenomenon that, according to industry sources, will continue to expand exponentially well into the next decade. This climate of change provides unprecedented opportunity for ADM to create a global company with substantial value.

ADM intends to launch full-scale sales operations in the United States, Europe and the Asia Pacific region during the next ____ months; it will also pursue opportunities to establish low-cost manufacturing operations in the Asia Pacific region during that period as demand for ADM products emerges from the sales efforts. Sales operations in the United States will be managed through a newly-formed subsidiary staffed by ADM managers and employees. Sales operations in Europe and the Asia Pacific region will be handled through independent sales representatives and a network of distribution alliances with original equipment manufacturers (OEMs). Initially, manufacturing will continue at the Company's headquarters facilities in Tel Aviv and products will be shipped on an "as needed" basis to Company affiliates and customers around the world. Customer service will be outsourced to a third party in each geographic region.

PROBLEMS AND OPPORTUNITIES

ADVISORY: Products are only important if they address a specific need or problem of an identified group of users. If a product has no value to a group of users, or the product does not solve a problem with existing competitive offerings, it will not generate the level of interest and revenues necessary to sustain the business. Accordingly, the business plan should always carefully and fully identify the problems that are being experienced by potential users of the company's products and the opportunities that can be seized by the company in executing its plan. In this case, the plan describes some of the broad changes in the technological environment (i.e., the convergence of digital media) and then goes on to discuss some of the specific problems with current products in the company's niche. The discussion should always lead nicely into a description of how the company's products will be able to provide "solutions" to these problems, as described in the next section.

CONVERGENCE OF DIGITAL MEDIA

The global telecommunications revolution started in the United States almost two decades ago and has created an increasing momentum in the conversion of analog television networks to all digital operation. Digital technology is now well established as the unifying element in modern media networks. The industry refers to this phenomenon as "convergence." Practically every aspect of the new media industry, from content creation, contribution and distribution to the end-user premises has been affected by this shift to efficient digital technology. Affected by this wide scale upgrade are the established media companies, such as the traditional broadcast networks in the United States and the United Kingdom, and new arrivals who are directing their resources at the development of new interactive television content for broadcasting over the Internet and other IP capable networks.

GLOBAL MARKET OPPORTUNITY

The movement from analog to digital technology in the delivery of television broadcasts, over the-air and by cable, is a multi-billion dollar global market. The conversion started in the early 1990's in the United States and Europe. It is predicted to expand exponentially over the next decade with the addition of new services and delivery methods by the world's major Telcos, including AT&T, BT, Deutsche Telekom and France Telecom, whose changing role has affected practically all aspects of modern communications, including entertainment.

In terms of technology, the conversion from analog operation and the implementation of digital media means a gradual progression from a mix of digital and analog services. For example, a digital set top box is provided but analog TV programs can still be received; over time, a transition will be made to digital service alone. Over the course of this progression, technologies and services will constantly change and become more complex. The industry will seek technology solutions that will allow frequent changes to their services and make the administration of these services easier once they are implemented.

Two significant, related trends are driving the move towards digital television distribution systems:

1. Competition between the major media companies, which is currently the leading factor.
2. A mandate by many governments to implement digital television, which is a longer term issue.

Therefore, to the world's leading media organizations, in both the short- and long-term, digital upgrades are a pressing issue. Digital systems are not "optional" for content distributors. They are a "must have" technology. The superior quality and number of services that digital technology can support will be a requirement for any player in the new media industry.

PROBLEMS WITH CURRENT TECHNOLOGIES

Television content producers and distribution companies require expensive and complex equipment for digital media signal processing, which fall generally into three main operations: 1) MPEG digital encoding, 2) Multiplexing / De-multiplexing, and 3) MPEG decoding. To perform these functions, companies need costly, high performance, digital-signal processing products, including encoders, decoders and multiplexers. The Company believes that there are significant problems with current technologies in this area, thereby creating new opportunities based on the Company's solutions.

Lack of Versatility. Current encoders, decoders and multiplexers are rarely combined within the same physical unit, so to meet the needs of complex multi-channel system requirements, companies must buy, connect, operate and maintain many separate units. This leads to high cost of ownership, inefficient use of space and reliability issues, because the more connections between separate units, the greater the chance of system malfunction. In addition, because many multi-channel systems are designed for large fixed purpose operations, where some of these considerations have been less important in the past, new media companies needing a less sophisticated system have no alternative and must accept this lack of versatility.

Lack of Adaptability. Currently available digital television (DTV) signal processing technologies can usually handle only a single fixed media source at any one time (e.g., satellite, cable, telco, DSL), and cannot support or convert between multi-standards (e.g., 625/50- PAL (European), 525/60-NTSC (USA)) on the same network. In today's rapidly developing digital media "convergence" market, there is a need for new technology products that can be easily adapted to a range of sources and standards, bringing greater efficiency to vital and time-consuming operations.

Lack of Reliability. Today's modern digital media networks are commonly designed with physically separate items of signal processing equipment. This system architecture does not provide the most efficient redundancy and service reliability. There is necessarily a pause between the failure of equipment in the system and the start of the backup system as an operator or automatic switchover sequence initiates the redundant equipment. This can result in signal disturbance that is detrimental to other equipment in the system and causes annoying program interruption.

Lack of Monitoring Ability. Television broadcasts must be monitored visually to detect service malfunction. Most digital TV signal processing technologies offer a limited number of channels, where only a single channel can be viewed at a time. This system is therefore quite labor intensive. The effect on the service provider is poorer quality of service or an increased expense to purchase, monitor, maintain and house large amounts of signal monitoring equipment.

The aforementioned problems are universal in nature and would apply wherever television broadcast and other media companies are operating. While there are wide variations in the scope and quality of the content available to consumers, the underlying technological problems are shared in each of the geographical regions targeted by the Company for market entry.

ADM'S SOLUTIONS

PLAN NOTE: This section includes a description of the technical solutions offered by the company's products. In this case, the description is a mere summary of the technology and it is likely that further detail would be provided in an actual plan. The level of detail will depend on the audience. For example, in the case of an internal business plan, the technology description would be fairly brief because it is assumed that readers are familiar with research and product developments within the company. On the other hand, when the plan is prepared for investors, it may be necessary to include a longer description, including a glossary of terms and charts and drawings that make it easier for the reader to understand. When describing technical solutions to outsiders, emphasis should be placed on demonstrating competitive advantages over products and technologies available from other sources.

Current digital decoders offered by leading suppliers are burdened with most, if not all, of the design deficiencies described above. ADM believes that major vendors of digital media transmission systems are looking for new solutions for their signal processing requirements. In its initial contracts, the Company has been able to provide customers with an innovative, cost efficient solution to the critical decoder requirement. The major problems of flexibility, adaptability, reliability and overall quality were overcome to their satisfaction, and the Company was able to achieve these results within a short design and prototype cycle made possible by the innovative, flexible technology and architecture of the engineering design.

The design efficiency of the Company's digital media products will provide it with better speed-to-market capability than the majority of its competitors. In addition, the Company's technology lends itself to the development of a comprehensive line of digital signal processing products that can satisfy the growing needs of new digital media.

ADM's core technology lies in its innovative system architecture that allows a unique combination of hardware and software to be accommodated within an efficient single main board assembly. It provides ADM with a significant competitive advantage against existing digital media products, and effectively eliminates many of the inconveniences of existing digital signal processing technologies.

ADM's digital signal processing technology and product architecture provides an order of magnitude improvement over currently available technology in MPEG2 multi-channel digital media systems. With its unique system architecture, the ADM product line sets new high performance standards at lower overall cost in multi-channel digital cable, satellite and Telco networks. In addition, the Company's proprietary technology for its initial line of products provide features that reduce overall operating costs, simplify operational control and improve system performance. These important advantages are not currently available from any other manufacturer of MPEG2 digital signal processing equipment. And, with the open architecture and standards based design, ADM's technology is simple to integrate into legacy networks.

PRODUCTS

PLAN TIP: While many companies pursue profitability through the sale or license of their technologies, it is more common for the business plan to be focused on leveraging technology that has been embodied in one or more of its products. In such situations, the plan should include a detailed description of the company's major products, as well as all planned future products that are in development or that are reasonably expected to be developed within the next 12-24 months. Again, the level of detail will vary depending on the reader, with outside investor candidates receiving far more information than inside readers. In many cases, reference might be made to product brochures and specification sheets prepared for distribution to customers. In this case, the plan anticipates expansion into two new markets. The text omits a detailed discussion of how current product offerings will be adapted for those markets. In the actual plan, this detail should be provided along with a complete analysis of those markets and the actual needs of prospective customers.

The Company's innovative technology has enabled it to create two initial products that have had an immediate application in the market. The two products are ADMX4, a four-channel digital media decoder with mosaic monitor, and the ADMX16, a sixteen-channel real-time monitoring decoder. These two products have created the foundation for an expanded product line that will in the future include decoders, encoders and multiplexers required by the world's new digital media networks. A description of these products, including full technical specifications, is included as Exhibit ____.

The development work expended in creating the ADMX4 and ADMX16 products has provided the Company with a pathway to additional products that will not involve extensive adaptations of the basic technology concept. The development goal for the ADMX series is to create derivatives of the basic product that will provide added system features and will allow users to factory-customize their system and scale it to meet specific channel requirements. A description of the initial anticipated follow-on products is included as Exhibit ____.

ADM plans to become a leader in performance improvement products for the digital media industry. This will commence with the ADMX series, allowing ADM to penetrate the professional and industrial markets. Thereafter, ADM plans to extend this reach into the prosumer and consumer markets using the same proprietary system architecture. A list of the products for those markets that will be derived from experience gained in the ADMX series, as well as a new product development schedule, is included as Exhibit ____.

MARKETS AND COMPETITION

PLAN NOTE: The market for this company's products is interesting in that the primary customers are large telecommunications and broadcast companies, as opposed to small- and medium-sized users. As such, the company is able to project significant revenues from landing just a few accounts, since each customer will require a number of units, plus ongoing service and maintenance. Market size and characteristics are often illustrated by information derived from independent market research firms, which should be identified in the plan. While this plan has a description of the market size included as an exhibit, it is also common to present this information in tables and charts in the body of the plan. While this company actually identified five or six target markets, the text highlights only three.

Industry analysts predict that the digital media market will expand rapidly in the next several years, offering significant opportunities for providers of technology elements that deliver feature rich, reliable performance. A description of the market size, according to a recent report from Digital Media Industry Analysts, an independent market research firm, is included as Exhibit ____.

NEW DIGITAL MEDIA SERVICES

Cable networks, Direct Broadcast Satellite (DBS) and traditional Over-the-Air (OTA) broadcasters are in fierce competition for subscribers or/and ratings. The result of this trend has been new investment in upgrading networks to provide more programs and improved signal quality through digital distribution. In an effort to retain customers, cable operators and DBS providers are offering bundled broadband services—one-stop shopping for program content, Internet and other communication services.

This is the start of digital media "convergence" that will provide consumers the ability to receive both paid and free services; a single service provider and common digital terminal equipment set-top-boxes (STB's) will support a variety of new services, including:

- Video-on-Demand (VOD) – No further need to rent videos.

- Interactive Television – Interact with game shows or edutainment programs.

- Digital VR – No need for a VCR, record and play from disc in the STB.

- Internet TV – Browse the world's TV stations through Internet video streaming.

- Communications – Phone, fax and videophone service through the STB.

Evidence of increased competitiveness to provide new services that go beyond television delivery is the strategic activity that has reshaped the cable industry over the past few years. In the United States, for example, mergers, acquisitions and partnerships between concerns such as AT&T and TCI, MediaOne and USWest, MediaOne and Comcast and numerous others, have created operations with access to significant proportions of the United States population. The prices paid for these deals cannot be justified by revenue from video alone. Instead, these companies are strategically positioning themselves to provide "bundled" media services, preparing their companies for a new digital infrastructure that will support "convergence" in digital media— delivering video, audio, voice and data services on the same local, regional and global network.

NETWORK AND CABLE SECTOR UPGRADES

Major television networks in the United States and Europe have been actively upgrading their networks to digital operation since the late 1990's and will continue with this work over the next several years. It is estimated that there are over ____ television channels around the world, and most of these will convert to all digital operation over the next decade. As a result, the need for digital signal processing equipment will expand rapidly, as older equipment will need to be replaced and analog equipment will cease to be manufactured.

Cable companies also face a need to upgrade to deliver new digital media services that can compete with the 200-500 channel satellite DBS services. The growing demand for cable services supporting "broadband digital media" and "convergence" has led cable operators to upgrade their infrastructure, mainly by adding optical fibers.

TELCO/INTERNET SECTOR

The Telco market sector is considered most important to the future of ADM, in it's enormous forecasted demand for both infrastructure elements (encoders, decoders and multiplexers) and for consumer and business terminals, or set-top-boxes (STBs), needed to support the convergence of video, audio, voice and data services offered by the telcos. Industry leaders predict that telco networks will be the predominant vehicle for delivery of all digital media in the future. Satellite and OTA will compete with more specialized services such as HDTV (high definition television) and mobile multi-media services.

Broadband networks are rapidly being built by major Telcos in the United States, Europe and Asia to support new digital media services, such as Video-on-Demand, Interactive TV, Fast Internet, etc. The expansion of broadband networks will create a substantial demand for digital media signal processing equipment. This significant opportunity can be addressed by the flexible, innovative digital media technology now being introduced by ADM.

Telcos present special marketing challenges for the Company and its competitors in that many large telecommunications companies in rapidly development markets are still heavily controlled and/or regulated by national and regional governments. As such, ADM and its competitors often will be confronted with complex procurement procedures, including significant interaction with a wide range of government agencies and administrators. The Company intends to identify and recruit senior governmental relations managers in each of the large target foreign markets identified herein to develop a strategy for communication with government agencies that have jurisdiction over telecommunications and other activities relevant to the business and products of the Company. In appropriate cases, the Company may seek out relationships with large systems integrators in foreign countries that have local knowledge of and experience with government agencies to promote sale of ADM products in conjunction with their systems.

COMPETITION

PLAN NOTE: In many cases, the description of the competition is one of the largest and most comprehensive sections of the business plan. The text in this example is quite short and relies on an exhibit that has not been included. This exhibit describes the key competitors by name, type of business, annual revenues, product line and sales strategy. The business plan should always identify the chief competitive factors that must be confronted by the company, along with an analysis of how the company intends to compete with respect to each factor.

As service providers move rapidly into the digital domain, many technology companies have moved to these markets. Some of these companies have a limited product line and offer little added value. Among these are companies with low-end consumer products, who lack the ability to develop products suitable for the high-end professional market. Information relating to some of the major companies engaged in the professional market segment is included as Exhibit ____. The Company believes that the chief competitive factors in the industry include the following: [list].

MANUFACTURING STRATEGY

PLAN NOTE: Many companies, such as the pet food and supply company featured in one of the other business plan examples in this book, rely on third parties for the manufacture of the products that are then sold to end-users. However, the firm highlighted in this plan is also the developer and manufacturer of its own products. As such, the plan must always include a thorough description of the how the company intends to produce the inventories necessary to meet the requirements of the marketplace. A wide array of alternatives may be available and the company will clearly be looking at several strategies, including internal manufacturing facilities, licensing arrangements with system integrators and other parties in the distribution chain, and establishment of offshore manufacturing facilities or relationships. When the offshore strategy is used, products may be exported from the foreign country back into the company's home market for distribution, thereby reducing the need for in-house manufacturing in the home market.

ADM's initial manufacturing requirements have been satisfied at its facilities in Israel. The Company has set aside a production and manufacturing area within its facilities that is operated in conjunction with new product development and research. Manufacturing activities are supervised by a senior manager with overall responsibility for manufacturing strategy and the coordination of procurement of necessary supplies and maintenance of inventories.

INITIAL EXPANSION STAGE

As ADM expands it operations into the United States and the other foreign markets, new manufacturing strategies will be required. Initially, it is anticipated that the United States facilities will include a new state-of-the-art manufacturing and production processing area with sufficient capacity to meet the initial unit requirements in the United States and in foreign markets for the next 12-18 months. Technology transfer from the Israeli facility has already begun and once completed, the manufacturing operations in Israel will be terminated. The manufacturing operations will continue to be operated by the same managerial personnel, all of whom have agreed to transfer to the United States. Non-managerial engineering and technical staff will be recruited locally and provided with rigorous training in the Company's technology and quality control standards.

Once the manufacturing operations have been completely moved to the United States, further work will continue on developing optimal production strategies for geographic regions outside of the United States as well as for dealing with expanding demand beyond the capacity of the United States facilities. Two specific alternatives will be investigated, including manufacturing by systems integrators under licenses to be granted by the Company and use of one or more low-cost manufacturing facilities outside of the United States.

SYSTEMS INTEGRATOR LICENSEES

As described below in the discussion of the Company's Marketing Strategy, ADM intends to rely on relationships with systems integrators to assist it in distribution of its products. These partners would integrate the Company's products into larger systems that would be distributed directly to the end-users in ADM's target markets. These relationships will allow the Company to take advantage of the large sales forces and existing client relationships of the system integrators, thereby accelerating the sales cycle and penetration of the Company's products.

In selected cases, the Company may grant a license to a system integrator to actually manufacture the Company's products that are to be included with the overall system. Such an arrangement can reduce the manufacturing burden on the Company and allows the system integrator to take over inventory controls. In some cases, a system integrator may also have a contract to manufacture products for the account of the Company in those cases where the economies of scale at the system integrator's facility are appropriate.

Terms of the licensing arrangement will vary depending on the scope of the relationship and the anticipated volume of products to be used by the system integrator. Generally, the Company will receive a royalty or per unit fee based on actual sales of the products by the system integrator. The compensation may increase or decrease based on the volume of sales. The Company would be required to provide adequate training and technology transfer assistance to the system integrator's personnel; and the parties will mutually determine responsibility for maintenance and service of the Company's products included in the integrator's systems. A license will be limited to manufacture of the products for use in the integrator's systems; therefore, the Company may consider awarding a partner exclusive rights for a specific geographic territory, industry and/or customer for so long as the relationship generates an agreed minimum level of revenues.

OFFSHORE MANUFACTURING FACILITIES

Another long-term alternative for the Company's manufacturing requirements is the use of offshore manufacturing facilities in one or more locations where low-cost facilities and skilled labor can be obtained. Offshore manufacturing can be accomplished in a variety of organizational formats, including manufacturing and supply agreements with established foreign firms, a joint venture with a foreign firm with the requisite technical expertise or the launch of a new wholly-owned manufacturing subsidiary. The decision as to choice of entry will be made based on a number of factors, including government regulations, proximity to customers and technical expertise of the local manufacturing industry. It is anticipated that some sort of offshore manufacturing strategy will be implemented within the next ____ months as the Company reaches full capacity in its proposed United States manufacturing facilities.

MARKETING STRATEGY

ADVISORY: Experience shows that the most important section of any international business plan is the marketing strategy, including the selection and execution of the appropriate method for entering and penetrating the chosen geographic or global industrial market. Since the plan is focusing on markets that are generally unfamiliar to the company, it is important to demonstrate that the company understands the distribution and communications channels for reaching the intended users in each market. In the case of a telecommunications-related product as discussed in this plan, this generally means learning how to deal with procurement procedures used by many of the large government-related telecommunications firms around the world. This is a special skill and often requires careful staffing with local experts.

ADM has significant expertise in marketing, sales and customer care, having been previously successful in marketing technology products to high profile customers in the professional media market. This experience will allow the Company to become a market leader in providing new and innovative products for digital media distribution.

At the core of ADM's marketing strategy is the development of "high value" products and solutions for the vertical market. After establishing itself in the corporate professional sector, the Company will leverage its brand equity to access the consumer sector. Consumers shopping for set-top-boxes often rely on the recommendation of their service provider, or have the box supplied as part of the service contract. Since ADM will already be established as the technology of choice for many service providers, these companies will have the confidence in ADM to make the Company's set-top-box their preferred choice.

In order to quickly penetrate the United States, European and Asia Pacific markets, ADM will employ a staff of technology-oriented marketing and sales experts. Their experience will allow them to team with their clients and provide solutions that deliver significant benefit through the adoption of ADM technology. The marketing staff will develop strategies for product lines, including pricing and demand forecasts according to client, industry and geography. Through close contact with clients, the marketing and sales staff also will influence product development.

During the Company's last fiscal year, it achieved sales of approximately $____ million from transactions with systems integrators in the United States and Europe. These sales were closed with a modest marketing and sales staff, including senior managers of the Company, operating from the Company's headquarters in Israel. In addition, ADM made an initial approach to various key media broadcasters in the United States, Europe and Asia Pacific with its solution. The response thus far has been very positive and has met expectations. Based on this response, the Company has been able to raise additional funds to develop its global marketing strategy, which will use a mix of direct sales channels, representatives, distributors and system integrators in the United States, Europe and the Asia Pacific region.

TARGET MARKETS

PLAN TIP: In this case, the company has identified several target markets for its products. Each target market is a discrete type of business within its own set of competitive conditions and procurement processes. As such, the company will need to develop a unique marketing and sales strategy for each market, often organizing sales forces for each market even though the underlying technological requirements are similar. In the earlier stages of implementation of the company's market strategy, it makes sense to establish priorities among the target market groups. In this way, the company can begin to approach customers in those markets that have the best promise for early success, thereby building brand recognition and quality acceptance that can be transferred to other markets.

ADM's initial target market is in "high value" professional products and systems for large media organizations. These firms often make procurements that involve millions of dollars worth of investment in equipment. The size and scope of these companies can generate sufficient revenue for ADM, even with only a few—or only one—client. However, in order to diversify the customer base and mitigate the risk caused by dependence on a few companies or sectors, the Company has set a goal of securing ____ customers within ____ to ____ years.

The Company will access target markets in this order:

- Cable system operators, which are rapidly moving from analog to digital, such as [list].

- Television broadcasters, which are currently involved in replacing old analog equipment with new digital systems. Examples include [list]. This also includes a secondary market of mobile broadcast trucks, which will provide additional revenue opportunities.

- Telcos, such as [list].

- Business television networks, such as those used for corporate media distribution and in distance education.

The most advanced markets for adoption of digital upgrade include the United States, Canada, the United Kingdom, Germany, France and the Asia Pacific region. The Asia Pacific region is an interesting opportunity in that it includes not only mature and developed economies, such as Australia, Japan, Singapore and Taiwan, but also emerging nations, such as China, that have made a policy decision to leapfrog traditional technologies in favor of digital systems.

ADM predicts that initially ____% of its customers will come from the United States and Canada, the remainder from Europe and the Asia Pacific region. Geographically, the United States market will be approached first. The Company already has experience dealing with this market, and has recently opened its central sales office there. With the recent infusion of capital based on early sales and technological achievements, the Company intends to expand its presence in the United States to the level of a wholly-owned subsidiary corporation with its own autonomous executive, financial and operational functions. The United States entity will have a large sales force of Company employees, and it will also enter into selective distribution relationships with systems integrators and other sales partners.

The Company will then move to Europe and the Asia Pacific region. These markets will be more challenging due to staffing requirements, government regulations and the need to understand marketing and distribution channels that are not as familiar to the Company as those in the United States. As such, it is likely that marketing strategies in these areas will be based on strategic relationships with local distributors until the Company is able to develop the critical customer mass necessary to support its own independent sales infrastructure in those regions.

MARKETING CHANNELS

The Company's initial target market is the high-end professional user within large corporate media organizations, such as _____, _____ and _____. This requires marketing and sales staff to deal directly with individuals at the highest levels in these large companies. Because of its prior extensive market experience, ADM has the necessary business relationships to secure business with the large corporate client group. Access to the wider market will be accomplished through the appointment of dealers and representatives, or through relationships with system integrators who supply complete system solutions to all sectors of the media business.

The Company will use basically three marketing channels:

Direct Sales. ADM will employ experienced sales professionals to address the large market opportunities. This channel generally requires a ____ to ____ month sales development cycle. The Company believes that approximately ____% of its early stage sales will occur through this channel. The direct sales force will be organized geographically to achieve the most efficient approach to the various target markets.

Initial sales in the United States will be made through a direct sales force organized by the Company's new wholly-owned United States subsidiary. The sales force will include not only full-time employees of the subsidiary, but also independent sales representative working on a commission basis. Sales efforts will be coordinated by one of the Company's current senior managers as Vice President of North American Sales Operations. In turn, several regional sales directors will be appointed to coordinate sales activities in particular geographic regions, including allocation of customer opportunities, customer service and promotional activities in the specific region.

Direct sales activities in Europe and the Asia Pacific region will be limited during the early stages of the marketing strategy. Eventually, however, the Company intends to establish a dedicated group of sales employees in those areas operating under the guidance of a senior regional sales executive. Initial direct sales activities outside of the United States will be managed through the United States subsidiary and will focus on accounts identified as good targets for initial sales, albeit at low volumes and revenue levels. In many cases, foreign sales targets will include affiliates of United States companies that have already purchased products from the Company. While sales to larger telecommunications organizations will necessarily have a longer sales cycle, and it is unlikely the Company will obtain significant revenues from sales to such organizations within the next ____ months, sales representatives will begin initial communications with key personnel in such organizations in order to position the Company for future opportunities once the Company brand has been established.

Small foreign sales offices will be established in key telecommunications centers in Europe and the Asia Pacific region, including Berlin, Hong Kong, London, Paris, Singapore and Tokyo. Directors of those offices will initially report to a global Vice President of Sales Operations. As sales activities expand, ADM anticipates the formation of one or more foreign regional sales subsidiaries organized in a fashion similar to the United States subsidiary and including staff to fulfill administrative, finance, operational and sales functions.

System Integrators. This channel generally requires a longer sales cycle than direct to end-user, as the system integrator must first be convinced that the product is superior to that being used in their current offerings. These partners can, however, deliver greater volume of business because they serve a wide spectrum of end-users ranging from very large companies to small applications in their local community. ADM already has established relationships with the following systems integrators in the indicated target markets: ____ (United States), ____ (United Kingdom), ____ (France) and ____ (Taiwan).

As indicated above, systems integrators will be the primary form of initial sales activity for the Company outside of North America, and directors of the foreign sales offices will be responsible for identifying potential candidates for strategic relationships and initiating contacts with those organizations that are headquartered in their geographic territory. Since many of these systems integrators sell their products on a global basis, it is likely that sales efforts will be carried out on a cooperative basis with account representatives in North America and elsewhere.

Dealers & Distributors. The sales decision is almost immediate in this sector, as most dealers and distributors are looking for new and innovative products to offer their customers. ADM already has established contact with the following distributors in the indicated target markets: ____ (United States), ____ (United Kingdom), ____ (Germany) and ____ (Japan). Relationships with dealers and distributors will be handled in the same manner as systems integrators above.

Marketing Communications

ADM recognizes the importance of highly professional marketing communications, including exhibitions at major trade shows. ADM has exhibited at industry trade events in Las Vegas, Los Angeles, New York, Singapore, London and Munich. In addition, the Company has secured affordable outsourced MARCOM services from an outside vendor that has worked successfully with digital media companies, providing a complete package of MARCOM services, including public relations, advertising, trade show management and other marketing collateral.

Customer Care

ADM's products are primarily software based and designed for ease of installation and operation. The Company does not believe that there will be a large requirement for product support, other than providing guidance to users in the flexibility of the configuration and in trouble-shooting using a telephone and Internet support structure.

Support has been provided directly by ADM from its headquarters in Israel. As the Company expands, it intends to develop a network of centrally located support offices in each of the major target market countries. Support for product sales made to various strategic partners will be provided by those companies. ADM's support organization will provide service on a 24x7 basis employing customer care professionals.

ADM will provide specific training for its larger customers and system integrators both on site and at the Company's offices. The attention to training of customer staff has proven to be an excellent marketing tool, retaining customer loyalty and preventing unnecessary costs related to product support caused by unfamiliarity with product features by customer personnel.

FINANCING STRATEGY

Based on its early successes in product development and closing initial accounts, the Company has been able to raise $____ million to continue its product development efforts and develop the sales and manufacturing infrastructure necessary for expansion of its business. ADM believes this amount will be sufficient to fund operations for the next ____ months. The proposed budget for operations of the Company's business during that period is included as Exhibit ____.

Funds for the initial expansion of sales efforts into Europe and the Asia Pacific region have already been allocated and the Company anticipates that expenditures will be limited to the costs of small field offices and direct sales personnel. As activities in those markets expand, the Company will consider additional fund-raising for the establishment of formal sales subsidiaries in those regions, including internal functional capabilities for administration, finance, operations, marketing and human resources. While ADM is mindful of the current downturn in general economic conditions, the telecommunications market is expected to continue to grow in the years to come; it will likely be one of the sectors that will attract substantial amounts of venture and other private capital. Funding for establishment of offshore manufacturing facilities may be available through local governments and affiliated commercial banks looking to provide incentives for new direct foreign investment. Systems integrators and other manufacturing and sales partners may also be willing to provide direct funding or trade credits that can be used to bolster the Company's cash flow and available cash resources.

Pro-forma results of operations for the next 24 months are included as Exhibit ____, including profit and loss statements, balance sheets, cash flow analysis and a description of material assumptions underlying the proforma figures.

CHAPTER 18

Sample Plan #3:
Goods & Services Retailer

HE WHO DOES NOT KNOW ONE THING, KNOWS

ANOTHER. — KENYAN PROVERB

THIS SAMPLE BUSINESS PLAN RELATES to a pet supply "superstore" chain in the United States that is expanding into new foreign markets. While not strictly a form of franchise operation, the success of the business is dependent on repeating the same outlet structure throughout the geographic areas served by the company. The plan raises several market research and analysis issues, including evaluation of the consumer behavior of "pet owners" and the company's ability to purchase pet food and supplies directly from manufacturers. The original plan upon which this example is based led to a rather successful commercial venture. While the plans focuses on sales activities in new foreign markets, including procurement of products in those markets, reference is also made to two other global strategies—low-cost manufacturing in foreign countries and e-commerce selling activities.

Opening Outlets in New Foreign Market

PET CLUB
INTERNATIONAL BUSINESS PLAN

PET CLUB (the "Company") is a leading provider of products for the lifetime needs of pets. The Company currently operates a chain of large-format pet supply specialty stores in the United States and Canada that offer an extensive line of pet foods, pet accessories and related services. In addition, the Company operates a popular e-commerce site for pet owners, as well as several major branded catalogs that market supplies for pets.

The concept for large-format pet supply specialty stores began with an effort by a California pet food milling company to create a retail outlet for its surplus manufactured inventory. The store was launched almost a decade ago and it soon became obvious that the store could justify its own existence and generate substantial profit by selling products from other sources. Other stores were opened and within three years, sales of the parent company products dropped to a small fraction of the total sales of the chain. The success and profitability of the stores was not surprising in that they share many of the same attributes of other well-known successful retail superstores.

PET CLUB was launched ____ years ago with the opening of ____ stores in the southwestern United States. Following the business and operating strategies outlined herein, the Company quickly expanded to other parts of the United States where large populations of pet enthusiasts could be reached and strong store locations and distribution outlets could be obtained. As of the end of its most recent fiscal year, PET CLUB was operating ____ stores in the continental United States and had outlets in ____ states. Exhibit ____ lists the locations of PET CLUB's existing stores, as well as the sites targeted for expansion or entry within the next 12-15 months.

The success of the Company's large-format pet supply specialty stores in the United States has led to interest in expanding operations into select foreign markets. Expansion is an important strategy given the potential saturation of the United States market. PET CLUB believes that its proprietary business and operational practices can be profitably deployed in foreign markets with demographic and economic characteristics similar to those found in the pet supply industry in the United States.

The Company entered the Canadian market ____ years ago, and was operating ____ stores in Canada as of the end of its most recent fiscal year. Given the geographic proximity of Canada to the United States and the similarity of demographic and cultural conditions in the major metropolitan areas of both countries, the PET CLUB format could be easily introduced into Canada with very little modification from the United States, apart from language and currency issues. The Company's current distribution channels and purchasing network could easily be extended to Canada and PET CLUB is also able to use existing advertising and promotional campaigns in this foreign market.

In addition to its Canadian operations, PET CLUB has also entered into several agreements to provide product sourcing and consulting services to major retailers in three other countries. These arrangements were intended to increase the Company's familiarity with the local markets and build relationships with established companies that have the facilities and distribution infrastructure to possibly support a chain of large-format pet supply specialty stores in those countries. In all but one case, these agreements have proven successful and PET CLUB is now faced with the decision as to whether or not to devote greater management and financial resources to new international operations. While the Company believes the opportunities are strong, it remains mindful of various risks, including fluctuations in currency exchange rates, changes in international staffing and employment issues, tariff and other trade barriers, the burden of complying with foreign laws and political and economic instability and developments.

Initially, PET CLUB intends to focus on foreign markets with high populations of pet enthusiasts concentrated in one or more metropolitan areas, easy access to manufacturers, distribution systems that are cost-effective and reliable and a history of acceptance of other types of retail superstores. Secondary considerations include the availability of experienced retail managers and the effect of local labor regulations on recruiting and wage levels. Based on these factors, and the knowledge gained through the consulting arrangements described above, PET CLUB plans to open up to ____ stores in France, Germany and the United Kingdom within the next 12-15 months. The launch strategy will follow the successful plans of the Company in the United States and target locations in and around such metropolitan areas as Berlin, Edinburgh, London, Munich and Paris. Development of the PET CLUB brand in Europe will be accelerated through catalog and e-commerce operations similar to those in North America. Exhibit lists the locations targeted for entry.

The expansion of the Company's activities into Europe will be conducted through a separate operating division to be called PET CLUB EUROPE. PET CLUB EUROPE will be based in a separate headquarters office in London. However, the senior management of PET CLUB EUROPE will report directly to the Chief Executive Officer of PET CLUB in the United States. The primary role of the executive staff of PET CLUB EUROPE is to ensure that market information is collected and analyzed and that initial store launches proceed smoothly. In some cases, global procurement decisions will be required as many pet products and supplies are suitable for resale in all markets to be covered by the Company's operations. PET CLUB

EUROPE will be responsible for developing and executing an advertising and promotional strategy in line with the budgetary levels previously used by the Company in its North American markets.

MARKET AND INDUSTRY BACKGROUND

PLAN NOTE: This example emphasizes market and industry background in the US, while providing less detail for the projected new markets in Europe. However, the description of the situation in the US illustrates the issues that should be addressed whenever the drafter is preparing a market analysis. Whenever applicable, reference should be made to market research reports from independent analysts and the presentation can be spiced up with charts and other graphical materials. The specific analysis of consumer behavior is unique among the plans in this book and demonstrates recognition of the need to think through the eyes of the consumer in each of the new foreign markets.

Information regarding market size and characteristics, consumer behavior and industry practices has been derived from a variety of sources, including published research reports and the proprietary surveys conducted by the Company of its customers in various areas of the United States. The pet food, supplies and services industries are relatively mature and the basic needs of consumers are well established. PET CLUB's strategy is based on the development of innovative methods that can be used to provide better service for consumers and attract market share away from traditional sellers, such as supermarkets and small pet store outlets. The challenge in establishing a strategy for PET CLUB EUROPE is understanding consumer behavior in a new market that is accustomed to distribution channels that often differ from those historically offered in the United States.

THE MARKETS

In the United States, the annual retail market for pet food is approximately $35 billion, based on aggregate sales during the last calendar year. During that period, owners of dogs and cats alone purchased $15 billion of pet food, which equaled 33% of pet food purchases. With a dog population of 5 million and a cat population of 8 million in the United States, industry figures show that over half of all households own a dog, cat or both. Viewed individually, 15% of United States households have dogs and 18% have cats. Demand for pets is primarily influenced by family formation, as most pets are owned by families with children between the ages of five and nineteen. Retail sales histories for dog and cat food show an average annual real dollar sales increase of between 25% and 33% over the last ten years.

Additionally, 11% of the nation's households own or regularly feed birds, fish and small animals (pet rodents and reptiles). Annual retail sales of foods for these pets is approximately $18 million.

A $5 billion pet accessory market has emerged to house, groom, entertain, make healthy, transport, train, clothe, control, clean up after, learn about and otherwise care for all these animals. Over 85% of these purchases are for feline or canine pets. The remaining market is divided among all other types of pets.

The sales dollar volume generated by each specie's market segment is driven by two logical parameters. The first parameter, the animal's size, determines the quantity of food eaten per animal as well as the size of the accessories needed to accommodate the pet. The second parameter, the specie's population, determines the number of related supply purchase transactions. PET CLUB stores address the needs of owners of animals that have sufficient population and physical size to create volume sales.

Because of changing lifestyles and demographic profiles in human populations, a few small, but noticeable, changes are occurring in the pet supply market in the United States. These trends stem from the move to smaller living quarters by many pet owners and the aging of the country's population. Most people who live in apartments and condominiums occupy housing units smaller in size than that of their house-dwelling counterparts. These more modest living quarters are suitable for smaller-sized pets. As the number of people living in apartments and condominiums increases, large dogs represent a smaller proportion of the pet population, while the cat population has soared. This trend is reflected by stalled dog food sales at the same time that high-margin cat food sales have increased.

Clearly, the aging of America's human population is positive for the industry. There are an increasing number of older citizens who may have lost spouses or close friends. A common method used to enrich the lives of those who have suffered such losses is the companionship of a pet. Market studies have shown that these pets are lavished with attention. Liberal spending on pet products characterizes this market segment. This trend is predicted to cause the pet supply market to grow to $____ billion by the end of the decade.

Beginning a little more than 10 years ago, sales increases of most grocery brand pet foods slowed. The exception in this market was the more expensive canned "gourmet" products. In the non-grocery channels, professional-grade dog foods have shown a compound annual growth rate of over 15% for the last three years. These trends, which presumably were caused by health consciousness and improved incomes, benefit the industry as a whole. The total sales dollar volume of pet food shipments is increasing faster than the total gross weight. Unit sale price is increasing. PET CLUB, as a major purveyor of professional-grade foods, expects to benefit from this trend.

Sales of pet supplies, including dog and cat toys, collars and leashes, cages and habitats, books, vitamins and supplements, shampoos, flea and tick control and aquatic supplies, were approximately $2 billion in the United States in 2000. Sales of pet services, including veterinary care, grooming, and obedience training, were estimated at $4 billion in the latest calendar year.

Historical buying patterns for pet foods and supplies in Canada, France, Germany and the United Kingdom are strikingly similar to those in the United States. For example, the annual reported market for pet food in the United Kingdom, which has approximately 66% of the population of the United States, was approximately $3 billion in the latest calendar year (as compared to $2.5 billion in the United States). Ownership of a dog or cat, expressed as a percentage of total households, exceeds 15% in each of the countries; annual real dollar sales increase in dog and cat food in those countries over the last five years has actually exceeded the rate of growth in the United States. Exhibit ____ lists comparative market data on the United States and each of the targeted foreign countries.

The demographic characteristics in the targeted foreign countries are also very interesting. For example, in many of the large metropolitan areas where the Company intends to launch its initial stores, a large proportion of the pet enthusiasts live in apartments as opposed to houses. Statistics indicate that apartment owners in these areas are much more likely to have one or more pets. In addition, each of the foreign countries has a similar percentage of its population in the over-50 age group as exists in the United States. Accordingly, the Company anticipates that senior citizens in these countries will show the same propensity for large expenditures on their pets as exists in the United States.

PET CLUB has also studied the level of expenditures on pet food and supplies in each of the targeted foreign countries as a percentage of disposable income in those households that have pets. The Company has discovered that pets in the targeted foreign markets actually command a significantly higher percentage of the household income than in the United States. At the same time, consumers have proven to be just as serious about obtaining value for their money in all of their expenditures as their counterparts in the United States. Each of these factors bode well for the value-driven strategies used by PET CLUB in launching its stores and pricing its offerings.

While the pet food and supply industry in Europe is well-established, market research information is not as well developed as in the United States. As one of the first companies to offer large format pet supply specialty stores in the market, PET CLUB EUROPE intends to establish a competitive advantage through a comprehensive database of consumer information derived from surveys to be taken at the initial stores and in secondary markets targeted as potential areas for the second wave of stores once the initial launch is completed.

CONSUMER BEHAVIOR

The success of PET CLUB and other large format pet supply specialty stores can be traced, in large part, to the consumer behavior that led to the success of predecessors in other industries (e.g., in the United States, Price Club, general merchandising and Toys-R-Us, toys). These companies had broad customer appeal and captured a share of the upper income consumer segments, as well as the less affluent, despite their no-frills approach to retailing.

For example, in the case of large format general merchandising stores, much of their well-priced assortment is composed of low-visibility, high-utility products. Examples are Michelin tires, Black and Decker power tools and office supplies. Performance and/or durability are fundamental to the consumer's decision to purchase these high-utility products. These useful, low-glamour products are not enhanced in the mind of the consumer by the selling "glitter" of high overhead stores. Thus, today's ever more sophisticated consumer, consciously or unconsciously, is shunning fancy retail settings for such utility products classes.

Many pet supply products share a similar profile. Pet food and accessories are low-profile utility products. For every well-liked animal there is also an owner who is concerned about their pet's nutrition and comfort. This pet supply customer seeks affordable "quality" products, preferring not to pay more than is absolutely necessary. Value-conscious grocery and general merchandise stores do not carry better quality pet supplies. In the consumer's quest for quality at reasonable prices, "low-frills" pet supply retailing was a natural evolutionary step.

Until the advent of stores like Toys-R-Us, consumers seldom had access to comprehensive assortments for any given product class. The results are self-evident—consumers will make stores with large specialized assortments a shopping destination. Large-scale specialty stores now exist for many product classes, including sporting goods, home improvement and records and tapes, to name a few. The same consumer logic applies to the pet supply market.

Animal lovers appreciate the abundance of specialty products that now exist for pets. However, customers were challenged to find a shop with a full assortment of accessories and/or food. Grocery stores did not carry pet food brands with the nutritional requirements recommended by veterinarians. Pet stores that did carry these superior products were expensive. In both cases, accessory lines were limited by retail space considerations. Consumer behavior substantiates the need for the comprehensive assortment of pet products available in large format specialty stores.

The new foreign markets have been selected due to the substantial similarity between consumer behavior in those countries and behavior in the United States. All of the target foreign countries are substantially familiar with the large scale specialty store format. In fact, retail superstores in these countries offering toys, sporting goods and records and tapes have been very successful in recent years. In addition, pet enthusiasts in the targeted foreign country also have not been able to easily access high-quality pet foods and supplies through grocery-type outlets; they are expected to appreciate the value and time savings offered by the comprehensive selection that will be available in the local PET CLUB stores.

In developing its initial launch strategy for the European markets, Company representatives have conducted extensive interviews at grocery outlets in each of the metropolitan areas targeted for the new stores. In addition, the Company has surveyed visitors to Toys-R-Us superstores in the area surrounding London, Munich and Paris to determine the level of satisfaction with the large format store concept. Based on these interviews and surveys, PET CLUB believes that it will find a good reception to its own stores. These interviews and surveys have also provided the Company with information on possible alteration in the layout of the stores that might be appropriate for the new markets, as well as possible changes in the product mix based on the type of pet and the historical buying patterns of European consumers.

INDUSTRY STRUCTURE

The pet food and pet supply retail business is highly competitive and can be categorized into four different segments: (i) supermarkets, warehouse clubs and other mass merchandisers, (ii) specialty pet supply chains and pet supply stores, (iii) independent pet stores and (iv) Internet retailers. The principal competitive factors in the United States in this industry include product selection and quality, convenience of store locations, customer service and price.

In the United States, supermarkets currently capture approximately ____% of the total market for pet food and accessories. In recent years, supermarkets' share of total pet food sales has steadily decreased as a result of increased competition from superstores, warehouse clubs, mass merchandisers, Internet retailers and specialty pet stores, as well as the growing proportion of sales of premium pet foods that are not generally found in supermarkets.

Manufacturers that sell directly to discount, drug and grocery chains represent the "efficient" side of the industry, with good value and adequate quality. Despite the economic value, these brands are generally lower in nutritional value or manufacturing quality than most specialty pet brands.

Further, the pet supplies sold in grocery, discount or drug stores are only a small portion of the store's broad selection of merchandise. These grocery, discount and drug stores have limited pet related assortments because they cannot devote more than a single aisle to pet supplies. While these chain stores maintain acceptable price levels, the customer is forced to chose from a limited selection of limited quality.

To purchase more specialized and/or better quality products, the pet owner must turn to less efficient market channels. Premium pet food brands, which offer higher levels of nutrition than non-premium brands, accounted for approximately ____% of total pet food sales in the Company's most recent fiscal year. Many premium pet foods currently are not sold through supermarkets, warehouse clubs and mass merchandisers due to manufacturers' restrictions and, until only a few years ago, they were sold primarily through small pet stores and veterinarians buying from a distributor who must stock the product. This purchasing process caused the end customer to overpay for pet-related items because of its two fundamental inefficiencies. First, the industry's product distributors added a "middleman's" mark-up to cover handling costs and profit. This mid-channel mark-up increased wholesale prices to retailers. Second, small stores with limited sales volume then had to add their considerable margins to retail prices. The end result was high retail prices yielding sub-optimal value to the customer.

PET CLUB and other superstores have capitalized on the inefficiencies in the traditional distribution chain by eliminating distributor's margins and increasing economies of scale at the store outlet. PET CLUB stores are operated as high-volume, low-overhead outlets, buying and shipping directly from manufacturers. The result has been substantial savings for customers purchasing through warehouse stores as opposed to the old high-markup outlets (veterinarians and neighborhood pet stores). This strategy has been extended beyond foods to include the sales of accessory items at pricing levels that will yield similar savings for customers.

In the United States, pet supplies are sold by many types of retailers, including supermarkets, discount stores and other mass merchandisers, specialty pet stores, direct mail houses, Internet retailers and veterinarians. Distribution channels for these goods are highly fragmented, with superstores and discount stores estimated to account for over ____% of sales volume in the United States. Similarly, the pet services industry in the United States is also highly fragmented. It significantly underserves many pet owners who do not regularly use pet services due to inconvenience, a lack of awareness or the cost of the services.

The industry structure in each of the new target foreign markets is substantially similar to that which exists in the United States. There are, however, some important exceptions to take into account. First, the range of pet products and supplies available through supermarkets and other mass merchandisers is not as broad in the foreign markets as in the United States. Accordingly, the competitive position of supermarkets in the foreign countries is less threatening to the Company than it might be in the United States. Second, specialty pet supply chains and pet supply stores are less active in the foreign markets. In many cases, pet enthusiasts will do most of their shopping at independent pet stores and accept pricing levels that are much higher due to the same sort of distribution issues described above. As consumers in the foreign markets begin to appreciate the convenience of shopping at large retail centers, including supermarkets and PET CLUB outlets, it is anticipated that buying habits will quickly change and that market share of independent pet stores will suffer.

MERCHANDISE AND SERVICES

PLAN NOTE: This company has assembled a broad array of service offerings that allows customers to do business with the company in several different ways. In addition to the actual store outlets, the company has launched a catalog business and has even arranged for products to be sold over the Internet. Although these valuable alternatives will be transported into the new foreign markets, the company has wisely opted for a "go slow" strategy, particularly in the e-commerce area. Attempts to successfully sell pet food and supplies over the Internet ran into significant problems in the United States, resulting in heavy losses and ultimate consolidation of a number of competitors. This company prefers to use the Internet to support its "brick and mortar" store outlets, at least for the early years of the new market initiative.

PET CLUB offers a wide array of merchandise and services to its customers in North America and, upon launch of PET CLUB EUROPE, selected areas in Europe. Through its store outlets, the Company offers pet foods and supplies, as well as training and veterinary services. In addition, as an adjunct to its stores and a special service to customers not able to access the store, the Company has established an e-commerce sales outlet and catalogs that appeal to specialized sectors of the Company's target markets. In general, the mix of merchandise and services is fairly standardized across each geographic area. However, it is likely that merchandise and services offered initially in PET CLUB EUROPE stores will be different due to local buying habits and the need to test demand for certain services not offered in the first United States stores; these will be added only as the Company becomes more familiar with customer behavior.

STORES

PET CLUB stores carry the largest pet supply assortment of any store in the market. The store inventory is typically composed of two classes of goods. The first product group, consumables, is comprised of food (including treats), litter and shavings. In the United States, the average annual inventory turnover rate on consumables is in excess of ____ times. Comparable turnover rates are also anticipated in the markets to be served by PET CLUB

EUROPE. Consumables generate regular repeat purchases. In contrast, supplies and accessories, the other class of goods, are occasional discretionary purchases. Supplies include such items as cages, kennels, beds, books, leashes, toys, treats, shampoos and many other related products. Their turnover is approximately _____ times per year. Total Company sales in United States outlets have generally broken down into _____% consumables and _____% accessories.

The two product categories are complementary. Consumable products lead customers past the supply selection. Much as grocery stores sell discretionary items (chips and beer) when their customers buy staples (milk and bread), the Company expects to sell cat toys when customers come in to buy kibble. The merchandise assortment is conducive to multiple-item sales to customers with a predisposition to reward their animals. Past experience has shown that a superior selection of pet supplies will draw customers from a wide radius. This provides an opportunity to introduce new customers to the store's line of consumables. Huge assortments of pet-related products have turned large format stores into proven customer-shopping destinations.

Unlike its principal competitors, PET CLUB also offers a wide range of services for the pet owner, including full-service grooming and pet training services. In addition, a growing number of PET CLUB stores have in-store veterinary clinics that generally offer a full range of services, including routine examinations and vaccinations, dental care, a pharmacy and routine and complex surgical procedures. Many stores without in-store clinics nonetheless offer routine vaccinations and wellness services. All in-store veterinary clinics are operated by a third-party operator of such clinics under the terms of a strategic partnering arrangement that divides the revenues and costs associated with the clinic between the parties.

PET CLUB stores use many proven merchandising methods pioneered by the large, low-frills specialty and "warehouse" retailers. Thus, PET CLUB stores more closely resemble large discount specialty stores (such as Toys-R-Us) and super warehouse stores (such as Price Club) than traditional neighborhood pet stores. The store environment will intentionally be kept Spartan to promote its low overhead image and, thus, maintain its credibility with customers. For example, large bags of kibbles and cases of canned pet food are displayed on pallets (moved directly to the selling floor by forklift). Concrete floors and industrial type shelving are standard.

Based on market surveys, and its experiences with various consulting agreements, the Company anticipates that the store formats in the new foreign countries will be similar to that used in the United States. In some cases, the size of the store will be slightly smaller than in the United States. This is a function of the available real estate in the new markets, as well as the relative unfamiliarity of consumers in those countries with large-scale retail stores. The size and layout of the stores in the foreign countries also will be impacted by the selection of local goods and the relative importance of a specific type of pet species. Finally, the Company anticipates that offerings of pet services in foreign countries will be relatively modest at the outset. For example, the ability of the Company to offer in-house veterinary clinics may be limited by applicable local laws and regulations.

In conducting its market research for the launch of new stores in Europe, PET CLUB has determined that the sales mix of consumables to supplies and accessories will likely be somewhat different in Europe than in the United States. While per capita spending on pets and their needs as a percentage of income in both markets is generally comparable, pet enthusiasts in Europe are likely to spend more on consumable than on the supplies and accessories, which are viewed as being more discretionary purchase items. While this behavior may change over time as customers begin to appreciate the cost savings on consumables and invest a portion of those savings in supplies and accessories, it does dictate changes in the initial product mix in the European outlets.

E-Commerce Shopping Opportunities

PET CLUB has recognized the growing popularity of the Internet and e-commerce by developing its own popular pet-related e-commerce site. Since the Web site was launched ____ years ago, it consistently has been rated as one of the most visited sites in its target market as rated by independent Internet sources. It features a broad range of merchandise, expert advice and community activities for consumers who care about pets. Although the Company's initial e-commerce efforts have been moderately successful, there can be no assurance that this will be a viable distribution strategy in the future. Among other things, the Company has noted that competitors have been forced to spend significant amounts of capital to fund their online shopping sites. Moreover, since e-commerce in general has been much slower to develop in the targeted foreign countries, the Company anticipates little future revenue from local Web site activities in those countries.

PET CLUB is planning on launching a PET CLUB EUROPE Web site to take advantage of e-commerce opportunities in Europe once the initial stores have been launched. Initially, the site will include largely informational materials and will lack the costly infrastructure necessary for the sale of large volume of online product sales. In fact, initial sales activities through the Web site likely will be to simply refer visitors to a telephone ordering system that takes orders and transfers them to the store location closest to the customer for processing. PET CLUB EUROPE will not have a separate European fulfillment center, nor will significant financial resources be devoted to the Web site, until brand recognition has been established. Once the store outlets have been launched and established, additional online services will be heavily promoted within the stores. In effect, the Company intends to take a cautious "wait-and-see" approach to e-commerce activities in Europe.

Catalogs

PET CLUB also engages in direct marketing of certain products in North America through its own catalog operation, which currently features four catalogs: [list]. Each of the catalogs is geared toward a specific line of products, generally segmented by the type of pet and the geographic location of the pet owner. The catalogs offer discounted brand-name products and promote the products offered through the Company's stores and Web site. Customers can order through the mail or take advantage of a toll-free telephone fulfillment service. As of the end of last year, more than ____ million catalogs were distributed in North America on a yearly basis; and PET CLUB's proprietary customer database contained the names of approximately ____ million customers who have made a purchase from PET CLUB catalogs within the past ____ months. The Company uses this marketing and customer database to attract new customers and generate additional sales.

The Company believes the catalogs also will be a valuable marketing tool in the new foreign markets. Based on market research, the Company believes that a high proportion of pet enthusiasts also have had satisfactory shopping experiences with catalogs for other goods. The Company is currently in negotiations with publication houses and fulfillment companies in each of the target markets to establish the infrastructure for its catalog business. Once the catalog operations are launched in the new foreign markets, the Company anticipates that it will be able to rapidly develop a substantial proprietary customer database in each country. The Company also believes that the catalog operations will allow it to create a foothold in neighboring geographic markets within the European Union that eventually can be targeted for the launch of actual store outlet operations.

While several of the foreign countries that initially are being targeted in Europe are not primarily English-speaking, PET CLUB EUROPE's first catalogs only will be in English. There are several good reasons for this approach. First, market research indicates that a high percentage of the potential customers can speak and read English and are used to receiving promotional materials directed primarily at English-speaking audiences. Second, use of a single language in preparation of the catalogs significantly reduces the costs of launching the European initiative; and allows the Company to adapt much of the content that already is prepared for North American versions of the catalogs. Obviously, as PET CLUB EUROPE expands into other countries, and into geographic areas that are farther from the central metropolitan areas, further resources will need to be devoted to localization of content and information.

BUSINESS STRATEGY

PET CLUB's strategy has been to be the preferred provider for the lifetime needs of pets. The Company's activities are focused on what it believes is the clearly identifiable market of "pet enthusiasts," which includes those persons and family units with a compassionate commitment to the well-being of their pets. As pets, and the compassion of their owners, are truly a universal phenomenon, PET CLUB is blessed with the opportunity to develop a core business strategy that can be adapted easily and quickly to a global marketplace.

PET CLUB constantly monitors the needs, desires and aspirations of pet enthusiasts and other key customer segments in developing its products, business strategy and operational techniques. Fundamental elements of the Company's business strategy include:

Provide Customer Value through Product Selection and Pricing. PET CLUB stores offer the most complete assortment of pet-related products in the marketplace, including the products that historically only could be found at small specialty stores at high prices. PET CLUB's ability to buy in large batches directly from manufacturers, coupled with the strategies for reducing and controlling store and administrative overhead, allows the Company to offer all of its products at everyday low prices. In addition to product selection, the Company also intends to build on its industry leading position in pet services through training and addition of resources.

PET CLUB EUROPE intends to follow the product selection and pricing practices of the Company's North American outlets. Key to this strategy is the ability to develop and maintain the same sort of relationships with local manufacturers and vendors as have existed in the United States and Canada. In many cases, European manufacturers are affiliated with companies in the United States that have been long-standing partners of PET CLUB in the United States. A number of preliminary inquiries have been made and the Company is confident that there will be no significant problems obtaining large volumes of product in Europe at attractive prices. In many ways, the launch of the European stores will be easier than the initial push in the United States, which occurred when the Company lacked business relationship history with manufacturers.

Consumer surveys in Europe also indicate a strong sensitivity to pricing, and it would appear that pet enthusiasts are willing to shift their buying patterns to realize significant savings. As noted in previous discussions, pet-related expenditures represent a material portion of distributable income in Europe, and it can be expected that consumers will want to maximize their value. The market in Europe for pet-related services, such as training and veterinary services, is more unclear, and it is likely that the initial stores will devote little or no resources to these areas until time has passed to measure the actual demand. Pet owners in Europe actually appear to have different expectations as to the level of training of their pets. The reasons are unclear, but they may have to do with the background of pet owners and their initial experiences with pets in the household during their childhood years.

Outstanding Customer Service. A significant and unique competitive supplement to product selection and pricing is PET CLUB's emphasis on outstanding customer service and enhancement of the customer's shopping experience. The Company conducts extensive employee training and creates incentives for employees to forge positive relationships with customers and become the trusted and informed source for advice. In addition, the store format has been overhauled to organize products by pet type, thereby enhancing sales productivity and making it quicker and easier for customers to find what they need.

The value of customer service in the new foreign markets will need to be determined during the first few months that the new stores are in operation. It is likely that customers will initially be attracted to the stores by the wide array of products and value-added pricing as opposed to any specific level of customer service. However, as the Company fully expects that one or more new competitors will eventually arise in Europe, customer service will be emphasized from the beginning of the initiative in anticipation that it will ultimately build a high level of loyalty to PET CLUB EUROPE. It is anticipated that PET CLUB EUROPE will develop a comprehensive human resources infrastructure that covers training, compensation and overall employee morale. The Company has discovered that its best employees are those that truly are "pet enthusiasts," and have a strong interest in the questions and concerns of customers. This attribute will be factored into staffing decisions in the new European stores.

Cost Controls. PET CLUB has been resolute in its efforts to control costs in order to pass savings on to its customers and accelerate controlled growth of the business. A number of strategies are in place to achieve this goal, including quantity buying direct from manufacturers, economies of scale at the store level, accelerating industry-normal inventory turnover, occupying economically-sensible real estate, use of advertising scale and many other cost conscious measures. In addition, the Company purposely maintains its strategic focus by avoiding adjunct investments in consumer credit or real estate.

The Company anticipates that most of the cost control strategies that have been used effectively in North America will also be applicable for its European operations. Realizing that it is moving into a new market with an unpredictable set of consumer behavior habits, PET CLUB EUROPE will be especially vigilant as to the level of overhead and avoidance of long-term commitments that might impair its ability to change locations or take advantage of new market opportunities.

Store Locations. In the United States, Company stores are generally located in sites co-anchored by strong destination superstores, and typically are in or near major regional shopping centers. Following selection of an appropriate geographic market, the Company strives to quickly attain a leadership position in the market by opening several stores. This strategy enhances customer service in the market through ease of access and also achieves operating efficiencies and economies in advertising, distribution and management.

While the targeted European locations do not necessarily include the number of regional shopping centers that have virtually saturated the market in many parts of the United States, they do exhibit a growing tendency toward clustering retail outlets in a single location that can be easily accessed by car or public transportation. These locations will be the primary targets for new company stores in Europe and it is anticipated that they will generate sufficient traffic in the same manner as stores in the United States. PET CLUB EUROPE also will consider the feasibility of opening one or more urban store locations in central shopping areas to provide access to pet enthusiasts that live within the cities; such consumers choose not to have a car due to traffic and parking problems and do most of their shopping in proximity to their apartments or houses as opposed to venturing to suburban areas.

Alternative Shopping Methods. While the Company's superstores have been, and will continue to be, the primary outlets for the sale of PET CLUB products, the Company intends to build on alternative shopping methods for the convenience of its customers. The Company has launched a popular and successful e-commerce Web site that offers the same in-store bargains for its products and a wide range of information regarding pets. In addition, PET CLUB's catalogs create opportunities for expanding the products available to the owners of specific types of pets. Each of these alternatives also broadens the reach of the Company to serve customers who live outside the immediate area of one of the Company's stores. As noted above, e-commerce and catalogs will ultimately be part of the sales activities in Europe. However, PET CLUB EUROPE will focus first on the successful launch of the retail store outlets and development of brand recognition and acceptance.

MARKETING STRATEGY

GEOGRAPHIC MARKETS

PET CLUB stores in the United States have always targeted large, middle- and upper-middle income suburban communities as the primary geographic market setting. This market type was chosen for its high pet populations (both absolute and proportional), lot sizes appropriate for larger dogs and frequent incidence of mature households. In addition to retail trade, PET CLUB stores have some "cash and carry" wholesale customers, including neighborhood pet stores, animal breeders and grooming salons and ranches.

The initial geographic markets in Europe share most, if not all, of the same desired market characteristics for North American stores. Metropolitan areas such as London, Paris and Munich not only offer large concentrations of pet owners, they also include affluent communities that are more likely to spend significant amounts on their pets and venture to the retail centers at which PET FOOD EUROPE will locate its outlets.

STORE LOCATIONS

A key element of the strategy to reach suburban pet owners is to place stores in high-traffic-count suburban shopping street locations. The history of large format pet supply stores proves the concept's ability to attract the "destination" type customer. The Company feels that accessible locations also are necessary to capture "convenience" motivated customers. In this manner, PET CLUB has been quite successful in taking market share from supermarkets.

The Company's management recognizes that a significant portion of pet food sales always will be "convenience" purchases and, therefore, many customers will continue to buy in grocery stores. However, locations on main artery/shopping streets have improved the competitiveness of PET CLUB's convenience dimension. In the United States, store placements generally require population counts of at least 200,000 within a five-mile radius. Depending upon the particulars of each market, stores are typically placed 10 to 15 miles apart. Placement in the European locations will depend on specific demographic factors and, in fact, it is likely that stores will be more heavily concentrated due to the higher density of suburban populations in certain areas.

ADVERTISING AND PROMOTION

PET CLUB uses print and electronic media advertising as its primary method of promotion, and advertising expenditures have generally run around ____% of sales. To further leverage the budget, multiple stores are geographically clustered within an advertising market and small groups of stores are opened simultaneously when possible.

Initial advertising in newly opened markets is somewhat institutional in nature. Television advertising is used to convey the stores' unique large product assortment. However, scenes of the huge, "low-frills" store, and powerful sale product tags on the advertisements, also convey a value message to consumers. Continuing promotional efforts include frequent use of customer coupons. The cost of coupon usage is borne by participating suppliers (most often, grocery pet food brands). Also, the store's promotional calendar includes semi-annual "Super Sale" events.

Advertising and promotional strategies for the new European locations will follow local practice and the mix generally used in the United States will be modified accordingly. For example, many of the potential consumers receive most of their news and information from print publications, including newspapers, as opposed to television and radio. Accordingly, it can be expected that PET CLUB EUROPE will devote a higher percentage of advertising resources to print media. Where television promotion is used, emphasis will be placed on placing advertisements on those channels that typically reach the more affluent customers, particularly cable customers. The development of the European Union and integration of telecommunications companies will allow the Company to reach multiple countries with its televised promotions as broadcasters transmit their signals across the whole of Europe.

Pricing

One of the key elements of PET CLUB's in-store marketing strategy is value-pricing practices. The pricing strategy varies across the major product categories. For example, in the United States, the Company prices accessories and professional-grade foods to yield margins greater than ____%. Despite these comfortable margins, these products will sell at prices that are substantially below those offered by the competition. This is possible because of the absence of "middleman" margins and retail economies of scale. The Company anticipates that similar margins will be available for sales made at the initial outlets in Europe.

Grocery store pet food brands are priced to compete with the most aggressive supermarkets. For example, in most areas, PET CLUB stores beat or at least share the "best price in town" on half of the items. The Company's grocery brand pricing provides a good value for customers. However, these prices will not produce similar percentage savings available with the purchase of the more nutritious professional brands (not sold in the supermarkets). Coupons are an important factor in grocery brand sales in the United States and PET CLUB makes extensive use of this marketing tool to lower prices. While the grocery brands are the lowest margin category in the store's assortment, they stimulate customer traffic beneficial to the sales of the remainder of the store's higher margin assortment. Coupons are not expected to be an important factor in PET CLUB EUROPE stores. The Company believes that the larger selections available in those stores will provide the requisite incentive for consumers to abandon traditional purchasing patterns.

Customer brand loyalty is weak for most pet products. This is an exploitable opportunity. PET CLUB store brands offer the customer excellent value on quality merchandise. Aided by quantity purchases and direct imports, this program increases margins and lowers retail prices. The Company has conducted preliminary surveys in the European markets regarding specific brands and has discovered that many consumers would be willing to change their current preferences if they are assured of good value and quality.

Store Design

PET CLUB stores are designed with image, shopping convenience and cross-selling in mind. To support the low overhead customer perception, the facilities have a "warehouse" decor. High ceilings, metal shelving, concrete floors, hand-lettered-look signs and packing-crate wood displays are all intended to provide consistent "low-frills" image reinforcement. Store floor plans call for merchandise to be laid out by pet type. For example, all dog-related products are shelved in their particular section of the store. This merchandise layout assists customers in finding their intended purchase while also exposing them to other products of potential interest.

PET CLUB EUROPE stores will have the same "look-and-feel" as the Company's outlets in the United States. While consumers in the target markets may be slightly less familiar with the format than those in the United States, broad acceptance is expected given that retail stores in Europe generally are less ornate than those in the United States.

CUSTOMER SERVICE

The last important aspect of in-store marketing is customer service. The Company keeps services to a bare minimum. There is no PET CLUB credit extended to retail or wholesale customers. However, PET CLUB does focus on a few service areas appreciated by customers. For example, checks and major credit cards are taken at all locations in the United States, and the same policy will be followed in the PET CLUB EUROPE stores. Point-of-sale systems and checkout procedures are designed to reduce waiting. Where possible, a package pickup is used to speed turnover in the parking lot, reduce shopping cart collection and loss expense and provide a "warm good-bye" to customers. Most importantly, sales associates in the stores will be mobile and available to answer any questions that customers may have and direct them to the proper location for the product that they need.

OPERATING STRATEGY

Today's shopper will seek out a specially retailer for the focused selection of merchandise if that store delivers good value. PET CLUB's corporate mission is to provide customers with the largest pet supply selection in the market, priced to give superior value. This mission is possible if the Company establishes itself as the lowest overhead, volume-specialty store operator in the pet supply industry. To fulfill the "largest selection, superior value" mission while delivering superior returns to shareholders, the Company must focus on a limited number of critical operational tasks.

STORE OPENINGS

PET CLUB currently operates stores in most of the major market areas in the United States and Canada, and the Company's plans for the next fiscal year include opening a net total of __ new stores in existing markets. While PET CLUB expects each new store to be profitable, it has been the Company's experience that opening new stores can result in some cannibalization of the sales of other PET CLUB stores already in operation in those markets. In addition, a number of the Company's stores are still relatively immature and are still enjoying above-average rates of growth with respect to sales. However, for these stores, it can be expected the average annual earnings will level off and that opportunities for substantial increases will diminish. This is one of the primary reasons that the Company is looking to enter new foreign markets with high growth opportunities that might not otherwise be available in the United States.

Operating margins are also expected to be impacted by new store openings because of the recognition of pre-opening expenses and the lower sales volumes characteristic of immature stores. In certain North American geographic regions, the Company has experienced lower comparable store sales increases and levels of store contribution compared to results achieved in other regions. In addition, certain operating costs, particularly those related to occupancy, are expected to be higher than historical levels in some of these newly entered geographic regions; also, tight labor markets in certain areas are expected to increase store personnel expenses more rapidly than historical trends. As a result of the expected slower overall rate of comparable store sales increase and the impact of these rising costs, the Company's total store contribution and operating margins may be lower than historical levels in future periods.

New store openings in the United States and Canada also are subject to several other factors, including adequate sources of capital for leasehold improvements, fixtures and inventory, pre-opening expenses and the training and retention of skilled managers and personnel. While the Company currently has sufficient cash equivalents and cash flow from operations to fund its existing expansion plans and maintain the preferred number of outlets, there is no guarantee that adequate resources will remain available. This may result in the closure of stores and/or the sale of selected assets or investments by the Company.

The Company anticipates that store openings in Europe will not be subject to the aforementioned limitations and constraints for at least several years. The Company has gained a substantial amount of knowledge and experience in the United States regarding the optimal pace for opening new stores and strategies for clustering multiple stores in a single metropolitan area. As noted above, the Company has targeted a handful of large metropolitan areas for the initial launch of PET CLUB EUROPE stores. In the near future, the Company expects to add stores to each of the original clusters and branch out into second-tier urban areas in the same countries. These areas have the same consumer density features as the larger areas and could support several stores, albeit not as many as the larger areas. Given the mobility of consumers within the European Union, it can be anticipated that the Company will be able to move into several new countries over the next ____ months, with success assured by the development of brand recognition in the initial countries and promotion strategies that reach all parts of Europe.

PURCHASING

The core of PET CLUB's business has been its purchasing strategy. As described above, the Company has been able to purchase large quantities of pet food and supplies directly from manufacturers, thereby taking advantage of bulk discounts and the ability to avoid a commission to a distributor that would otherwise be in the middle of the chain. In turn, this has allowed PET CLUB stores to offer the best value and selection in relation to competitors.

While the Company has no long-term supply commitments from its premium food or other product vendors in the United States, its position as a recognized industry leader with substantial buying clout has allowed it to secure access to key manufacturers and negotiate attractive deals due to volume purchases. Sales of premium pet food for dogs and cats make up a significant portion of the Company's revenues. Currently, most of the major vendors of premium pet foods do not permit these products to be sold in supermarkets, warehouse clubs or through other mass merchandisers. However, these practices may change in the future and may adversely impact the traffic through the Company's stores.

The Company uses "forward buying" practices to lock in manufacture "deal" prices. If offered 8% off list price, the Company may "forward"- buy a ten-week supply rather than simply buy a lesser quantity sufficient for current needs. PET CLUB also will buy in-transit distress merchandise. For example, a truckload of pet food that is refused by an overstocked supermarket may be available at half the normal price. PET CLUB regularly uses these buying practices.

The volume requirements for the Company's line of supplies and accessory items means that a large amount of purchasing must be done directly from overseas manufacturers. In particular, the Company has targeted certain products where substantial gross margin improvements are possible with imports. However, there can be no assurance the Company's overseas vendors will be able to satisfy the Company's needs in terms of timeliness of delivery, acceptable product quality and packaging and labeling requirements.

The pet food and supply manufacturing market in Europe is much more fragmented than in the United States and there are only a handful of large vendors. In addition, a number of United States-based manufacturers have established subsidiaries in Europe that either produce their own products or process and distribute products imported from their parent companies. The Company already has commenced negotiations with a wide range of vendors in Europe and is confident that it will be able to gain access to a large inventory of products on attractive terms and conditions.

As part of its expansion into new foreign markets, the Company is also investigating opportunities for developing strategic arrangements with overseas manufacturers who can supply accessories directly to the European market. The form of these arrangements is yet to be determined. For example, the Company may enter into a supply agreement directly with a foreign manufacturer that includes volume discounts on top of the already generous cost savings that can be realized by importing these items. In other cases, the Company may actually consider a joint venture with a foreign manufacturer that will allow the Company to exercise greater control over the quality of the accessories and the operations of the manufacturing plant. In the case of a joint venture, output would be shipped to North America as well as Europe.

DISTRIBUTION

In the United States, PET CLUB uses a variety of integrated distribution strategies for delivery of products to its stores, including, as appropriate, full truckload shipments to individual stores, the splitting of full truckloads among several closely located stores, consolidation centers to service regional clusters of stores and central distribution centers.

The Company leases and operates a ____ square-foot distribution center outside Springfield, Illinois, which began operations ____ years ago, and a ____ square-foot distribution center in Las Vegas, Nevada. The Company also has a ____ square-foot leased facility just outside Fort Worth, Texas, which was redesigned a year ago as a forward distribution center (FDC). The FDC handles consumables that require rapid replenishment, improving inventory productivity in an efficient, cost-effective manner. The FDC format allows for a more efficient use of store inventory, store labor, reduced transportation costs, improved in-stock position and distribution center productivity and vendor support. PET CLUB also owns and operates a ____ square-foot fulfillment and distribution center in upstate New York that meets the needs of the Company's e-commerce and catalog customers.

The Company anticipates that distribution in the new foreign markets will be handled through central distribution centers in each country coupled with delivery of goods to several closely located stories in each metropolitan area. The Company has done a preliminary survey of available warehouse space in each major foreign metropolitan area and has concluded that suitable locations can be found on attractive terms and conditions. Initially, the Company will be leasing its distribution and storage facilities in foreign markets. However, it is anticipated that the Company eventually will construct its own distribution centers in each country. The Company also is satisfied that it can lease a fleet of trucks in each country to move goods from its distribution centers to the stores.

DATA SYSTEMS AND INVENTORY CONTROL

PET CLUB has always believed that sophisticated management information systems are best used as feedback mechanisms for responding to customers. The Company uses modern data systems to fine-tune its purchases, distribute its merchandise to stores with pinpoint accuracy and make profit-optimizing pricing decisions. These elaborate systems must be viewed as important weapons in the market, allowing companies thus equipped to do what their competition cannot. In the last year, the Company has installed new in-store point of sale and support systems, warehousing systems, communication systems and SAP retail management information systems. It is anticipated that the data systems and inventory control procedures utilized by the Company in the United States can be easily transferred to the operations in the new foreign countries.

REAL ESTATE

The importance of location to the success of stores is well-known. The PET CLUB real estate strategy takes advantage of scientific siting methods to secure locations that "serve the market" within workable budgetary limitations. The Company always has worked with retail real estate specialists in its target geographic markets to build a successful store location profile with the experience gained in each location. The Company will use the best available demographic data to assess each location.

Two unusual recent trends in the United States offered potential benefits to the Company's real estate acquisition efforts. Nationwide, supermarkets began to abandon 20,000 square-foot locations on shopping streets in favor of larger locations. Many of these sites satisfied the requirements for a PET CLUB store in areas where build-to-suit locations were unavailable. The other trend was a direct result of changes in United States tax laws. Since less building of all kinds was done on a speculative basis, developers and builders competed aggressively for build-to-suit jobs. A build-to-suit location offers several advantages to the Company. A store constructed to the specifications of the Company saves labor expense in operation. The Company also was able to accelerate expansion using building-to-suit locations as they require no leasehold improvement cash-outlays prior to occupancy.

The Company believes that it will be able to locate satisfactory real estate for its initial stores in the new foreign markets. However, expansion in those markets, and the opening of additional stores, will present certain challenges that do not confront the Company in the United States. For example, the foreign countries do not have the inventory of abandoned supermarket locations that currently exists in the United States. Accordingly, it will be necessary for the Company to either construct its own build-to-suite buildings or incur substantial leasehold improvement expenses to modify existing warehouse space. Either strategy is potentially risky due to local building regulations and construction costs that tend to run higher than in the United States.

GOVERNMENT REGULATION

PET CLUB is subject to laws governing its relationship with employees, including minimum wage requirements, overtime, working conditions and citizenship requirements. In addition, there are statutes and regulations in certain states and Canadian provinces that affect the ownership of veterinary practices or the operation of veterinary clinics in retail stores. The Company has surveyed the legal and regulatory requirements that would apply to the stores to be opened in the new foreign markets and has determined that all required permits and licenses can be obtained on a timely and cost-effective basis. However, the costs of compliance with labor laws and other regulations adopted for the protection of employees will be marginally greater in the new foreign markets than in the United States.

HUMAN RESOURCES

As of the end of its last fiscal year, the Company employed _____ associates in the United States and Canada, _____ of whom were employed full time. The Company's associates receive wages and benefits competitive with those of the local retail community. The Company is not subject to any collective bargaining agreements and has not experienced any work stoppages.

PET CLUB always has operated with limited corporate staff. The Company's management philosophy values "flat" entrepreneurial management structures. Companies organized in this manner tend to be more flexible and have lower costs than multi-layered bureaucracies. They also produce better managers. PET CLUB has avoided excessive middle-management layers. Monitoring geographically dispersed operations can be done more efficiently and less intrusively with modern management information systems.

PET CLUB management uses several incentive systems to encourage attainment of the Company's goals. Every employee in the Company has objectives supported by recognition systems. Store staffing is structured with several on-the-job training positions, and promotions are offered as realistic incentives given the rapid growth of the Company. In addition, Company employees are expected to participate in operating decisions and honor the common themes of respect for all of the Company's customers and fellow employees.

The human resource strategies for the operation of PET CLUB EUROPE will be handled by a professional staff located at PET CLUB EUROPE's headquarters. Senior management staff will include a president or chief operating officer and top-level managers with responsibility for each of the following functions: finance, procurement, distribution, logistics, human resources and marketing. While each of these functional managers will consult with their counterparts in North America on a regular basis, executive and strategic decisions for the entire organization will initially continue to be made in the United States. Consultative topics will focus primarily on integration of activities that can be operated across the organization, including procurement from manufacturers active in North America and Europe and information systems that can provide real-time information on store performance throughout the world. PET CLUB EUROPE managers will be given substantial autonomy for execution of strategies with budgetary standards established in consultation with United States executive staff.

PET CLUB EUROPE senior managers will be selected from a pool of local professionals, as opposed to transferring personnel from North American operations. This strategy will be used for several reasons. First, as noted above, North American operations are generally run in a very lean fashion and it is not practical to move substantial numbers of management personnel to Europe on a permanent basis. Second, while PET CLUB stores follow a franchise-like format, their success is ultimately dependent on development of local relationships with customers and a keen understanding of their specific needs. This requires managers with experience in the local market and the ability to continuously monitor consumer behavior in the new countries.

The Company has engaged an executive search firm based in ____ to locate appropriate candidates. Once selected, they will spend three months in the United States learning about the operations strategy of the Company and meeting with senior managers to develop the personal relationships necessary for successful global communications. Once the European operations are ready for launch, management staff from North America will spend relatively short periods (no more than two weeks at a time) in Europe to provide consultation on store launch and organization.

The human resources manager for PET CLUB EUROPE, who has already been selected, will be working with local search firms to locate suitable candidates for in-store sale associate positions and also will be responsible for development of associate training and incentive programs. The PET CLUB EUROPE human resources manager already has completed initial training in North America and has worked with colleagues in the United States to develop an associate manual and specific rules and procedures that have been adapted to the unique cultural environment in the new foreign markets.

A detailed description of the responsibilities of each senior manager for PET CLUB EUROPE, as well the preliminary staff headcount for each function, is included as Exhibit ____ .

FINANCIAL STRATEGY

The Company currently anticipates that its existing capital resources and cash flows from operations will enable it to maintain its currently planned operations for the foreseeable future, including the planned opening of the initial stores in the new foreign markets.

In general, the Company can open new stores with a minimal investment of cash since the outlets will be leased, store fixtures are kept to a minimum and inventories generally turn over very rapidly. Further savings can be realized by occupancy of build-to-suit locations, which avoids the costly up-front investment in leasehold improvements. Other opening cash investments are small relative to store volume. Equipment costs per store are conservatively estimated at $____. Based on experience, opening year advertisement requires only $____ per store (____% of sales). The ad budget can be leveraged further with co-op money from manufacturers. In addition, PET CLUB does not compete by extending credit, thereby avoiding the expense of running a credit department and carrying accounts receivable.

The Company has assessed its initial capitalization requirements for PET CLUB EUROPE based largely on the cost of opening the initial stores. For each store, the Company has established a budget for opening inventories, equipment costs, leasehold improvements and personnel. In addition, for each geographic area where two or more stores are to be opened contemporaneously, the Company has set aside funds to cover opening advertising and certain other pre-opening expenses, including legal and accounting fees. Finally, certain costs will be incurred in connection with the formation and organization of the legal and organizational structure for PET CLUB EUROPE. Taken together, the aggregate amount required for the launch of PET FOOD EUROPE will be approximately $____ million.

Funding for future stores in the European market will come from three primary sources. The first source of funding is in the form of trade credit which has the effect of reducing the company's net investment in inventory. Once the Company has its initial stores online, cash from operations is expected to provide funding for additional stores in the markets. A third source of capital for expansion could come from equipment financing. Since most of the equipment used in PET CLUB stores is generic in nature, it provides a safe asset base for borrowing. Once European operations are fully established, other bank borrowings can be used as needed. The Company does not anticipate substantial use of bank credit. If the opportunity presents itself, the Company might also accept private investment financing from European financial sources.

RISKS AND UNCERTAINTIES

PLAN NOTE: Any business plan, particularly one used to raise money from investors, should include a discussion of the risk factors that might endanger the company's ability to meet the goals outlined in the plan. These items can be referred to in the context of the discussion of each applicable functional area (e.g., risks of shortages of raw materials in the description of manufacturing) or in a separate section in the plan. In offering documents, the risk factors section (sometimes called "certain factors" so as to not scare investors) can be quite long and heavy on legal jargon. This section is an example of another approach, albeit one not often taken. It uses a simple "question-and-answer" format to take on potential problems that might arise in the mind of a reader. This format was taken from the original stock offering document for this company, which was circulated to a number of small investors who were unfamiliar with formal offerings and might be put off by a more detailed presentation.

QUESTION: What would be the impact of an economic downturn on PET CLUB's business strategy?

ANSWER: There are very few industries in the economy with less seasonal or cyclical variation. People seldom fire their pet in a recession. However, recessions generally cause an increase in consumer "bargain hunting." As a price leader, PET CLUB actually believes that its business could improve during difficult economic times. The Company may be economically counter-cyclical.

QUESTION: If the industry stops growing, how seriously will PET CLUB's prospects be affected?
ANSWER: If the pet supply industry stopped expanding, this would certainly slow the growth of PET CLUB but probably not stop it. The store concept is based upon taking market share from competitors in a very large industry by being more efficient. The Company feels that it has a solid and innovative business model that will capture market share for many years regardless of the rate of overall industry growth. The Company also believes that industry growth rates in Europe will continue to exceed those in North America over the next decade, which means that expansion of PET CLUB EUROPE during that period will reduce the impact of an industry slowdown in the Company's traditional geographic markets.

QUESTION: How will PET CLUB be able to continue to convince manufacturers to sell directly to it?
ANSWER: Several members of PET CLUB's senior management team have long relationships with key suppliers and have established the requisite level of trust and sales success to ensure that the Company is able to strike attractive deals with manufacturers. In addition, the Company's ability to make large volume purchases to stock a number of stores makes PET CLUB an important account for even the biggest manufacturer. The launch of PET CLUB EUROPE should bolster the Company's overall position with global manufacturers that see expanding opportunities to sell products to the Company from a number of foreign subsidiaries.

QUESTION: How is PET CLUB able to convince people who shop at supermarkets to shop at the Company's outlets?
ANSWER: PET CLUB is based on the proposition that it offers significant value-added products for its customers, including a vastly superior selection at very aggressive prices. In addition, convenient locations make the stop easy for customers. Unlike supermarkets, the Company's advertising budget is devoted exclusively to pet-related products. PET CLUB requires a ___% market share to achieve its projections. Accordingly, only one out of ___ customers needs to prefer the Company's pet product offerings over the supermarket's selection.

QUESTION: How does PET CLUB assess the danger of supermarkets undercutting its prices on the grocery brand foods?
ANSWER: It is not logical for them to do so on a sustained basis. If they sell eight cans for every one that PET CLUB sells, taking a loss on all eight cans does not replace the profit on the one sale lost.

QUESTION: Can PET CLUB's business model be copied by a larger and better-funded competitor?
ANSWER: This is a very serious danger. Management can only hope that such a competitor would seek to improve their start-up results by launching in a non-PET CLUB market. In general, PET CLUB always attempts to look big to its customers and gathers regional strength through a strategy of clustering stores in a new market. Local dominance is also aided by being first to saturate a market. By aggressively maintaining a very low-cost structure, competition will be prevented from entering the market from below. Most industry players (potential competitors with pet supply expertise) have large investments in the status quo. This has led to a mostly static industry dynamic that reduces the chance of such competition.

CHAPTER 19

Sample Non-Disclosure Agreement

WHAT ONE KNOWS IT IS SOMETIMES USEFUL TO

FORGET. — ROMAN PROVERB

IN MANY SITUATIONS, a company will find itself in a situation where it wants, or needs, to disclose confidential information regarding its business activities to a prospective business partner. However, a firm will not want to get bogged down in negotiations over the terms and conditions of a long-form confidentiality agreement. In such cases, the company should present the receiving party with a "short-form" non-disclosure agreement, which covers all of the basic issues necessary to protect the company's rights. This would include such items as the definition of the protected information or receiving party's obligations to protect the confidential information and return it to the company upon request. If, after initial disclosures, it appears that a great deal of confidential information will be disclosed, then a new long-form agreement might be appropriate, provided that the new agreement also covers information which was disclosed under the umbrella of the short-form agreement.

ADVISORY: Planners should bear in mind the previous caveats regarding the reluctance of some readers to sign any such documents, and the legal enforceability of non-disclosure agreements in cross-border situations.

NOTE: Consideration should be given to the fact that non-disclosure agreements may be either invalid or not carry much weight in cross-border situations. Also, the relevant governing law may be that of an administrative division of a country rather than that of the country itself.

For example, in this sample agreement, clause 10 refers to the "Governing Law" of a state. You will need to modify your agreement to include the correct legal administrative division of either country, state, province, etc.

NON-DISCLOSURE AGREEMENT

THIS AGREEMENT is made by and between [*Name of company*], a [*State or Country of incorporation*] corporation (hereinafter the "Company"), and the undersigned (hereinafter the "Receiving Party").

RECITALS

Company is in the business of [*Type of Business*] and Receiving Party is in the business of [*Type of Business*]. Company and Receiving Party desire to enter into confidential negotiations with respect to [*Purpose of Negotiations*] (the "Business Purpose"). In order to pursue the mutual Business Purpose,

Company and Receiving Party recognize that there is a need for the Company to disclose to Receiving Party certain of its confidential information to be used only for the Business Purpose and a need for Receiving Party to protect the Company's confidential information from unauthorized use and disclosure.

NOW, THEREFORE, in consideration of the mutual covenants and conditions herein contained, and the association with the Company of Receiving Party, the parties hereto agree as follows:

1. DEFINITION OF CONFIDENTIAL INFORMATION

"Confidential Information" shall mean information relating to [*Type of Product*] or other products or the business affairs of the Company of a proprietary or confidential nature, whether communicated orally or in writing, including by way of illustration and not limitation, (i) information concerning research and development activities, (ii) manufacturing and processing techniques and know-how, (iii) software, firmware and computer programs and elements of design relating thereto (including, for example, programming techniques, algorithms, inference structures and the construction of knowledge bases), (iv) designs, drawings and formulae, (v) cost, profit and market information, (vi) financial and other business information with respect to the Company that the Company has not made publicly available, (vii) customer business information, including products of the Company ordered, prices and delivery schedules, and (viii) any information disclosed to the Company by any third party which the Company has agreed, or is otherwise obligated, to treat as confidential or proprietary.

2. EXCLUSIONS

Receiving Party, however, shall have no liability to the other party, under this Agreement with respect to the disclosure and/or use of any such Confidential Information that it can establish:

(a) Has become generally known or available to the public without breach of this Agreement by the Receiving Party

(b) Was known by the Receiving Party before receiving such information from the Company

(c) Has become known by or available to Receiving Party from a source other than the Company, without any breach of any obligation of confidentiality owed to the Company, subsequent to disclosure of such information to it by the Company

(d) Has been disclosed to persons regularly employed by the Receiving Party who have previously agreed in writing not to disclose such information or to use such information for any purpose other than to assist it to determine whether to pursue the Business Purpose

(e) Has been independently developed by the Receiving Party without use of or reference to the Confidential Information by persons who had no access to the Confidential Information

(f) Has been provided to the Receiving Party with a written statement that it is provided without restriction on disclosures

(g) Has been approved for release or use by written authorization of the Company

3. OBLIGATIONS OF RECEIVING PARTY

The Receiving Party acknowledges that irreparable injury and damage will result from disclosure to third parties, or utilization for purposes other than those connected with the proposed acquisition or other business relationship, of any of the Confidential Information. Receiving Party agrees:

(a) To hold the Confidential Information in strict confidence

(b) Not to disclose such Confidential Information to any third party except as specifically authorized herein or as specifically authorized by the Company in writing

(c) To use all reasonable precautions, consistent with the Receiving Party's treatment of its own confidential information of a similar nature, to prevent the unauthorized disclosure of the Confidential Information, including, without limitation, protection of documents from theft, unauthorized duplication and discovery of contents, and restrictions on access by other persons to such Confidential Information

(d) Not to make or use any copies, synopses or summaries of oral or written material, photographs or any other documentation or information made available or supplied by the Company to Receiving Party except such as are necessary for Receiving Party's internal communications in connection with the Business Purpose

(e) Not to use any Confidential Information for any purpose other than the Business Purpose

3. ALTERNATIVE: DETAILED ENUMERATION OF RECEIVING PARTY'S OBLIGATIONS

The Receiving Party represents, warrants and covenants to the Company, each of the following:

The Receiving Party shall, indefinitely, hold any Confidential Information in the strictest confidence and will not disclose any Confidential Information to any person or entity whatsoever, absent the prior express written instruction, signed by the president or chief executive officer of the Company. The Receiving Party shall exercise all steps necessary to ensure that any Confidential Information is held in the strictest confidence and that the terms and conditions of this Agreement are strictly adhered to by the Receiving Party and its employees and agents.

The Receiving Party may provide access to the Confidential Information to its authorized officers and employees on, and only on, a need to know basis which is directly and solely for the authorized purposes under this Agreement. Provided, however, that prior to any such access, Company shall provide to the Receiving Party the identity of any such individual and a written listing of the material to which that person will have access is maintained and provided to the Company prior to access. In any event, any such person being provided with access to any of the Confidential Information shall have executed a Confidentiality and Non-Disclosure Agreement in a form acceptable to the Company, and its legal counsel, prior to obtaining access and a copy thereof shall be provided to the Company.

Notwithstanding the provisions of Section [Number], except as to authorized officers and employees employed by the Receiving Party and as to whom the Receiving Party is in compliance with the provisions of Section [Name], in no event shall the Receiving Party provide, inadvertently or otherwise, any of the Confidential Information to any person or entity who is directly or indirectly engaged, or who is planning to directly or indirectly engage in competition with the Company.

Neither the Receiving Party, nor any person to whom any of the Confidential Information is directly or indirectly disclosed by Receiving Party, will make, have made, use or sell, whether for its own purposes or for any other, any copies of Confidential Information, or any part of the contents thereof, unless express written instruction, signed by the president or chief executive officer of the Company, has been given prior to any such action or use by Receiving Party.

Receiving Party will maintain a log of any written Confidential Information provided to it by the Company and shall provide a copy thereof to the Company immediately upon request, with a certification that it is an accurate and complete listing thereof. Such log shall show the description of the Confidential Information provided, the date upon which such Confidential Information was received, the identification of any persons to whom access to such Confidential Information has been granted and the number, if any, of copies made of such Confidential Information, as well as the exact whereabouts of each such copy and all notations, compilations or similar work product generated through use of the Confidential Information.

The standard of care to be utilized by the Receiving Party in the performance of its representations, warranties, covenants and obligations set forth in this Agreement relative to its treatment of the Confidential Information shall be the standard of care, but in no event less than a reasonable standard of care, utilized by Receiving Party in treating its own most proprietary, secret and confidential information, and such information shall not be Confidential to any right of waiver.

Receiving Party further agrees to indemnify the Company against any loss or liability resulting from, or arising in connection with, unauthorized use or disclosure of the Confidential Information by the Receiving Party or its directors, employees or other representatives.

4. REQUIRED DISCLOSURES

Receiving Party may disclose the Confidential Information if and to the extent that such disclosure is required by applicable law, provided that the Receiving Party uses reasonable efforts to limit the disclosure by means of a protective order or a request for confidential treatment and provides the Company a reasonable opportunity to review the disclosure before it is made and to interpose its own objection to the disclosure.

5. RETURN OF CONFIDENTIAL INFORMATION

Receiving Party shall return all written material, photographs and all other documentation made available or supplied by the Company to Receiving Party, and all copies and reproductions thereof, on request.

6. RETENTION OF LEGAL RIGHTS

The Company retains all rights and remedies afforded it under the patent and other laws of the United States and the States thereof, including without limitation any laws designed to protect proprietary or confidential information.

7. INJUNCTIVE RELIEF

Receiving Party acknowledges that the unauthorized use or disclosure of the Confidential Information would cause irreparable harm to the Company. Accordingly, the Receiving Party agrees that the Company will have the right to obtain an immediate injunction against any breach or threatened breach of this Agreement, as well as the right to pursue any and all other rights and remedies available at law or in equity for such a breach.

8. TERM OF AGREEMENT

This Agreement applies to all Confidential Information that is disclosed by the Company to the Receiving Party during the period that begins on the date set forth below and ends [*Six*] months thereafter. The obligations of this Agreement will remain in effect for [*Five*] years after the date of the last disclosure of Confidential Information hereunder, at which time this Agreement will terminate.

9. ENTIRE AGREEMENT

This Agreement sets forth the entire agreement and understanding of the parties and merges all prior discussions between them as to Confidential Information. Neither party may be bound by any definition, condition, representation or waiver other than as expressly stated in this Agreement or as subsequently set forth in writing signed by the parties hereto.

10. GOVERNING LAW

This Agreement shall be governed by the laws of the State [or Country] of [*State or Country*] as applied to contracts entered into and to be performed entirely within the State [or Country] of [*State or Country*].

11. SUCCESSORS AND ASSIGNS

This Agreement shall be binding upon and inure to the benefit of the parties hereto and their respective heirs, administrators, executors, successors and assigns.

IN WITNESS WHEREOF, the parties hereto have executed this Agreement this [*Date*] day of [*Month*], [*Year*].

[*Name of Company*]

By [*signature*]

[*name and title of person signing*]

[*Name of Receiving Party*]

By [*signature*]

[*name and title of person signing*]

Sample Financial Statements

THE CREDITOR HAS A BETTER MEMORY THAN THE

DEBTOR. — JAMES HOWELL

THE FOLLOWING DOCUMENTS are offered as samples of financial statements. The layout of such documents will be dictated by local standards and by the software used to compile the statements. All financial statements used in the main body of the plan should be done in the condensed report format so as to facilitate the reader's grasp of the main points. Detailed financial data can be included in appendices.

A.D.I. Video Technologies Ltd.
Profit & Loss Forecast ($,000)

	Q1/01	Q2/01	Q3/01	Q4/01	2001	Q1/02	Q2/02	Q3/02	Q4/02	2002	2003	2004
Income:												
MX4	378	546	714	840	2,478	1,030	1,091	1,235	1,307	4,662	9,504	13,939
MX16	180	252	288	288	1,008	360	610	1,040	1,800	3,810	7,040	11,616
MCE12	0	0	300	600	900	840	1,008	1,176	1,176	4,200	4,435	4,684
MPEG-4	0	0	0	0	0	0	0	0	120	240	253	268
ADlvue/ADInet	0	0	0	0	0	0	0	0	0	0	970	11,792
	568	798	1,302	1,728	4,386	2,230	2,709	3,571	4,403	12,912	22,203	42,298
Discounts	140	200	326	432	1,097	557	677	893	1,101	3,228	5,308	7,627
Total Income	**419**	**599**	**977**	**1,296**	**3,290**	**1,672**	**2,032**	**2,678**	**3,302**	**9,684**	**16,894**	**34,672**
Cost of Sales												
BOM costs	171	245	373	478	1,267	576	674	863	1,059	3,171	6,605	17,204
One time dev. Adaptation	0	0	0	0	0	15	5	15	35	35	0	0
Operations & Logistics - Salaries	62	81	81	81	306	81	81	110	110	383	507	637
	233	327	454	559	1,573	672	760	989	1,169	3,589	7,111	17,841
Gross Profit	**186**	**272**	**523**	**737**	**1,717**	**1,000**	**1,272**	**1,690**	**2,133**	**6,096**	**9,783**	**16,831**
	33%	34%	40%	43%	39%	45%	47%	47%	48%	47%	44%	40%
Research and Development												
Salaries	302	430	443	443	1,619	443	443	443	443	1,773	2,011	2,499
Depreciation	5	21	32	32	89	39	47	49	49	183	284	315
Other	20	20	30	30	100	40	40	50	50	180	200	230
	327	471	505	505	1,808	522	531	542	542	2,137	2,495	3,045
Marketing	312	282	466	429	1,490	580	456	553	489	2,078	2,647	3,525
General & Administrative	128	129	132	138	527	156	161	171	176	663	768	876
Operating Profit (loss)	**(581)**	**(611)**	**(681)**	**(335)**	**(2,108)**	**(268)**	**124**	**424**	**927**	**1,217**	**3,874**	**9,385**
	-104%	-77%	-45%	-19%	-48%	-12%	5%	12%	21%	9%	17%	22%
EBIT	**(581)**	**(611)**	**(681)**	**(335)**	**(2,108)**	**(268)**	**124**	**424**	**927**	**1,217**	**3,874**	**9,385**
Income Tax	0	0	0	0	0	0	0	0	0	0	1,074	3,379
Net Profit (loss)	**(581)**	**(611)**	**(681)**	**(335)**	**(2,108)**	**(268)**	**124**	**424**	**927**	**1,217**	**2,800**	**6,006**
	-104%	-77%	-45%	-19%	-48%	-12%	5%	12%	21%	9%	13%	14%
Accumulated Net Profit	**(581)**	**(1,192)**	**(1,772)**	**(2,108)**	**(2,108)**	**(2,366)**	**(2,242)**	**(1,817)**	**(890)**	**(890)**	**1,909**	**7,916**

A.D.I. Video Technologies Ltd.
Sales Forecast ($, 000)

	Q1/01	Q2/01	Q3/01	Q4/01	2001	Q1/02	Q2/02	Q3/02	Q4/02	2002	2003	2004	2005
MX4													
Number of units	90	130	170	200	590	286	303	343	363	1,295	3,000	5,000	10,000
Price per unit	4.2	4.2	4.2	4.2	4.2	3.6	3.6	3.6	3.6	3.6	3.2	2.8	2.5
MX4 Revenues	378	546	714	840	2,478	1,030	1,091	1,235	1,307	4,662	9,504	13,939	24,533
	68%	68%	55%	49%	56%	46%	40%	35%	30%	36%	43%	33%	23%
MX16													
Number of units	15	21	24	24	84	36	61	104	180	381	800	1,500	3,000
Price per unit	12.0	12.0	12.0	12.0	12.0	10.0	10.0	10.0	10.0	10.0	8.8	7.7	6.8
MX16 Revenues	180	252	288	288	1,008	360	610	1,040	1,800	3,810	7,040	11,616	20,444
	32%	32%	22%	17%	23%	16%	23%	29%	41%	30%	32%	27%	19%
MCE12													
Number of units			10	20	30	30	36	42	42	150	180	216	259
Price per unit			30.0	30.0	30.0	28.0	28.0	28.0	28.0	28.0	24.6	21.7	19.1
MCE12 Revenues			300	600	900	840	1,008	1,176	1,176	4,200	4,435	4,684	4,946
			23%	35%	21%	38%	37%	33%	27%	33%	20%	11%	5%
MPEG-4													
Number of units								5	5	10	12	14	17
Price per unit								24.0	24.0	24.0	21.1	18.6	16.4
MPEG-4 Revenues								120	120	240	253	268	283
								3%	3%	2%	1%	1%	0%
HEC													
ADIvue													
Number of units											1,500	20,000	120,000
Price per unit											0.46	0.40	0.36
											690	8,096	42,747
ADInet													
Number of units											2,000	30,000	120,000
Price per unit											0.14	0.12	0.11
											280	3,696	13,010
HEC Revenues											970	11,792	55,757
											4%	28%	53%
Total Revenues before discounts	558	798	1,302	1,728	4,386	2,230	2,709	3,571	4,403	12,912	22,203	42,298	105,962
Discount (25%)*	140	200	326	432	1,097	557	677	893	1,101	3,228	5,308	7,627	12,551
Total Revenues	419	599	977	1,296	3,290	1,672	2,032	2,678	3,302	9,684	16,894	34,672	93,411

(*) Excluding HEC discounts.

A.D.I. Video Technologies Ltd.
Marketing Budget ($,000)

	Q1/01	Q2/01	Q3/01	Q4/01	2001	Q1/02	Q2/02	Q3/02	Q4/02	2002	2003	2004	2005
Salaries - Israel	67	92	108	108	375	117	117	132	132	498	639	753	938
Commissions (3% of HEC sales)	0	0	0	0	0	0	0	0	0	0	29	354	1,673
Exhibitions	120	0	60	0	180	120	0	60	0	180	200	220	240
Advertising	5	5	10	5	25	10	10	10	10	40	60	70	80
Internet Site	4		4		8	4		4		8	10	15	20
Foreign Travel	30	30	30	30	120	30	30	30	30	120	130	140	150
USA Subsidiary	76	145	244	276	742	285	285	302	302	1,172	1,509	1,893	2,329
Others	10	10	10	10	40	15	15	15	15	60	70	80	100
Total Marketing Costs	312	282	466	429	1,490	580	456	553	489	2,078	2,647	3,525	5,529

A.D.I. Video Technologies Ltd.
US Subsidiary Expenses ($,000)

	Q1/01	Q2/01	Q3/01	Q4/01	2001	Q1/02	Q2/02	Q3/02	Q4/02	2002	2003	2004	2005
Salaries	41	82	128	161	410	170	170	170	170	678	759	943	1,089
Rental & Taxes	3	12	24	30	69	30	30	30	30	120	140	160	180
Office Maintenance	1	2	3	4	10	5	5	5	5	20	50	70	100
Advertising	22	22	53	33	130	30	30	40	40	140	200	250	350
Communication	1	3	7	8	19	8	8	10	10	36	80	100	130
Transportation		1	1	1	3	1	1	1	1	4	30	40	50
Legal	3	6	6	6	21	6	6	6	6	24	30	40	50
Foreign Travel	5	12	12	21	50	20	20	25	25	90	120	150	200
Other		5	11	13	29	15	15	15	15	60	100	140	180
Total	76	145	244	276	742	285	285	302	302	1,172	1,509	1,893	2,329

A.D.I. Video Technologies Ltd.
Cash Flow Forecast ($,000)

	Q1/01	Q2/01	Q3/01	Q4/01	2001	Q1/02	Q2/02	Q3/02	Q4/02	2002	2003	2004	2005
Net Profit	(581)	(611)	(581)	(335)	(2,108)	(258)	124	424	927	1,217	2,800	6,006	17,960
Change in Working Capital	(80)	(92)	(293)	(278)	(743)	(170)	(304)	(499)	(454)	(1,427)	(619)	(2,930)	(9,486)
Depreciation	10	28	39	40	116	53	61	62	62	237	362	421	533
Total Cash Flow From Operations	**(651)**	**(675)**	**(835)**	**(574)**	**(2,735)**	**(376)**	**(120)**	**(12)**	**535**	**27**	**2,543**	**3,497**	**9,007**
Investments in Fixed Assets	(165)	(221)	(135)	(19)	(539)	(200)	(98)	(16)	0	(314)	(390)	(500)	(700)
Cash (Requirements) Surplus	**(816)**	**(896)**	**(970)**	**(592)**	**(3,274)**	**(576)**	**(218)**	**(28)**	**535**	**(287)**	**2,153**	**2,997**	**8,307**
Accumulated Cash (Req.) Surplus	**(816)**	**(1,711)**	**(2,682)**	**(3,274)**	**(3,274)**	**(3,850)**	**(4,067)**	**(4,095)**	**(3,560)**	**(3,560)**	**(1,408)**	**1,590**	**9,897**

CHAPTER 21

Sample Cover Page and Legends

DRESS A GOAT IN SILK AND IT IS STILL A GOAT.

— CELTIC PROVERB

DEPENDING ON THE INTENDED USE OF THE BUSINESS PLAN, one or more legends or disclaimers should be prominently displayed on the inside cover pages of the plan and, as appropriate, within the body of the plan itself. For example, financial projections should be accompanied by assumptions and disclaimers that the projections will actually be achieved. The following legends are based on compliance with securities laws in the United States. However, the plan writer can expect that similar regulations may be applicable in other countries. In addition to securities law compliance, legends to protect the confidentiality of any of the information in the plan should also be included regardless of the intended use of the plan, and recipients should be required to sign some form of nondisclosure agreement similar to that included elsewhere in this book.

SAMPLE COVER PAGE FOR BUSINESS PLAN

CONFIDENTIAL AND PROPRIETARY

Copy Number: _____

Recipient: _____

[*Company Name*]

[*Company Address*]

[*Date of Business Plan*]

The information contained in this Business Plan is confidential and is intended only for use by the person listed above to whom it has been transmitted by [*Name of company*] (the "Company"). Any reproduction of this Plan, in whole or in part, or the divulgence of any of its contents, without the prior written consent of the Company, is prohibited. See inside for further restrictions on the use of this Plan.

SAMPLE LEGENDS

The following is a sample securities legend for the inside cover pages of a business plan.

NO PERSON HAS BEEN AUTHORIZED TO GIVE ANY INFORMATION OR TO MAKE ANY REPRESENTATIONS OTHER THAN THOSE CONTAINED IN THIS BUSINESS PLAN IN CONNECTION WITH THE TRANSACTIONS DESCRIBED HEREIN, AND, IF GIVEN OR MADE, SUCH OTHER INFORMATION OR REPRESENTATIONS MUST NOT BE RELIED UPON AS HAVING BEEN AUTHORIZED BY THE COMPANY.

THIS BUSINESS PLAN DOES NOT CONSTITUTE AN OFFER TO SELL OR SOLICITATION OF AN OFFER TO BUY ANY SECURITIES OTHER THAN THE SECURITIES SPECIFICALLY OFFERED HEREBY, NOR DOES IT CONSTITUTE AN OFFER TO SELL OR SOLICITATION OF AN OFFER TO BUY FROM ANY PERSON IN ANY STATE OR OTHER JURISDICTION IN WHICH SUCH OFFER WOULD BE UNLAWFUL. THE OFFERING OF THE SECURITIES DESCRIBED IN THIS PLAN HAS NOT BEEN REGISTERED WITH THE FEDERAL SECURITIES AND EXCHANGE COMMISSION IN RELIANCE UPON AN EXEMPTION FROM THE REGISTRATION REQUIREMENTS OF THE SECURITIES ACT OF 1933, AS AMENDED.

NEITHER THE DELIVERY OF THIS BUSINESS PLAN AT ANY TIME, NOR ANY SALE OF SECURITIES HEREUNDER, SHALL UNDER ANY CIRCUMSTANCES CREATE AN IMPLICATION THAT THE INFORMATION CONTAINED HEREIN IS CORRECT AS OF ANY TIME SUBSEQUENT TO ITS DATE. OFFERS AND SALES WILL ONLY BE MADE TO PERSONS WHO HAVE THE KNOWLEDGE AND EXPERIENCE TO EVALUATE THE MERITS AND RISKS OF THE INVESTMENT AND WHO HAVE THE ECONOMIC MEANS TO AFFORD THE ILLIQUIDITY OF THE SECURITIES OFFERED HEREBY.

THE INFORMATION SET FORTH HEREIN IS BELIEVED BY THE COMPANY TO BE RELIABLE. IT MUST BE RECOGNIZED, HOWEVER, THAT PREDICTIONS AND PROJECTIONS AS TO THE COMPANY'S FUTURE PERFORMANCE ARE NECESSARILY SUBJECT TO A HIGH DEGREE OF UNCERTAINTY AND NO WARRANTY OF SUCH PROJECTIONS IS EXPRESSED OR IMPLIED HEREBY.

CHAPTER 22

Glossary

ACCESSORY GOODS Products used in operations, for example, office copiers, auxiliary power supplies and air compressors.

ACCOUNTS PAYABLE Short-term debts incurred as the result of day-to-day operations such as the purchase of goods for resale.

ACCOUNTS RECEIVABLE Monies owed to a company as the result of day-to-day operations such as from the sale of goods.

ACCRUAL BASED ACCOUNTING An accounting method that records income and expenses at the time of contract rather than when payment is received or expenses paid.

AMORTIZATION Allocation of a fraction of the original cost of long-term intangible assets to those periods benefited.

ANGEL INVESTOR A private investor willing to advance funds to an enterprise under favorable terms and conditions.

ASSETS Tangible and intangible property having positive financial value.

B2B Acronym for business-to-business. A company that provides goods or services to other businesses.

B2C Acronym for business-to-consumer. A company that provides goods or services to ultimate consumers.

BALANCE SHEET Also called Statement of Financial Position. A company's primary financial statement showing resources of a business on a particular date as well as claims against those resources on that same date (Assets, Liabilities, Owner's Equity).

BARRIERS TO ENTRY Conditions that make it difficulty for competitors to enter a market, for example, copyrights, trademarks, patents, exclusive distribution channels and high initial investment requirements.

BREAK-EVEN POINT The point at which revenues equal expenses.

BRICKS AND MORTAR A business with a physical location (building) open to the public; especially a retail business location.

BURN RATE The rate at which a start-up company spends its investment capital before it becomes profitable.

CAPITAL Financial investment used to start and operate a business.

CASH BASED ACCOUNTING An accounting method that records income and expenses at time payment is received or expenses paid (opposite of Accrual Accounting).

CASH FLOW STATEMENT Schedule of expected cash receipts and disbursements during a stated period of time.

CASH PIT Slang term used to describe an enterprise that requires a great deal of investment capital prior to its making a profit.

CHIEF EXECUTIVE OFFICER (CEO) The individual who is responsible for the day-to-day management of a business enterprise. In some countries called a MANAGING DIRECTOR.

CHIEF FINANCIAL OFFICER (CFO) The individual responsible for the day-to-day management of financial issues for a business enterprise.

CHIEF INFORMATION OFFICER (CIO) The individual responsible for the day-to-day management of information technology for a business enterprise.

COLLATERAL ASSETS Assets pledged to guarantee a loan.

CONFIDENTIALITY AGREEMENT An obligation to protect the confidentiality of proprietary information exchanged between parties exploring a commercial relationship. Also referred to as a nondisclosure agreement (NDA). Use of a confidentiality agreement is generally a condition to the availability of trade secret protection in most countries.

CONVENIENCE GOODS Products purchased by consumers who are generally willing to pay a premium for easy purchase access. For example, candy, cigarettes, drugs, newspapers, magazines and many grocery products.

CORPORATE CULTURE The social and traditional bonds that hold an organization together. It incorporates an organization's values, norms of behavior, policies and procedures, and is heavily influenced by national cultural values, ownership structure and the nature of the industry in which the corporation operates.

COST OF GOODS Direct costs to produce goods or services, including labor and materials.

COST OF SALES Cost of goods plus expenses involved in selling and delivering a product.

COUNTRY RISK (economics) The financial risks of a transaction that relate to the political, economic or social instability of a country.

CURRENT ASSETS Financial assets that can be converted quickly to cash, usually within 12 months.

CURRENT LIABILITIES Financial liabilities incurred in normal day-to-day business and due within 12 months.

DEBT An obligation to repay a lender the principal and interest due on a loan.

DEBT SERVICE The amount due on regularly scheduled payments that keep a loan current.

DEPRECIATION Allocation of a fraction of the original cost of long-term tangible assets to those periods benefited.

DIRECT SALES Sales made directly to end-users.

DISPOSABLE INCOME The amount of money a consumer has that is available to spend on products after necessary expenditures (e.g., rent, food, clothing) have been paid.

DISTRIBUTOR Purchaser of products for resale at a higher price to customers, who are usually retail outlets.

DISTRIBUTION CHANNEL (1) The path a product follows from manufacturer to end-user. For example, manufacturer–distributor–wholesaler–retailer–end-user. (2) The different types of paths a product can take to get from the manufacturer to the end-user. For example, retail outlets, Internet sales, self service outlets, vending machines, telephone sales and direct mail sales.

DOCUMENTATION The financial, commercial and legal documents relating to a transaction.

DUE DILIGENCE INVESTIGATION Preliminary research and exchange of data between parties contemplating a commercial transaction such as a potential joint venture. The data covers each party's business and affairs and specific matters relating to the proposed business plan. See CONFIDENTIALITY AGREEMENT.

ESCROW A written agreement wherein documents, money or other assets are placed on deposit with a third party to be delivered upon fulfillment or non-fulfillment of certain conditions or obligations.

EXHIBIT A document attached to a contract, agreement or plan. For example, a document entitled "Exhibit A" might list product specifications attached to a purchase order.

EXIT STRATEGY A component of a business plan that defines the possible methodologies for investors in a company to recoup their investment after a stated period by selling the enterprise.

FASHION GOODS Products whose style is important and price is secondary. For example, certain items of clothing, jewelry, furniture, draperies and dishes.

FINANCIALS The financial documents of a company including, balance sheet, income (profit and loss) statement and cash flow statement. Also included are budgets.

FIXED ASSETS Also called long-term assets; assets held for more than 12 months on the balance sheet date that are integral to the day-to-day operation of an enterprise. For example, real estate, equipment, patents and furniture.

FIXED COSTS The day-to-day costs of operating an enterprise that are not a function of sales volume, for example, salaries, insurance, lease expenses and utilities.

FULL SERVICE RETAIL SALES Sales resulting from a sales outlet at retail prices directly to the end-user.

GOING CONCERN A company that is actively engaged in commercial operations.

GOVERNING LAW CLAUSE A contract provision that specifies the law that the parties have selected for the interpretation of their contract. Whether a court respects the choice of the parties is discretionary, because parties are not permitted to deprive a court of jurisdiction.

GROSS MARGIN Positive difference between net sales revenues and cost of goods sold.

GROSS PROFIT Revenues less cost of sales.

HUMAN RESOURCES The "human capital" or employees of a company. The term typically includes considerations related to their hiring, firing, training and management. Often simply referred to as HR.

IMPERSONAL SERVICE AT CUSTOMER'S SITE Service provided to a client at client's location, but without dealing with factors that customer deems confidential. Examples include lawn service, copier repairs, office cleaning and trucking services.

IMPERSONAL SERVICE AT PROVIDER'S SITE Service provided at the service provider's location to a client's property, but without dealing with factors that customer deems confidential. For example, service to an automobile or television.

IMPERSONAL SERVICE, VOLUME Service that satisfies needs of a large number of customers, with service provider and customer never meeting, for example, classified ads, storage lockers and cash machines.

INCOME STATEMENT Also called Profit & Loss Statement or Statement of Earnings. The primary financial statement that summarizes revenues generated, expenses incurred, and gains or losses of business during a period of time.

INSTALLATION GOODS Products with long service life requiring large and expensive capital investment. For example, office buildings, manufacturing facilities and equipment such as tractors, printing presses, cranes and robotics.

INTANGIBLE ASSETS The non-physical assets of an enterprise that include goodwill, copyrights, trademarks, patents and trade recognition.

JOINT VENTURE (1) The combination of two or more legal entities who together undertake a transaction for mutual gain or engage in a commercial enterprise with mutual sharing of profits and losses. (2) A form of business partnership involving joint management and the sharing of risks and profits as between enterprises based in different countries.

LIABILITIES Financial obligations of a business to external creditors.

LICENSING AGREEMENT A contract by which the holder of a trademark, patent or copyright transfers a limited right to use a process, sell or manufacture an article, or furnish specialized services or information covered by the trademark, patent, or copyright to another firm for a stated period and for stated compensation.

LIQUIDITY Percentage of assets that can be quickly converted into cash.

LONG-TERM ASSETS Assets expected to be held for more than 12 months of the balance sheet date that are integral to day-to-day operation of an enterprise. For example, manufacturing plants, equipment, patents, furniture and real estate. Also called fixed assets.

LONG-TERM LIABILITIES Portions of external debt not deemed payable for 12 months from the date of the balance sheet.

MANAGING DIRECTOR The individual responsible for the day-to-day management of a business enterprise. Also called a chief executive officer in some countries.

MARKET LIFE CYCLE The time period during which consumers of a product are willing to purchase the product before it becomes obsolete, out of style or otherwise undesirable.

MARKET PENETRATION PRICING STRATEGY A pricing strategy where introductory pricing is low in order to achieve maximize market penetration.

MARKET SHARE (1) The percentage of an enterprise's sales of a given product compared to the total sales of like products in a specified market. For example, market share of an automaker's compact cars. (2) The percentage of an enterprise's total sales compared to total sales of a given product market. For example, market share of an automaker in a given country.

MATERIAL GOODS Raw or processed materials used in the manufacturing of finished goods. For example, steel that will become part of an automobile.

M.O.U. OR MEMORANDUM OF UNDERSTANDING A preliminary contract that expresses the interest of two or more parties in continuing negotiations with the goal of forming a joint venture or other commercial contractual agreements.

NET PROFIT Total revenues less total expenses.

NET WORTH See OWNER'S EQUITY.

NONDISCLOSURE AGREEMENT See CONFIDENTIALITY AGREEMENT.

ON-SITE SALES METHOD Selling directly to end-users using a sales force that calls on customers at their place of business.

OPERATING EXPENSE A cost incurred in the course of the day-to-day operation of a business enterprise.

OUTSOURCE The external purchase of goods and services.

OWNER'S EQUITY A statement of a business owner's value in an enterprise as stated in the equation
ASSETS − LIABILITIES = OWNER'S EQUITY.

PARTS/SUB ASSEMBLY GOODS Unfinished manufactured items that become part of a finished product. For example, screws, bolts, transistors, printed circuits, electric motors and castings.

PERSONAL SERVICE AT CUSTOMER'S SITE One-to-one or one-to-many relationship between a service provider and customer, provided at customer's site, sometimes dealing with factors customer deems confidential. For example, tutoring and consulting.

PERSONAL SERVICE AT SERVICE PROVIDER'S SITE One-to-one interaction between customer and service provider at service provider's site, sometimes dealing with factors customer deems confidential. For example, doctor, lawyer, accountant and educational institution.

PERSONAL SERVICE, VOLUME Services dealing with very high volumes that still require "personal touch." For example, airline services or a parcel delivery service such as United Parcel Service (UPS).

PREPAID EXPENSE An asset that takes the form of a payment made in advance for items normally charged to expense.

PROFORMA Financial forms (for example, balance sheet, income statement, cash flow statement and budget) based on future expectations.

PRODUCT A general term that denotes either goods or services offered by a company for sale.

PRODUCT BENEFITS ADVERTISING Advertising that focuses on the strengths of a product and benefits resulting from those strengths.

PRODUCT COMPARISON ADVERTISING Advertising that compares features of a product to detriment of competitors.

PRODUCTION CAPACITY The volume of products that can be produced by a business using current resources.

PROFIT MARGIN Total revenues less total expenses.

PROPRIETARY TECHNOLOGY Any technology that is unique and/or legally owned by a business enterprise that is incorporated in or used to produce a product.

PULL PROMOTIONAL STRATEGY Direct interface by seller with end-user of product that minimizes channels of distribution during first stages of promotion but maximizes advertising. Objective is to "pull" product into the various channel outlets creating a demand that channels cannot ignore.

PUSH PROMOTIONAL STRATEGY Maximum use of available distribution channels to "push" product into the marketplace. Usually requires significant incentives to distribution channels to promote product, but minimum advertising.

RAMP-UP PERIOD The period it takes a company to reach full production level for a start-up venture or a new product line.

RECEIVABLES (1) Money due from customers for products sold on credit terms. (2) Money due from or money loaned.

ROI Acronym for Return on Investment. A calculation of operating income (profit) divided by the operating assets utilized. Expressed as a percentage.

SALES PITCH Business slang for making a sales presentation. More specifically, refers to a short, energetic presentation of the benefits to a sale or transaction.

SELF-SERVICE RETAIL SALES METHOD Selling from sales outlet directly to end-users, usually at prices less than full list price and with few or no sales personnel.

SERVICE GOODS Products viewed by consumers as basically similar, so they "shop" to get the best price, for example, lawn mowers, refrigerators, television sets and automobiles.

SERVICE/GOODS MIX Business enterprise that combines the sale of products and follow on services, often where service quality is more important than the goods. For example, fast food, catering and telecommunications services.

STOCKHOLDERS' EQUITY A statement of shareholder ownership interest in a business enterprise as stated in the equation
ASSETS – LIABILITIES = SHAREHOLDER'S EQUITY.

STRATEGIC RELATIONSHIP Agreement between two or more businesses jointly to conduct specified business, usually related to technology development and/or marketing and distribution efforts.

SUPPLIES GOODS Products that will not become a part of purchaser's end product. For example, drill bits, chemicals, pencils, paper and paper clips.

SWOT Acronym for and process of analyzing a company's Strengths, Weaknesses, Opportunities and Threats.

TRACK RECORD Historical financial performance of a company.

TRADEMARK The name of a product that has been legally registered.

TRANSPARENCY The extent to which laws, regulations, agreements and practices affecting international trade and local business are open, clear, measurable and verifiable.

UNSOUGHT GOODS OR SERVICES Products usually purchased under adversity rather than desire, for example, coffins, medicine, life insurance and encyclopedias. Since consumer seldom goes out looking for such product, a constant, aggressive selling process is required.

VENTURE CAPITAL Financing provided to found and support a business, particularly one that is considered innovative or untested such that there is a relatively significant risk of losing the investment, but also a promise of unusually high return in the event the venture succeeds.

VERTICAL INTEGRATION The expansion, acquisition or merger of firms or business activities into different points of the same production and/or distribution path. For example, a leather shoe manufacturer who acquires a leather manufacturer and a retail shoe chain. In theory, the greater the vertical integration, the less vulnerable business is to outside forces.

WHOLESALE SALES METHOD Selling at significantly discounted prices to distributors who in turn sell to full-service or self-service retail outlets.

WORKING CAPITAL Cash available to business for day-to-day operations.

CHAPTER 23

Resources

Resource Directory for Small Business Management, Small Business Administration

Business Plans For Dummies, Paul Tiffany, Steven D. Peterson (1997)

Business Plans Handbook, Kristin Kahrs, Angela Shupe (Editor) (1997)

Business Plans to Game Plans: A Practical System for Turning Strategies into Action, Jan B. King (2000)

Model Business Plans for Product Businesses, William A. Cohen (1995)

Model Business Plans for Service Businesses, William A.,Cohen (1995)

On Target: The Book on Marketing Plans, Tim Berry, Doug Wilson (2000)

The Prentice Hall Encyclopedia of Model Business Plans, Wilbur Cross, Alice M. Richey (1998)

Writing Business Plans That Get Results: A Step-By-Step Guide, Michael O'Donnell (1991)

The Authors

ROBERT BROWN, MBA, J.D., PH.D.

Robert Brown is a member of Greenebaum Doll & McDonald PLLC. He has a Ph.D. from Cambridge University and a Masters degree from Jochi University in Tokyo. During three years of law school, he earned J.D., M.B.A. and Masters Degree from the University of Louisville. Dr. Brown is admitted as an attorney in New York, Washington D.C., California and Kentucky, and is qualified as a solicitor in England and Wales and in Hong Kong. For the past 25 years, he has worked closely with start-up companies as an investment banker and attorney, serving both in-house and as an outside advisor. His previous experience includes assignments in London, New York City, Tokyo, San Francisco and San Diego. Dr. Brown has taught law and economics courses at the law schools of the University of San Francisco and University of California Berkeley, as well as business plan, managerial finance and economic courses at the school of business of Bellarmine University. Dr. Brown is the author or editor of several books in the area, including *Equity Finance* (2001 Suppl.), *Financing Start-Ups* (now going into its fifth edition), *Doing Business on the Internet*, *Managing Your E-Business Singapore*, *Commercial Laws of East Asia*, *Intellectual Property Laws of East Asia*, and *Asian Economic and Legal Development*. He can be contacted at rlb@gdm.com.

ALAN S. GUTTERMAN, MBA, J.D., PH.D.

Alan S. Gutterman is a writer, attorney and consultant in the San Francisco Bay Area. He has over 20 years experience representing entrepreneurs, businesses and investors in a wide range of domestic and international transactions. He has authored books on cross-border transactions, strategic alliances and technology transfer and has taught graduate level courses on mergers and acquisitions, law and economic development and doing business in Asian markets. His current research and publication interests include development and management of growth-oriented firms in the United States and Europe. He is also the author of *A Short Course in International Joint Ventures*, also by World Trade Press.